MISSIONS
by the Spirit

Learning from Quaker Examples

BY RON STANSELL

BARCLAY PRESS

211 N. Meridian St., #101, Newberg, OR 97132
www.barclaypress.com

Missions by the Spirit
Learning from Quaker Examples

© 2009 by Ron Stansell

BARCLAY PRESS
Newberg, OR 97132
www.barclaypress.com

cover design by Darryl Brown

ISBN 978-1-59498-020-6

Contents

Early Friends and Missionary Theory

DESPITE RECEIVING much criticism during the twentieth century, Christian missions of this era made a huge cultural and societal impact around the world. *Missions by the Spirit* looks specifically at Friends (Quakers) and their theory and practice of missions as demonstrated during the twentieth century.

The earliest of seventeenth-century Quakers in the north of England became famous for their bold witness. Some of them traveled far afield to Europe, Turkey, the Caribbean, and the British colonies of North America. Yet their first missionary efforts were primarily monocultural and that monoculturalism characterized their efforts for about two hundred years; they reflected little on cross-cultural ministry.

George Fox, founder of the Quaker (Friends) movement, taught biblically about the equality of all human beings, the work of God in the hearts of people everywhere, loyalty to Scripture, the centrality of Christ, the possibility of transforming culture, and the personal guidance of the Holy Spirit. These basic teachings were powerfully important to missions and positioned Friends for expansion, despite Friends' generally unarticulated theology of cross-cultural missions. For whatever reasons, these early Friends did not go much beyond their Anglo-Saxon roots in large numbers (as the Moravians did one hundred years later), but when the time and opportunity came to reach out around the world, they found historic resources from Fox and earlier Quakers to encourage them. It wasn't until after the dawn of the evangelical Protestant movement led by William Carey in 1792 that Quaker practice began catching up with its missionary theory.

In the early nineteenth century, British Friend Daniel Wheeler and others witnessed in Russia and the South Sea islands. Other British Friends supported the work of the Bible societies, and some struggled through cultural barriers to witness for Christ. Still others, like Briton George Richardson (1859), remembered from their roots in Scripture and the theology of George Fox "to promote the extension of the kingdom of our Lord Jesus Christ in heathen lands."[1] But in the United States, shaking Quakers into a world awareness did not begin until after 1860, and required the ministry of Quaker aristocrat Joseph John Gurney, the Sunday School Movement, the Wesleyan Holiness revivals, and the evangelical missionary movement. Quaker missions efforts grew far deeper roots after 1900 when the subjects of this book began their missionary ministries.

I hope this book will assist contemporary missionaries in learning from the missionary theory and practice of Friends of the twentieth century. Friends have done some things differently than other evangelicals. At times they marched to a different drummer. Consciously and unconsciously they were influenced by traditions and beliefs about the Holy Spirit, interpersonal relationships of peace and harmony, convictions that the human condition involves both physical and spiritual needs, and the belief that a passionately holy life full of integrity was required of them as missionaries.

Theory and Practice as Shown by Example

How can a writer best get to the meat of missiology? What was my process in writing this book? When possible I gathered personal letters and diaries, and interviewed friends and family. I combed archival materials and personal writings, and then considered secondary sources about the missionaries and their times. I also drew from my own awareness of and contacts with the Friends movements of Africa, Asia, and Latin America, and from contact with Evangelical Friends Church International, of which I am a part. Finally, I worked to synthesize into a limited number of categories the theories and practices these Friends followed, and as I present these concepts I enliven them with life events. The best missionary theory cooks in the stew of culture and the spice of ordinary living.

But these are not comprehensive biographies. Many important events and people I never mention. But I hope clear statements of theory and practice might combine to show their power through these brief biographical sketches.

There are always stones unturned and stories not discovered. Readers will notice that these four figures, and no others, appear to receive all the credit. I purposely keep the scope of this book narrow, but I do believe the lives of other powerful workers reinforce many of these lessons.

The writer always runs the risk of reading his or her concerns back into the lives of others. So be it. I accept the risk and invite the reader to exercise discernment, especially when reading the "Reflections" section at the end of each chapter.

Where twenty-first-century applications are not obvious, I have endeavored to make them explicit so Friends and others in the West can improve current practice. Evangelical Christians in the West still play an important role on the stage of global missions. I also believe Friends, specifically, have something to teach other Christians.

Friends missionaries were certainly not the only orthodox Christians of their day, nor were the four missionaries highlighted here the only outstanding missionaries among Friends. Yet these individuals were respected by their peers, frequently mingled in interdenominational circles, and each in their way influenced a wider circle of mission leaders. By exposing that influence and broadening it, I encourage readers to learn from the past—the past of a small Christian movement whose impact has been far greater than its numbers.

Non-Western Missionaries

Through this book I want to speak not only to the Western church, but to a new generation of non-Western missionaries now spreading around the globe. I believe these missionaries have some significant advantages over Western missionaries in their abilities to meet people, to understand human needs, and to speak grace to a world in great need. We live in a wonderful day when once again the locus of the worldwide Christian church resides in the Global South and the East, as it did until about A.D. 1000 when the churches of Africa and Asia began to weaken and wither. Now, one thousand years later, the majority of Christians are once again from the Global South and East. These Christians—from Asia and Africa and Latin America—will not do missions like Westerners, who often ministered from an imperial position of power and prestige. Although approaches are different, this new generation of non-Western missionaries can learn from the errors and successes of their Western spiritual ancestors.

I hope missionaries from the Global South will be blessed by this book's examples of courage and fortitude. These missionaries will need courage in great measure in coming years. I hope they discover how easy it is to get fatigued and shocked by another culture, even when the culture seems so much like their own. I hope workers from the Global South may be better equipped to smell out the dangers of dependency, and will join this book's cry for trained indigenous leaders. I hope they will grapple with how to disciple new believers for the fullest development of the Christian life and the influence of the church in society. I believe the Spirit will at times lead them to new answers, but a study of the past will help them sense the right questions to ask.

Missionary Stereotypes

Who hasn't seen a movie or read a book portraying the stereotype of the rugged missionary of one hundred years ago—Kathryn Hepburn in *The African Queen*, James Michener's "Abner Hale" of *Hawaii*, or more recently Barbara Kingsolver's description of a egocentric and culturally oblivious missionary in *The Poisonwood Bible*? Such a missionary wears heavy, dark clothes topped by a white pith helmet for protection against the blazing tropical sun. His narrow, pinched face recoils from fearsome and hostile natives brandishing spears. Or she clutches a Bible with one hand and points to the sky as she preaches under the spreading and gently swaying limbs of a banyan tree, all the while trying to avoid the boiling pot!

The stereotype has not entirely faded, and with reason: One hundred years ago the picture was at least partially true. The four subjects of this book never had to dodge cannibalism, but in the first half of the twentieth century, spears, deceit, and bullets were not unknown, and traveling through the tropics was accompanied by malaria, typhoid, and bone-achingly hard physical labor. The missionaries weren't all sour and shriveled people, but some of them were certainly intense! The social sciences were just developing, and

4

missionaries made mistakes, but the evangelical missionaries of the early twentieth century tended to be far more culturally sensitive and politically savvy than the colonialists and empire-builders with whom they are usually lumped.[2] The same claims to greater-than-average cultural sensitivity can be made for Friends (Quakers) at the beginning of the last century, despite their weaknesses and their insensitivities.

Nigerian writer Lamin Sanneh defends the missionaries of one hundred years ago on the grounds that they actually worked to preserve culture far more than destroy it. By learning the vernacular languages of their regions, missionaries honored their new friends. They upheld cultural uniqueness, and by creating new church structures, the missionaries contributed greatly to the de-Westernization of Christianity.[3] As the missionary learned a language, he or she tended to grow in appreciation of the culture and became increasingly unsure that Western culture actually answered the questions being asked.[4] Sanneh maintains that more recent scholars have found the missionaries genuinely aligned with the common people. In contrast with earlier anti-missionary writers, scholars like Sanneh have discovered striking and persistent rifts between missionaries and the colonial powers that secular historians had judged to be their natural allies.[5] For example, most of the first nationalists (and anti-colonialists) in Africa and Asia were educated in Christian mission schools.[6] Rather than suppress independence movements, missions tended to foster them even though they generally claimed to be apolitical. Furthermore, by planting autonomous Christian bodies, Christianity in the non-Western world directly and indirectly promoted national self-determination rather than subservience to the West. That which Sanneh says of American evangelicals in general will be shown to be true of these four American Quakers in particular.

The Truth in the Stereotypes

Part of the stereotype rings true: These missionaries were strong people hardened by work, but there was more to their work than manual labor and rugged living. One of the subjects of this book scratched roads out of the tropical forest. Another road mule-back for days at a time. At least three were adept at outdoor living. Even more draining than the long hours of physical stress endured by the stereotypical missionary, however, were the years spent tediously learning new languages; coping with strange customs, cultures and diseases; and carefully teaching about the love of Christ, sometimes in the face of little or no response. Yes, some missionaries died or left because of accidents or disease, but others left their fields because of emotional or spiritual breakdown. A missionary without a strong self-image didn't last long. A missionary without some sort of a functioning support system either fled for home quickly or went "over the edge" into emotional or mental imbalance. We will see our four Friends subjects to be focused and determined people, yet "connected" people who valued others. Had they not been strong willed, they would not have lasted long enough to make the contributions they did.

Andrew Walls strikingly proclaims both the "immense energy, resourcefulness and inventiveness"[7] of American missionaries of the era and their "first-rate technology."[8] Walls's adjectives aptly describe the four Quakers of this book, all of them creating legends of long hours and hard work. Sometimes they were not only inventing *lifestyles* as they went, but also leadership and church structures. Of course, the only patterns they knew were American patterns, so we must be forgiving if they didn't always see how those patterns might have been better adapted. Perhaps what is more amazing is how many times they sensed the need for something new and went looking for it!

Beneath the Surface

If the missionary movement at the beginning of the twentieth century required great commitment and hard work, it also required great faith and vision as it faced the non-Christian, largely rural masses of Asia and Africa and the nominal Christianity of Latin America. Mission efforts face similar challenges in burgeoning, non-Western, industrialized cities in the twenty-first century. On the surface, today's terrain and technology have changed, but deeper down the demands for personal vulnerability, courage, and vision demanded by new cultures seem amazingly the same as in earlier years. *Missions by the Spirit* attempts to capture the unseen stories of these four Quaker leaders who founded and developed significant national movements and contributed greatly to preserving and extending the Friends movement around the world. It is a serious attempt to learn from them and to help propel evangelical Friends and others in the West into still untouched fields, and to help non-Western Quakers better understand their spiritual roots. Perhaps a closer look will even help daughter churches in the non-Western world learn from the successes and errors of their spiritual parents and grandparents.

Beneath their stolid Victorian appearances, Friends at the end of the nineteenth century were saturated in a spiritual gospel and enlivened by Wesleyan revivals. This made them a part of the hugely significant missionary movement that would profoundly alter world cultures and color the geo-political picture for decades to come. Our four subjects followed a holy Jesus of love who they believed had compassion for the poor and a power to transform rich and poor alike. Without the contributions of these missionaries and others who either worked with them or extended their efforts after their deaths, the Friends denomination would likely be a mere fraction of its current size. In other words, without these early-twentieth-century missions, the Friends movement might have come close to death. The same can be said for a number of other Western evangelical denominations. Instead of dying, however, Friends have joined other evangelical movements in a major harvest around the world that has reestablished Christianity as a largely non-Western religious movement.[9] And for the first time in their relatively short history, Quakers at the beginning of the twenty-first century are clearly more non-Western than Western in culture.

The following chapters claim that such international Christian workers not only saved the Quaker movement from a great eclipse, but that they displayed certain insights of the Spirit that are profitable for fellow evangelicals to consider. As with missionaries from other denominations, these Quakers did not have it all put together.

7

They failed in some ways when others succeeded. Their unique insights from the Holy Spirit, however, made significant contributions to the theory and practice of cross-cultural ministry that must be pondered and employed. The way they made decisions, the way they showed compassion, their concern for the spirituality and purity of the church, and their vision for an empowered and independent church can be profitably studied.

Four Friends Doing Missions by the Spirit

I invite you, then, into the world of Arthur B. Chilson, R. Esther Smith, Everett L. Cattell, and Jack L. Willcuts—four Quaker missionaries who were founders, statespersons, and visionaries. Arthur B. Chilson was a Midwestern "mechanic" from Iowa, Ohio, and Kansas who thought he could repair and build almost anything in east Africa, and he was mostly right. R. Esther Smith was from Indiana and Kansas, trained as a teacher, and became an inner-city mission worker in California. Her mission work went down in shambles and up in smoke in the great San Francisco earthquake and fire of 1906, but she responded to what she thought was God's voice to give her life away in Central America. Everett Cattell was a brilliant young pastor and administrator from a region of Ohio that was quick to become industrialized. Church leaders wanted him to attempt the impossible—to revive a nearly dead mission work in an unresponsive region of north India. They laid hands on him and prayed and he answered God's call, going on to become a world statesman for Friends and evangelicals in general. Jack Willcuts grew up in rural Kansas and Idaho with something of a nervous disposition, but found his niche in cities in Oregon and South America as a self-trained theologian/writer. An advocate for the truly self-governing church, his friendly spirit and gentle good humor helped him burrow his way into hearts everywhere.

Within the Friends movement, all four of these individuals became well known as speakers, and across the United States they were acknowledged as leaders even before their deaths. Each of them recruited and directed others to become missionaries. The three men married and raised families, and they passed down strong international interests to their children and grandchildren. R. Esther Smith became known and celebrated as "Mother of us all" to generations of Guatemalan Quakers.

The four people selected for study represent considerable differences in personalities, spiritual gifts, and geography (where they came from and where they served). Some were humorous and some not so much! Not all were charismatic leaders, although all four may have been catalytic apostles—self-starters who knew instinctively what needed to be done and found innovative ways to accomplish it. Not all were superior intellectuals, but at least two were careful systematic thinkers. Not all were successful cross-cultural evangelistic church planters, but at least three contributed hugely to church planting, and the fourth, Everett Cattell, moved into a strategic support role for church planters and evangelists across all of India. These four missionaries were not of one mind in their attitude toward culture, and neither were they of one practice in how they tried to build churches independent of missionary supervision. They also came from four different Friends communities (yearly meetings) in the United States (Mid-America, Southwest, Eastern Region, and Northwest) and went to serve in four distinct regions of the world—Africa, Central America, Asia, and South America. But all were stunningly committed to sacrificial service, honestly believed the Spirit of God would lead them, and trusted the Spirit would transform individuals and societies through their efforts.

As our story opens in the American West of 1900, Friends had just experienced fifty years of revolutionary revival and the creation of a pastoral system—the first pastoral system in their 250 years of history. Friends had already begun efforts to break out of their Anglo-Saxon cultural cocoon inherited from Great Britain. They started permanent ministry in places like Palestine, Jamaica, Mexico, Alaska, Japan, Madagascar, China, and India *before* 1900, but the number of new Christians in those locations was still small and most of those works were not destined to permanently leave large numbers of Friends Christians. It wasn't until after the turn of the century that new efforts took deeper root and the Friends Church greatly extended itself. For Friends, the "great century" of increase was the twentieth century, with nations entered between 1900 and 1930 experiencing the greatest growth. And contacts made much earlier—especially in China, India, and South Asia—began to bear greater fruit in the latter half of the twentieth century.

This is a story, then, drawn from the American Friends missionary movement of the early twentieth century. It's a story saturated by holiness revival, consumed by a belief that God changes hearts and lifestyles, convinced that women are equal to men, and confident of the human potential found in all cultures touched by the Spirit. This is a story of three men and one woman who preached salvation by faith, lived out a full consecration to the work of the Holy Spirit in the heart, believed in and promoted social justice and compassion, prayed for physical healing, and exhibited an enthusiasm for the soon return of Christ.

Of course, they were creatures of their times, with foibles and limitations. They may have, on occasion, naïvely confused Western civilization with conversion. Even so, they recognized (and lamented) some of the evil encroachments from outside cultures and looked for ways to affirm some of the old, disappearing non-Western ways. They sometimes failed to be fully sensitive to the work of the Spirit in and through indigenous cultures; they did not have the advantage of the social sciences to analyze cultures that one hundred years later we Christians employ. At times they may have even argued harshly with their colleagues, blindly missed God-given open doors, and wasted time on a few fruitless enterprises. But they loved God, they persisted, they carried a vision for spiritual transformation, and they did not attempt to build personal empires. They were rugged individuals, but not lone-ranger individualists who drove people away from Christ. They were ethical people who knew their public and private lives mattered and that their silent testimonies counted more than the elegance of their words. They were pastoral people who loved others deeply, leaders unafraid to lean forward into pain and conflict on behalf of the flock.

Many fascinating aspects of these people's lives still lie unstated or undiscovered; this is a series of stories about missionary theory and practice, not a series of biographies. But common themes emerge from their lives—core message, integrity of life, equal concern for faith *and* practice, and belief that a spiritual gospel radiates from a personal Spirit who communicates Jesus Christ to individuals and to societies. Their stories express a concept of conversion as a spiritual transformation and a commitment to evangelization as reconciliation and peace with God and neighbor. Their lives exhibit similarities in leadership expressed through sensitivity to consensus and community. They practiced equality and defense of the poor and oppressed in surprising ways. They carried a concern that new churches might reach their full, independent, and autonomous potentials—free of dependency upon the West. Self-aware as Quakers, they believed Friends needed to contribute to the mosaic of an emerging, Christ-centered community of faith in the non-Western world.

Only as we look back can we categorize these four as something of pioneers. Not one of the four was the first evangelical in his or her nation of service. All four were aware that the "real pioneers" had already appeared on the scene, and that they were—to a large degree—following in the tracks of others. Each of them, however, was a *pioneer for Friends* and honored a call to fresh evangelism. The Quaker traits they carried into their ministry lent a certain character to their work.

Reflections:

Why do you think Friends (Quakers) were relatively slow to join the movement of world missions?

To what degree do you think the negative stereotypes of missionaries have been fair or unfair? How does the author seem to defend the work of twentieth-century missions?

Which Friends values does the author believe colored the missionary theory and practice of Quakers serving internationally? Which of these values seem especially necessary in today's world?

Arthur B. Chilson

chapter 1

Called to Africa

Childhood and Waiting

ARTHUR BENTON CHILSON was born near Marshalltown and
LeGrand, Iowa, on June 16, 1872, and divided his childhood
between school and the workshop of his father's hardware business.
He didn't learn much about faith from his father; he looked to his
pious mother for that part of his identity and values. From his father
he learned mechanics, and by the time he was a teenager he was
adept at metal work, plumbing, carpentry, brickwork, wheel repair,
and road construction, as well as grain milling and the growing of
Midwestern grain crops. A photograph of seventeen-year-old Arthur
shows a chiseled chin and strikingly deep-set eyes beneath a wide,
handsome forehead. In a snapshot showing him at age thirty (still
unmarried), he is onboard a ship bound for Africa and is formally
dressed (with hat in hand), leaning casually between his two com-
panions and smiling broadly into the sea breeze while an American
flag flutters in the background.

His good humor and bright spirits were formed in a Midwestern America where people wrested a living from the open plains and
brought a settled existence to terrain largely unsettled only a generation earlier. Perhaps by coincidence, perhaps by divine appointment,
Arthur took on the task of changing the terrain of Africa to make it
more livable.

Although he grew up in a community influenced by a local
Friends meeting and his mother had ties with Friends, Arthur's life
became more intimately linked with the things of the Spirit when he
was sixteen and he felt drawn to Christ through the Wesleyan and
Holiness revivalism sweeping Iowa Friends in the 1880s. A Quaker
pastoral system took shape and was adopted by Iowa Friends to
disciple the large numbers of nontraditional Friends who had just
become believers and followers of Christ. Initially his conversion
came during a revival series of "protracted meetings," as they were

called among Friends. It seemed to bring no great emotion, but he accepted exhortations to wait patiently for the "witness of the Spirit," which then came in a few days with a flood of joy. During morning worship not long after his conversion—perhaps during open worship—he felt he heard a clear voice asking if he was willing to be a missionary in Africa. A few years later, the call to full surrender and a life of holiness came forcefully to Arthur.[1]

Arthur's sister spoke of "his shining face [and] beautiful smile" shortly after his conversion.[2] Three years later when he experienced what he would call a "second work of grace," he came to feel the Holy Spirit had filled his life and was his companion and friend for life. This was a "personal acquaintance, not some vague experience, not a mere professed 'second blessing,' but a living reality, a walking and talking with God."[3] His gift in public ministry was recorded by Friends in 1899 when he was twenty-seven years old, three years before he undertook his first missionary journey of discovery to Africa with colleagues Edgar Hole and Willis Hotchkiss.

Despite his joyous, early experiences of the Spirit, Arthur's journey into public ministry wasn't without hurdles. Arthur faced a crisis with his father, who longed for Arthur to join him in business. Arthur prayed frequently for his father, and felt responsible for a "good testimony" before him. Even though father Harry Chilson staunchly opposed his son's talk of missionary service, Arthur enrolled at William Penn College in Iowa and began work in a nearby "city mission" where one convert under his youthful preaching went on to become superintendent of the mission.[4]

Arthur later accepted employment in a factory near Chicago where he learned to "make anything, from a hoe to a threshing machine,"[5] and then went back to Iowa to a large hardware store where he combined "secular" employment with weekend preaching in country churches with his brother Carl.[6] In time Arthur moved up to weeklong preaching at revivals and continued to do so for much of his life between the mid-1890s and his departure for Africa in 1902.

Holiness and Missions

A decisive turn came when Arthur Chilson decided he needed better theological and biblical training and moved east to Cleveland, Ohio, to enter the newly founded Cleveland Bible Training School (known later as Cleveland Bible College, then Malone College, and eventually Malone University) under the direction of wealthy Ohio Quakers Walter and Emma B. Malone. In Cleveland he once again joined the inner-city mission work, which was considered standard preparation for anyone planning for pastoral or cross-cultural service.[7] Arthur formed lifelong friendships in Cleveland, and Friends from the area welcomed him home as one of their own for years to come, and for a while his financial support was underwritten by the Training School.[8]

Arthur pursued his theological and biblical education at the height of the so-called "Bible-school movement" in American evangelicalism, stirred by revivalists like D. L. Moody. The sharp focus on "training for Christian workers" tended to give way to more comprehensive liberal-arts Christian education later in the twentieth century, but in 1900, Midwestern and Western Friends were deeply involved in "Bible schools" in Huntington Park, California, and in Cleveland, Ohio. Similar schools arose later in Chicago (later Vennard College); Portland, Oregon, (Portland Bible Institute, later Cascade College); and in central Kansas (Friends Bible College, later Barclay College). A network of Quaker educators like William Pinkham, Dougan Clark, the Malones, Edward Mott, Esther Frame, and others maintained a strong vision of salvation by grace indissolubly linked with individual moral transformation, social uplift, and care for the oppressed. They proclaimed the necessity of a total consecration in order to have the power to carry a gospel to a world languishing in sin and darkness.

Salvation Army-style rescue missions looked for jobs for the unemployed and for prostitutes, cooked food, and handed out clothing, as well as provided rent money and beds for homeless wanderers and families, and vocational training for men, women, and children in a context of warm evangelical faith. The American urban waste-land of a rapidly industrializing society at the end of the nineteenth century contained pits of despair and social ills. Wealthy Friends visiting Cleveland Bible Institute workers on the streets of Brooklyn, New York, sniffed at the workers' naïveté. They took exception to their theology and evangelism, but allowed that they were brave and well meaning, suggesting that their "minds were cramped by too much Bible study."[9] Whether or not such inner-city ministry was always effective, it was the crucible in which Arthur Chilson and other missionary candidates of his day were formed, and where they learned to touch the lowest of society and attempted to connect them with hope in Christ.

The message of "a second definite work of grace" was preached, prayed, and embraced enthusiastically. This second defi-nite work of grace was sanctification capable of establishing a full and willing consecration to the Holy Spirit, and at times this was preached to be the eradication of the root of sin. Being sold out to God meant having victory over petty self-centeredness and a capacity for love that is impossible without the fullness of the Spirit—"helping [the] friendless, in visiting the shut-ins, and in being all things to all men."[10]

It was at Cleveland Bible Institute that Arthur's theological temperament was clearly established and where he met a young businessman named Edgar Hole and a furloughing African mission-ary named Willis Hotchkiss. Edgar Hole and Arthur Chilson were strongly drawn to the exotic stories and pioneering adventures of the older man, Willis Hotchkiss, an alumnus of Cleveland Bible Training School, who had just returned from a term of service with Africa Inland Mission in British East Africa, Kenya Colony.

Together the three young men made plans for Africa and for an organization they began calling Friends Africa Industrial Mission. With Willis Hotchkiss taking the lead, they spoke broadly among many Friends yearly meetings about their vision, raising both finan-cial and prayer support. Nine yearly meetings appointed representa-tives for a board that was propelled forward by Walter and Emma

Malone, who encouraged them in every way possible. Emma Malone served as first secretary of the board, and her vision of Wesleyan and Quaker holiness and social transformation through the preaching of a biblical gospel was deeply impressed upon the three new workers destined for Africa.[11]

The Great Adventure

The diaries of Arthur Chilson and the memoirs written by his wife together paint a picture of high adventure and humble service as the three young men—two of them married and leaving families behind (only Arthur Chilson, age thirty, was single)—embarked on the S.S. St. Paul from New York to London. The Malones and others went to New York City to see them off, and the men set out to find a location for Friends in Africa. The deep sense of commitment to God and love for the Savior led them to active witness on board the ship. "We seem to be attracting considerable attention on board," Arthur wrote.[12] "The everlasting arms of God are round about me and His glory fills my soul even though . . . it may be, I will never see [my loved ones] again here [on this earth]."[13] Given the abysmal mortality rate for Europeans in nineteenth-century Africa, the threat of death was real.

The three men's visit in the British Isles included Dublin Yearly Meeting sessions, where Arthur spoke of the moral degradation of Africans he had not yet met: "While the moral condition is beastly, God is abundantly able to transform it."[14] They stayed on for two weeks to attend London Yearly Meeting in hopes of stirring up interest in missions and to be a blessing by preaching holiness. Wealthy Friends in both Dublin and London treated them royally, despite their strange American accents and their confusion over British teas, currencies, and protocols. It was, after all, Arthur and Edgar's first time outside the United States and their cross-cultural training had been limited to the inner cities of America. Arthur appreciated British generosity, but sensed at the Woodbrooke missionary training school in Birmingham a different kind of spirituality from what he knew back home in Cleveland.[15] "With all their money and brains, they [the British] can't save souls without the Holy Ghost," he wrote.[16] His abiding concern, repeated over and over in the diary of his journey, was to win souls and proclaim the holy life in the Spirit.

On other occasions, however, he enjoyed spiritual fellowship and warmth of reception with some British Friends. For example, the cordial way the British Mission Board received Arthur and his colleagues was "so unlike England!" Arthur quipped.[17] He felt many in the Yearly Meeting sessions, however, had not been converted to Christ, and most had not experienced the fullness of the Holy Spirit. He knew this was partially English reticence—perhaps even hiding true spiritual depth. He acknowledged that "the English are hard to get started, but when started are hard to stop."[18]

George Cadbury, the Quaker industrialist and a part of the Cadbury chocolate empire, entertained the missionary trio at his palatial estate near London, yet Arthur saw him and his family as "real simple and Christians."[19] Perhaps as much as anything, Arthur's accounts of the visit to England reinforce an image of him as a fervent evangelical, eager to win souls, eager to preach the baptism of the Holy Spirit, and basking in every opportunity of public ministry. He brims with joy and the presence of the Spirit. "Our God is with us." "Emanuel." "I am rejoicing in my Savior tonight." "I am resting sweetly in my Master's arms."[20]

The time with the British paid off. Within two years, British Quakers sent off to Kenya a dismantled superstructure of an iron building that was erected at the Kaimosi compound and that formed the shell of one of the first permanent buildings there. Various British Friends supported Arthur in his missionary and industrial efforts in Africa over the years, even sending a medical doctor and major donations to the mission in Burundi close to the end of Arthur's life. Arthur's correspondence with British Friends continued into the mid-1930s. From separate correspondence, we know that George A. Fox, the founder and leader of the British Evangelistic Band in the early twentieth century, met Arthur in later years and thought highly of him.[21]

Arthur celebrated his thirtieth birthday in the British port of Aden, now modern Yemen. He was single, ardently Christian, bound for Africa for an undetermined length of time, and ready to forego family status, comforts of home, and who knows what else! He wrote longingly of a dear friend back in America he thought might become his wife some day. Family life eventually became extremely important to him, but at this point his commitment was to ministry as a bachelor.

Willis Hotchkiss

While the three were still in England, Willis Hotchkiss's words and behavior began to grate on Arthur. Willis's competitiveness with his younger colleagues was annoying, and he found it difficult to be second at anything.[22] In Arthur's opinion, Willis always pressed his own judgment forward.[23] Willis thought to invite Fred Krieger, a British acquaintance from his Africa Inland Mission days, to join them for the survey trip, but Edgar and Arthur objected. Willis submitted to their views, however, and Arthur was pleased with Willis's decision. Thus, the initial party of investigation was only American.[24]

On other occasions, Arthur appreciated Willis Hotchkiss's preaching and the British response to him. During the sea journey, Willis instructed Arthur and Edgar in Kiswahili, the unifying trade language of East Africa, and the language Arthur came to use most commonly in preaching. But Arthur struggled to overcome a spirit of criticism toward Willis when, for instance, Willis shaved his beard, apparently prompted by the presence of young ladies on board. "Will the Lord bless him? I am glad to commit him and all his faults to the dear Lord. I expect Willis sees more faults in me than I do and I suspect he don't [sic] see nearly all."[25]

Willis Hotchkiss was a somewhat controversial figure, probably dashing and exciting in his presentations about the "Dark Continent" and about his four years of experience (1895–1899) with the newly formed Africa Inland Mission (AIM). Arthur met him at the turn of the century, when Willis was back in the United States after having been a part of the AIM pioneering group of seven led by mission founder Peter Cameron Scott. Scott himself died in Africa within the first year, leaving Willis and others in confusion and disarray. By all accounts, those four years with AIM were wracked by threats from hostile Africans, fever and disease, cultural estrangement, and discouragement.[26]

Willis's first book, *Sketches From the Dark Continent*, was read broadly among Friends from Ohio to California and sparked Arthur Chilson's interest in Africa. It became the rallying call for the cause of Christ in Africa among Friends, as Willis separated himself from AIM for the purpose of establishing a Friends mission to Africa. The Africa that Willis Hotchkiss first experienced and wrote about had suffered at the exploitative hands of outsiders and unscrupulous insiders, but he had few resources and little experience to interpret the causes of what he saw. Willis spoke to a comfortable Victorian world and showed appalling contrasts between African and Western culture. He seemed to assume that those cut off from Christian influence had lost all cultural values and sensibilities and that the degradation of the African heart, mind, and spirit was supreme—no respect for life, for women, for children, for industry, for economic planning, or for social organization. He wrote,

> The African's history is one long record of war and carnage, rapine and murder, horrid superstition and frightful abomination . . . . Tribe arrayed against tribe, the conflict goes on: the weaker crushed out of existence or assimilated with the stronger. . . . Melancholy sight! Slaughtered manhood; enslaved womanhood; blighted childhood; burned villages; ruined fields; charred and blackened valleys where once was peace and plenty![27]

Who were the culprits of this devastation? Willis Hotchkiss blamed fratricidal conflicts among Africans themselves and Arab slavers, but also the European "leeches of humanity which have been sucking the native's life blood."[28] There seems to have been plenty of blame to pass around.

Africans initially looked upon Willis as an agent of the white British government. It took time for Africans to observe that Willis did not surround himself with an army contingent to maintain his safety. His Quaker sensibilities demanded that he not "fight, and kill and devour, in the effort to extend His kingdom."[29] He knew he had to "win patiently the confidence of the Africans," a refrain also commonly found in the diaries of Arthur Chilson. Specifically, Willis tried to gain African confidence by sowing kindness and healing to violent enemies.[30] Even though the relationship between Willis and Arthur began to sour before the three young men set foot off the transatlantic steamer, Willis's approach to the African people to ministry in Africa contributed to the formative influences upon Arthur Chilson.

Another influence upon Arthur was Willis's view that the African mission was not so much charitable and philanthropic as it was spiritual. He did, however, describe it as an audacious civilizing enterprise, placing his confidence in "a divine potency in the gospel of Christ to reach down to the lowest depths of African beastliness and transform it, creating these lost ones anew in the image of God."[31] There is no reference to tools to analyze and appreciate culture, but he longed for a transformation and felt assured he knew how that transformation would come about.

Arthur Chilson's mentor believed Africans had a moral conscience. He knew, for example, they were hungry to end warfare and that God was not pleased with killing. Additionally, he attributed to special saving grace the Africans' appreciation for the beauty and fragrance of a flower, something he declared was not part of African sensibilities before the gospel touched them.[32] (Contemporary observers would not agree with him.)

The culture gap between African culture and Willis Hotchkiss, Arthur Chilson, and Edgar Hole was wide indeed. During his first term in Africa with AIM, Willis encountered ceremonies of demonic trance and the work of the witch doctor. Although he was aware of some Semitic influences at work in the history of East Africa, resembling Old Testament practices,[33] the specter of African animism was a shock. He wrote that the African imagination was filled with "vague, terrible shapes, ever ready to pounce upon them and rend them with pain or disease...so the weary round of sacrifice, and offering, and dance must need be in order to stay the evil."[34]

Once in Africa, Arthur and Willis came to be increasingly at odds with one another. Arthur felt this was due to a spiritual problem in his colleague's life, and on one occasion felt "led to speak plainly" to him about it, "and the Lord blessed us in it. It was hard to do but I believe it was right. May he die to self."[35] The conversation with Willis stayed on Arthur's mind into the next day, but Arthur felt he had done his duty, felt the burden lifted, and reiterated to his journal once again that there "is certainly a work of grace for him he has never received."[36] The following day, Willis was once again out of sorts ("pouting"), but by evening was more congenial.[37] And so it went. The relationship continued up and down for months, and consistently Arthur felt Edgar Hole was on his side in opposition to Willis Hotchkiss.

One could easily interpret from the accounts of the first months together that Willis was not so much unsanctified as he was suffering from depression and probably missing his family back in the United States, something Arthur Chilson could hardly understand. The relationship between the two was not helped by the fact that the younger missionary, who had less experience with the culture of Africa, may have had superior experience in industry and labor.

After one particularly bad day of glumness and tension, Arthur writes, "O, I wish [Willis] could get saved from himself."[38] The next day Willis was still upset, saying "many mean little cutting things." Arthur attempted to keep sweet; instead of replying he wrote in his journal about how wrong he felt it was of Willis to act one way back home and quite another in Africa.[39] This did not look like holiness to Arthur Chilson.

Arthur had developed a great deal of mechanical, industrial, and "hands-on" experience since childhood, so he had much self-confidence on matters of construction. Willis, on the other hand knew "very little about building houses, but thinks he knows it all,

22

of course." Arthur admitted to himself that Willis knew how to build grass houses and he did not, but that Willis moved ahead on things that to Arthur looked mistaken. "It is mighty trying," wrote Arthur, the would-be "engineer" who was eager to do it the American way.[40]

Arthur was an orderly person, and his experience in Midwestern business and farming helped him form strong opinions. Willis managed to put in a garden "every which way"—not in the neat rows Arthur favored. Arthur spoke to Willis about it.

> O how mad he got. His face got white with anger and he said a lot of mean cutting things and has kept it up all day on every occasion, but I simply let him talk and O how I bless God for keeping me. These things are all for my good. It's as good as being in a red hot revival....I know God sanctifies and keeps, bless his name. This diary would be a mighty revelation to a good many people.[41]

"A revelation to whom?" we might ask. Perhaps it would have been a revelation to hoodwinked supporters back home who naïvely trusted Willis Hotchkiss. Or perhaps Arthur felt his thoughts on Willis's loss of temper and lack of holiness would be a revelation to Willis. Or perhaps could it have also been a revelation to any young missionary who was learning how to deal tactfully with a more experienced missionary.

The group disagreed over the conducting of devotions with African workers, over common worship among the missionaries, over the placement of buildings, and over the conduct of mission business. Arthur favored decision making according to the Friends concept of consensus around the will of God; Willis Hotchkiss favored parliamentary procedure.[42] Edgar Hole wondered about the rightness of the workers using tobacco, but Willis strongly opposed doing more than to use moral reasoning with the workers. On this Arthur agreed that they ought not to make a ruling against paid workers using tobacco, "so it rests for the time being."[43] Willis Hotchkiss had liberal ideas about purchases and indebtedness; Arthur and Edgar opposed debt. Willis built a "fearfully ungainly outhouse," and while he was gone one day, Edgar and Arthur tore it down and rebuilt it more to their liking, "a neat little round one that is a real ornament to the place."[44]

With the passage of the weeks and months of their first year together, Willis Hotchkiss increasingly took on the symptoms of emotional depression—he was withdrawn, silent, moody, prone to anger and fits of temper. By late January he announced to Edgar and Arthur he was leaving within a month. The home board did not want him to leave, but Arthur felt Willis did not want to be subject to others.[45] In Edgar's tent, Arthur and Edgar prayed together for Willis.[46]

The Final Break

Willis Hotchkiss left Kaimosi on February 20, 1903, less than a year after sailing for Africa. He was ready to return to his wife and child. Wrote Arthur: "My heart is heavy for Willis. He left for home this morning. I tremble for his future."[47] Despite the troubled relations and frequent clashes of opinion that marked their ten months together, Arthur came to move beyond thoughts of Willis's lack of spirituality to express a deep sadness and sense of loss as Willis left. "My heart has felt rather lonely here on the station alone [Edgar Hole was gone briefly], but the Lord has been with me and has blessed the work of my hands."[48] They had bonded in some ways as Arthur nursed Willis through bouts with fever and dysentery. Yet Arthur never came to trust Willis and kept him at arm's length, even in later years.

When Willis returned to Kenya in late 1905, he established another "industrial mission" at Lumbwa among a neighboring ethnic group. One of his biographers refers to Willis Hotchkiss as a loner[49] and others initially attracted to him left Willis's work and joined with Arthur after only a few months with Willis.[50] Months after his departure, the field council dealt with charges against Willis and counter charges from Willis back in the United States and in letters from the mission board.

Although conflicts surrounding him were sharp, Willis deeply influenced Arthur. They shared core doctrines from the Holiness

Movement and believed world mission was an outworking of God's transforming power in the world. In this we can see traces of the postmillennial optimism of the age—an emphasis that Arthur later repudiated in favor of the premillennial return of Christ, or "the soon return of Christ." Arthur Chilson responded to the call, the great adventure was launched, but interpersonal tension had broken the team.

Reflections:

What important experiences and learning do you see in the preparation of Arthur Chilson for a lifetime of missions? Are there lessons to be learned?

How do you evaluate the emphasis upon holiness? Why was it so important to Arthur Chilson?

How do you deal with shortcomings in a leader like Willis Hotchkiss who seems to have accomplished so much?

What lessons can you learn from tensions among Christian workers?

chapter 2

A Great People to Be Gathered

DESPITE DISUNITY AND SOME SADNESS over interpersonal relationships, the three young men from Cleveland Bible Institute maintained a vision of a great many people to be gathered to Christ. They set out to accomplish this goal by using Western industrial arts to win a hearing for the gospel—a strategy they declared to be suitable to meet the unique needs of Africa. Theirs was an industrial project, but "controlled" by the impulse for evangelism among all people.[1] They did not seek to only change social conditions, but to create a "self-supporting, self-propagating native church" as effectively as possible.[2]

The Industrial Mission

Willis Hotchkiss's vision for an industrial mission had been quite clear back home in America, and was never seriously challenged by Arthur Chilson or Edgar Hole. Wrote Willis:

> Now [this] is precisely what we mean by Industrial Missionary work. Not converts merely, but strong *healthy* converts: not life merely, but enough life to *propagate* itself; a life that can stretch...and make them feel. We mean to help the African so to change the conditions that surround him as to realize the highest possible ideal in the Christian life, and so make him a positive force in the advancement of the Kingdom of Christ.[3]

Those words themselves do not necessarily make it clear that Willis and Arthur intended to carry Western social norms and lifestyles into Africa. Willis goes on, however, to draw a contrast between missions to Africa and missions to the cultures of India, China, or Turkey. In those other locations, "the acceptance of Christ in individual lives must be left to work itself out in the social environment."[4] Africa, on the other hand, was not a "semi-civilized people with subtle philosophies [and] social structure based upon law....[Rather it is] barbarism pure and simple, with its social anarchy, lawlessness and consequent instability of character."[5] It would seem Willis Hotchkiss at least, felt Africa was especially deprived of civilization.

As painful as it is to admit, Willis's view of African culture likely had a formative influence upon Arthur Chilson. At the beginning of their work, the men had little or no understanding of animistic culture, its forms, its virtues, or ideals. In later years, Willis came to appreciate the sense of community in animism, the capacity for loyal friendship, the respect for nature, and the love of family. But initially, Arthur heard from Willis mostly about African "idleness and ignorance…frightful cruelty, unparalleled suffering, and hideous atrocity."[6] The Hotchkiss solution to the problems he perceived was careful training in habits of industry to overcome the "usually weak, vacillating character" of the African.[7]

At this stage of his experience Willis felt that once he and the other missionaries established friendships with Africans, they were "quite ready to work for the white man, and especially the missionary,"[8] and that industrial work was quite superior to itinerating preaching, bringing "speedier results and…more permanent results.[9] There was no question: These Quaker missionaries believed it necessary that civilization be carried along with the gospel for the church to prosper.

The problems with this approach were many, of course. The true depth and nature of African civilization went largely ignored. The strategy to extricate converts from the target culture and its darkness tended to alienate the new believers from their culture. The witness of a new convert to his ethnic unit was not directly encouraged at first, and in practice was at times actually hindered by the African's close association with the missionary. Cultural overhang (that is, what today we would consider unnecessary cultural change) was not considered a problem. In essence, the industrial mission was defended not in biblical or theological terms, but rather in practical and "commonsense" terms. It was more efficient than itinerate preaching and more rapid than waiting on the Spirit to work its changes from within. Willis Hotchkiss specified he did not want "to wait until the reception of gospel wrought the change," which, he noted would take unnecessary "years of time."[10] The concept was quite clear that while the gospel has power to change from within, an industrial mission would speed things up and bring the church to maturity faster and more permanently.

Africans and non-Africans would later beg to differ with Willis Hotchkiss, so much so that in the 1960s and 1970s, some called for a moratorium on Western missionaries to Africa. Andrew Walls, a Scottish missionary statesman from West Africa, later cried out for patience in the West while Africans sorted through their own priorities theologically and culturally, much like the West did in the second and third centuries in the Roman Empire as the gospel moved from a Hebrew cultural base to a Greek cultural base.[11]

Cultural Imperialism?

Given Willis Hotchkiss's approach, do we need to say that the Friends Africa Industrial Mission was an unmitigated fiasco of cultural imperialism? While Willis declared, "We do *not* believe in the theory that a man must be civilized before he can be Christianized," he went on to assert, "We do insist that Christianity and civilization go hand in hand."[12] The civilization to which he referred, of course, was *Western* civilization, the only civilization with which he had had much contact. While the industrial mission was laudably concerned for the whole person, it was explicitly a vehicle for Western ways. This ideal dominated Friends ministry in Kenya for two decades and in some ways is present still today, as seen in Friends involvement in secular education in western Kenya.

How could such cultural imperialism have possibly produced a sizable church, the spiritual body of Christ, and speak to the deepest longings of the human spirit? For one thing, even though the Friends Africa Industrial Mission was a fatherly model of bringing Africans out of their "childlike slumber," as some called it, there was also a deep confidence that Africans had potential and were fully capable of a significant change of heart and lifestyle. In 1937, thirty-five years after the mission was founded, Willis wrote that "Africa is

29

growing up."[13] Second, the goals of self-support and self-propagation established the belief that Africans were capable of great achievements.[14] Third, these missionaries were compassionate men who genuinely wanted to express love and care for mind, body, and spirit. Fourth, and perhaps most important, western Kenya contained a burgeoning population highly receptive to social and political change, open to listen to the preaching. In the Christian message of these Quaker missionaries, the people of Western Kenya found a deep spiritual satisfaction.

What does it mean that the population was receptive? Many Kenyans were looking outside themselves. They were smart enough to see the winds of change worldwide and "began to understand the full implications of the colonial situations," that is, that East Africa was becoming a "white man's world" and if they were going to cope, they needed the white people's tools.[15] The white people had the power, and here were some white men willing and eager to share technology that was believed to be the road to power. Furthermore, the African population was large and the number of converts grew rapidly enough that cultural overhang by a relatively small number of missionaries did not have nearly as great a negative impact as it might have. African culture remained far more intact than one might have expected.

And in some ways, these three Quaker missionaries did not conform to the "secular" Western white people's culture they were thought to represent. By prioritizing spiritual needs over physical needs, they gave space for the Holy Spirit to work in hearts, and they had an abiding concern for the elevation of the status of women, mentioned frequently by both Willis and Arthur.[16] Neither the spiritual concern nor the concern for human equality was on the radarscope of the colonial administrators. Certainly, the ultimate goal of the industrial mission was conversion to Christ, and the programs of education, industry, and medicine were often permeated with opportunities to proclaim Christ as Lord. Acceptance of Christ was the goal, not *simply* Westernization. Perhaps it's only the wisdom of hindsight a century later that allows us to be critical of cultural insensitivity.

In his final years, Willis Hotchkiss defended missionaries against the charge of unnecessarily changing cultures: "Missionaries are often blamed for introducing innovations for which they are in no way responsible. Most missionaries want the African Christians to remain essentially African rather than to become an imitation European."[17] Yet we can wag our critical finger back at Willis and note that his own accounts of transformation by the gospel are essentially accounts of changing culture—seen in mention of clothes, permanent brick buildings, and settled agriculture, with occasional references to the opposition to polygamy, beer, warfare, and the oppression of women. Quarries, roads, buildings, mills, farms, and clothing were seen to support and encourage sexual morality, business integrity, better health, and longer life,[18] and to some degree he was right. Willis was culturally alert enough to recognize years later, however, that the benefits of Western culture were not all salubrious, and that Western vice had been accepted along with Western virtue.[19]

Perhaps we can breathe freer when we come toward the end of Willis Hotchkiss's life and find he openly admitted to the patience Africans had with him over his cultural errors. "I was [at times] glad at things that ought to have made me sad, and I was chagrined over things that ought to have delighted me....[I] did learn after awhile. And one's mortification is modified by the knowledge that those were the days of ignorance concerning native customs generally."[20]

We can only speculate how closely Arthur Chilson followed Willis Hotchkiss in his developing attitudes about African culture, but we see there may have been some differences. Soon after arriving in Kenya, Arthur fretted over the danger of the industrial feature "becoming too prominent."[21] Yet he was attracted to the self-support issue, not so much self-support for a church that did not yet exist, as self-support for their own mission efforts. He believed the industries they were introducing would allow interpersonal relationships that would commend their teachings. He believed in holy living, integrity, the power of the Spirit, and living victoriously in hard circumstances: "I am proving some of my own preaching these days and it stands the test it was the truth."[22] Fair treatment of Africans, he felt, would commend their beliefs and help win their trust.

The Founding of Kaimosi

The trust toward white men that Arthur was looking for was in short supply as the threesome wound their way upcountry from the coastal town of Mombasa, taking the first passenger train on the newly completed Mombasa-Nairobi-Kisumu route, ending on the shores of Lake Victoria in western Kenya. On the human level Willis, Arthur, and Edgar had valuable contacts with AIM workers and British colonial administrators. They needed all the help they could get dealing with malaria, the hostile Nandi ethnic group, unreliable hired porters who occasionally abandoned them, and disagreements among themselves. They also prayed regularly for divine guidance and protection, and Arthur particularly longed for a deeper spiritual fellowship and a shared devotional life with Willis.

After traveling and camping for about six weeks from Kisumu north into what was known as Maragoli territory and among the Kavirondo people, both Willis and Edgar were feverish and ill. The only able-bodied man of the three, Arthur was frantic to find a healthy camping place for his comrades and the porters, and finally climbed a tree and spied a grassy slope at a distance. They set up camp and within a few days of further consideration it became quite clear that the place qualified as a location for their industrial mission. It was a tract of unoccupied land with a stream of water that had a good falls and rapids providing good drinking water. And there was heavy timber nearby—all of this located at a healthy 5,300-foot elevation.[23] On August 11, 1902, Arthur recorded, "I guess we are at last located, glory be to God. Of course it isn't final yet."[24]

Within three weeks they settled in with their extensive personal belongings brought from the railhead at Port Florence and nearby Kisumu. The sense of God's guidance was strong: "I feel that this is my home and my wanderings for years is over, for the Lord has brought me to the place he promised me and he is going to give me souls for my hire. O, I do love him tonight,"[25] Arthur wrote in his journal.

Language Learning

The three young men had settled among Luragoli-speaking people, most of whom did not speak Kiswahili, the trade language Willis Hotchkiss had studied. Arthur wanted devotional meetings for the newly hired porters and workers at Kaimosi, even if their understanding of Kiswahili was minimal. The task of winning the confidence of the Africans was difficult, but Arthur wanted to get started. His commitment was to be "filled with the Holy Ghost so that they [the porters] will see Jesus in me."[26] Nevertheless some of those very porters abandoned their loads along the way and new porters had to be secured.[27] With very little shared language, the barriers were high between the two cultures and misunderstandings were frequent.

Arthur early began praying that God would "give them [him and the other missionaries] the language," specifically the gift of tongues to communicate to the people. He felt if they could unite in prayer God would answer, but they found it hard "to unite on anything."[28] The pleas to God for help with language continued a week later: "I wonder why the Lord don't [sic] give me the language. I am still trusting him for it."[29] Later yet, he called in his helper and read a portion of the Kiswahili scripture to him and talked, fulfilling a deep longing to proclaim Jesus. This was quickly followed by a number of other individual teaching times and his first steps in language learning, both of Kiswahili and Luhya.[30] "O how I wish the Lord would give me the gift of tongues," he prayed once again after five months in Africa.[31]

Language never came to Arthur Chilson supernaturally, but by February 1903, he was leading mid-day devotions with the workers in Kiswahili and enjoying it immensely. He preached his first sermon in the language on February 22, 1903, "and the dear Lord graciously blessed me in it. O it is such a privilege to tell the story even in such a lame faulty way."[32] For a mature man past thirty years of age, his language learning was going well.

On March 2, 1903, after Willis's departure, Arthur and Edgar received the heartening word that missionary reinforcements were on their way from the United States: a medical doctor and his family;

Edgar's wife, Adelaide, and their young daughter; and Emory and Deborah Reese, talented linguists with training in African languages in South Africa. This rather sophisticated team approach meant the Reeses were henceforth assigned primarily to language learning and translation, Dr. Elisha Blackburn to medicine, and Edgar and Arthur to industrial work and evangelism. With the passage of time, Arthur leaned more and more toward public preaching in evangelism and revival, so language was crucial for him and his Kiswahili abilities increased.[33]

Recognizing the importance of going beyond Kiswahili, Arthur very early valued the mother tongue Luhya language. Still he wished for a supernatural gift: "O, if He would give the...language. I can't understand why He don't [sic] unless it is because of Edgar's unbelief for it."[34]

A year after the Reeses' arrival, Arthur began studying language more seriously with Emory and Deborah. They talked over the language situation and Arthur was impressed by Emory Reese's good judgment and spiritual life: "I believe he is in living touch with God and He will lead him in the Truth."[35] Emory and Arthur spent evenings together reducing the language to writing—a big job but intensely interesting to both of them. His diary at this point no longer mentions his team "getting the language," but says in fact they are "getting it" through linguistic studies[36] as they set about gathering vocabulary and bits and pieces of grammar, surely under the strong influence of Emory Reese.[37] Two months later he also spent time with a Kiswahili teacher who came to their aid in Kaimosi. "I do want to learn to speak it correctly,"[38] Arthur wrote. He humbly declared that he spoke it "so frightfully incorrect, Swahili even worse than my English."[39] His journal regularly mentioned language study from this point forward.

Winning Confidence

For most of the time, the task of winning the trust of Africans went in a very practical direction, accomplished through Arthur's working alongside his African neighbors. He regularly oversaw construction of homes, storerooms, and roads, and as the industrial mission took shape, he tackled any number of other mechanical and agricultural tasks. He kept himself consistently busy even when, after an injury, he could not use his own hands. His capacity for hard work may have intimidated and even irritated those closest to him,[40] but in his journals he asked God, "keep me sweet," and he asked God to help him see everyday labors of life as "for the Lord" in the presence of the African observers.

His journals frequently recorded irritation with fellow workers, probably because no one could keep up with him and his joy for hard labor. He worked so hard physically that his clothes were constantly wearing out and needing repairs. He patched his trousers on the knees and groused to himself that "Edgar is so stiff and prim that he doesn't wear out his clothes much, and Willis does very little work and of course his clothes don't wear out much."[41] Yet he often recorded a sense of blessedness in his work, no matter what it was,[42] and all the while he was rubbing shoulders with Africans, directing them, correcting them, and supervising their manual projects.

Arthur's strong and certain opinions may have irritated even Edgar on occasion but their relationship was such that they could confront one another. While working on the construction of the iron house shipped from England, Edgar talked with Arthur about being "too positive." Wrote Arthur, "and I expect possibly I am and I am going to with the help of the Lord be less so....I am so glad Edgar loves me enough to tell me my faults for I know I must be O so faulty but I want to constantly get less so."[43] By "positive" Edgar seems to have meant opinionated and strong willed. How did this play out with the Africans? In later years Arthur became known as "Shiganga," probably literally referring to his strong shoulders and neck, but variously interpreted as "benefactor" or "protector."[44] While this clearly referred to the paternal relationship Arthur had with the Africans, it also indicated a respect for his caring work and his willingness to go shoot the threatening leopard or the marauding baboons as a favor for friends. His hard work made friends and built relationships.

35

Loneliness and Marriage

Arthur had another issue to face during the earliest days in Kaimosi, this one very personal. He was unmarried and lonely. Regularly he pined for mail day in Kisumu and then the arrival of a courier after the eight-hour walk to Kaimosi. Some days a letter from his friend Sulu would arrive with banter about family and friends. One day she sent word she was leaving the millinery business, and he was glad for that. At Christmas time, Sulu sent a hand painted calendar for the year 1903, which he treasured.[45] On other mail days, nothing arrived. He longed for Sulu's companionship and for marriage to her, and he expressed trust in the Lord for that to happen.

In May 1904 Virginia Blackburn, Dr. Elisha Blackburn's wife, gave birth to a baby girl. This seems to have exacerbated Arthur's loneliness and awareness of his lack of family. "I hope the Lord will give me a wife and children some day."[46] Ten weeks after penning these words, his longings emerged once again: "I have longed for loved ones today, for one with whom I could visit. I need to get married. God only knows how hungry my heart gets for the companionship of one who is a very part of me. Dr. Blackburn's boy's wife gave birth to a child today. I am so glad for it will have a good influence on the natives."[47] On August 31, 1904, he expressed great disappointment, although he did not disclose the cause: "I am sad at heart today. While I know keen disappointment will come, still it does hurt."[48]

Arthur's journals never mention Sulu again. But about two years later in Wichita, Kansas, Arthur renewed a casual friendship with the stately, charming, and musically gifted Edna Hill during his first furlough in the United States. They had known each other briefly at Cleveland Bible Institute when Edna was a student and Arthur was being commissioned for Africa.

After a rather whirlwind courtship in late 1905 and early 1906, while Arthur was visiting churches and recovering from a number of illnesses, they married in Indiana. Married at last! Arthur and Edna then interviewed with the mission board in nearby Richmond and received the board's "stamp of approval" for them to return to Kenya together.

Nandi Opposition

Back in Africa during Arthur's first stretch of service before his furlough, the neighboring Nandi tribe became hostile to European encroachment. They tried to exercise sovereignty over the region by sending raiding parties to steal cattle from the Kavirondo people among whom the Friends missionaries lived. Crossing through Nandi territory was somewhat precarious. The British offered armed guards to the missionaries, but they refused, wanting to place their trust in God, not in human weapons; they desired to leave a less warlike impression.[49] At one point, Arthur felt led to go out to meet some of the Nandi, and eventually found them receptive and friendly; they were even childlike in pulling each other's hair with curiosity and laughter.[50]

At one point the missionaries received a credible threat that a hostile band of Nandi might come and attack Kaimosi with the purpose of killing the white people.[51] Three weeks passed and threats continued. Nandi were seen lurking in the forest around the station. Arthur felt that divine protection kept the missionaries from harm.[52]

A month later some of the Kavirondo workers quit out of fear of the neighboring Nandi,[53] and a few months later fighting broke out again.[54]

In April 1904, a year later, war talk intensified. The colonial government sent armed African soldiers to punish lawbreakers.[55] "It is sad but from the government's standpoint necessary, but it is barbarous,"[56] Arthur wrote. A month before that, a young pacifist Friend from Boston named William Wendte came to Kaimosi to explore how Friends peace principles might work among hostile peoples. Although Arthur felt uncomfortable with Williams's brand of spirituality and wondered if he really knew the Lord, Arthur welcomed William to travel with him and to observe activities.

During one particularly sharp battle between colonial police and the Nandi, William wandered into the forest in the direction the fighting. He and one of the armed guards were killed by the Nandi, their bodies left mutilated in the open forest. The next day, Arthur went searching and found the bloodied and hacked bodies full of arrows, and returned them to Kaimosi for burial. Conversations in later years made it clear the Nandi did not truly understand what was happening—why the armed officials had chased them and looked upon them all as thieves trying to steal "their" cattle. William Wendte was thought by the Nandi to have been one of the colonial officials, not a guest at Kaimosi.[57]

Arthur felt confused and sad about William. He had prayed with him and for him and they traveled together. After his death, however, Arthur found evidence that William was harshly critical of their work and of him personally, even while receiving their hospitality. In papers Arthur found among William's belongings, William accused Arthur of being "intolerant and uncharitable" while Arthur looked upon William as mentally unbalanced, having walked into the line of fire.[58] The interchange is telling. Unprogrammed and non-evangelical pacifist William thoroughly disapproved of Arthur and the evangelistic focus of the mission. By this time in Friends history, the divide between evangelical and non-evangelical strategy was fairly wide. Although the Chilson diaries lament the loss of life and barbarities committed on both sides, the missionary band engaged the African culture differently than did William. Arthur did not directly oppose William's pacifism, but felt "none but a crazy man would have done what he did," and that he suffered from "a disorganized brain."[59]

William Wendte's death was followed by further days of turmoil and government investigation. The killing of a white man was taken seriously. Up to two hundred soldiers and three government officials moved into Kaimosi. This did not please the missionary staff,[60] nor did the government suggestion that the missionaries get armed soldiers to protect themselves. Said Arthur, "This is asking what we cannot do. It would be an insult to God but we must refuse in such a way as not to offend the government. O, I wish they would stay away with their soldiers and leave us alone. Our Lord can protect us vastly better than the government can."[61] Quaker pacifism was alive and well among these evangelicals who saw their primary task to be that of winning confidence and sharing faith without resorting to armed protection.

Faith Healing and Arthur Chilson

During the exploratory journey and for years later, Arthur Chilson prayed for the gift of healing. Shortly before discovering the campsite at Kaimosi, Arthur felt discouraged about prayer for healing. He could not "get hold of the Lord to heal [Willis]," but attributed it to Willis having a lack of faith to believe for his own healing.[62] Porters carried Willis twelve miles during his illness, and Edgar, too, fell ill with a fever. Arthur prayed for Edgar and he began to improve quickly, while Willis continued to improve only slowly.[63] Later, as the malarial cycle once again took its toll on Edgar's body, he spent most of the day in a malarial sleep. In Willis's opinion, Edgar would not make it in Africa. Arthur defended Edgar, feeling firmly convinced that Willis was looking for an excuse to send Edgar home because he had blocked Willis's desires at times. Although Arthur wanted them to trust in God alone for Edgar's healing, Willis called a European doctor from Kisumu. Arthur accused Willis in his journal of praying outwardly for Edgar without actually believing God would help him.[64]

The doctor arrived and worked with Edgar, who was in a stupor again. Writes Arthur, "If God don't [sic] touch him, he isn't long for this world."[65] Willis talked about sending Edgar home even if he did recover from the fever, but Arthur felt that was not God's will. Deeply troubled, Arthur spent most of the night in prayer for Edgar. By the next day, Arthur was still trying to hold on in faith, but Willis's words discouraged him. Willis blamed Edgar's illness on heat exhaustion and an inability to adjust to the climate, but the doctor declared it was a very severe case of malaria.

At a point when Arthur was alone with his friend Edgar, he felt led to lay his hands on Edgar and command the fever to go away in Jesus' name. Edgar seemed to improve from that time.[66]

The day after Arthur laid hands on Edgar, Edgar was conscious and improving. Arthur was assured the Lord had touched him, and Willis stopped talking about sending Edgar home. Arthur wrote that Willis "is praising God for answering **our** prayers" (emphasis by Arthur). He went on to say that he thought Willis

> had no faith in his or my prayers and even talked so discouraging that it was hard for me to get hold of the Lord. I believe if he and I could have unitedly laid our hands on Edgar and prayed in Jesus' name that the Lord would have heard and we wouldn't have needed a Doctor. Jesus is my healer as well as Savior and coming King.[67]

Six days later, Edgar continued to improve. The doctor said he was improving ahead of schedule and didn't understand his quick recovery. But Arthur understood: "It is the Lord answering prayer, bless his name."[68]

Edgar Hole, the recipient of Arthur's prayers, did not fully agree with Arthur's aspirations for faith healing. About a year into their Africa adventure they had a "plain talk...about Divine Healing," Arthur wrote, "and I find I am really alone in it. O may God keep me true [that] he and the others and these natives may see the power of God."[69] In Athur's defense, his great concern was for witness, and while the term *power encounter* had not yet grown popular in missionary circles, that was the burden he carried. He wanted God's power to be visibly seen by Africans. Furthermore, Arthur never seemed to reject the use of medicines or doctors and had excellent fellowship with the mission's Dr. Blackburn, but he clearly longed for the visible expressions of the power of God. At one point he refused quinine and preferred "to trust Jesus."[70]

In his earliest years, Arthur Chilson used the language of the Pentecostal Movement that had grown out of the Holiness Movement he knew so well. His expectations, however, came to be different from Pentecostalism. God did not always heal, but sometimes he did, and Arthur came to accept that the outcome was not merely a matter of one's faith and unity of belief, but depended also upon the sovereignty of God. Every day of good health and no injuries was a cause for rejoicing. Rather than a meaningless repetition of thanks for health, he saw daily prayer for the body as a vital part of living in a dangerous place where every day one faced heavy manual labor and the potential for injury and disease.

The first five years of Arthur Chilson's missionary career allowed him to launch his career, learn one new language well, and experience the personal turmoil of establishing a new cross-cultural ministry. Willis Hotchkiss's influence was without doubt important, but Arthur clearly stood apart from Willis while maintaining commitment to an industrial mission and to the Holiness Movement. Before returning to America and marrying, Arthur had helped establish a beachhead in Kaimosi for a large ministry, despite many obstacles, and had built a reputation for hard work and self-sacrifice.

Reflections:

In twenty-first-century terms, the Friends Africa Industrial Mission in Kenya was attempting to be "holistic," combining economic and lifestyle betterment with evangelism. As popular and attractive as holism is, can you see potential problems with this approach?

Arthur Chilson and the Friends pioneers in Kenya did not always see eye-to-eye with other Europeans there. What differences did they have? Is it important to maintain "independence" from political powers?

What do you think were the key methods Arthur Chilson used to build relationships with Africans?

chapter 3

Chilson and Evangelism

MARRIAGE WAS A MILESTONE in the life of Arthur Chilson in many ways. At thirty-four, he was no longer quite so young! His first three years in Africa (1902–1905) took a toll physically, but renewed by rest, secure financial support, and a lifelong companion, he returned to Kenya in 1907 with great enthusiasm. Arthur and Edna Hill Chilson, who left America as well-known speakers among Eastern and Midwestern Quakers, formed a strong team as preachers and musicians. Although they worked and sang together, Edna served as a preacher and teacher in her own right as a recorded Friends minister.

Arthur and Edna's supporting board was still known as the Friends Africa Industrial Mission, although financial support and interest was drawn largely from what was known as Five Years Meeting of Friends (now Friends United Meeting). The American Friends Board of Foreign Missions of Five Years Meeting was incorporated in Richmond, Indiana, in 1901, but at first served mostly in a consultative capacity. By 1913 the Kenya mission (the industrial mission) that had functioned independently but drew support almost exclusively from among Friends, was officially handed over to the Five Years Meeting. The Chilsons' ties with Five Years Meeting continued until 1928.

First Steps in Evangelism

During the first two decades of the twentieth century, "civilizing efforts" in Kenya reigned supreme and culture changed rapidly. Simply building a road produced a fascinating chain reaction. By building roads, Europeans encouraged oxcarts. By introducing carts, oxen and not women became beasts of burden and oxen could be used for industry rather than for dowries.[1] On other fronts, the common people turned away from witch doctors and tried Western medicine, which in turn changed leadership patterns in village communities. On a spiritual level, the missionaries believed they saw the power of Christ surpassing the power of darkness.[2] Geographically, the people of western Kenya were also on the move. The area around Kaimosi that in 1902 was relatively unpopulated became home to hundreds in the next few years. These recently relocated Africans were receptive to new ideas of all kinds.[3]

The Chilsons did not work alone but were members of a talented team of educators, medical people, builders, teachers, industrialists—and evangelistic preachers. Small thatched chapels sprouted up, followed by more substantial, permanent meetinghouses. Arthur continued arduous work in the building of roads, dams, and houses, but very early he began a pattern of itineration to African villages on Saturdays.[4] He met head chiefs, exchanged gifts, made friendly conversation, and requested permission for public gatherings. Some chiefs were friendly; others were less so. Some requested schools for their children, and across the years some sons of chiefs were received into boarding arrangements on mission stations.

Before his second term of service, Arthur's first witnessing opportunities to Africans were most often one-on-one in his tent or room in the evenings after work. For example, his helper Faragui began asking for nightly lessons, at least partially in Kiswahili.[5] Another evening three young men and the cook came to read the Bible with him.[6] "The boys" (probably the working men) would slip into his room at night to listen to Scripture and to talk, always building Arthur's hope they would soon accept Christ.[7] As language proficiency increased, so did the witnessing and preaching. When on his feet preaching, Arthur never felt "more sure of [his] call,"[8] and he felt his call was to preach.

Earlier, one of the first tensions between Willis Hotchkiss and Arthur Chilson had to do with teaching the African employees. We don't have Willis's side of the story, but Arthur eagerly accepted all such opportunities for teaching and tried to create new opportunities. But according to Arthur, Willis objected to the morning devotional gatherings. One might suspect Willis's objection was due to the work relationships; perhaps he felt the workers would feel pressured to convert merely to please their white bosses. Certainly there were conduct problems with the workers and the missionaries responded with punishment. One worker lied, another was caught stealing beans from a native field, and another was accused of killing a sheep.[9] One young man was caught with a young girl in one of the huts and was discharged.[10] Arthur's helper Faragui took a second wife under pressure from his first wife and a non-Christian interpreter employed on the station. Arthur told Faragui in no uncertain terms, "If he wanted two wives he would have to take them and go. [But] he wanted to stay. The interpreter took the other wife for himself."[11]

Between the major industrial and building projects undertaken, Arthur also mended gashes, cleaned ulcers, and pulled teeth. A simple school was started and passed off to Edgar Hole, giving Arthur more time for manual labor and weekend itineration,[12] a pattern he continued for years to come.

Arthur and others used the African custom of *shauri,* a sort of community council or conference of elders, to discuss official matters and to take first steps in more public witness. Sometimes the *shauri* was initiated by an African or a colonial official. Sometimes Arthur or a missionary used the same method to share their faith or to solve disputes.[13] On one occasion Arthur tried to use the *shauri* to make peace among non-employees.[14]

Slowly but surely, village itineration paid off, even though Arthur wore out a pair of shoes in two or three months.[15] With time the mission council united with Arthur in his concern for itineration and relieved him of some mission-station chores to give time for travel.[16] Arthur found himself learning to love the people more and more,[17] and occasionally an African would speak his heart to him about having experienced God's forgiveness.[18] Beginning after about two years in Kenya and continuing on through 1928, Arthur gave preaching responsibilities to some of his closest Kenyan worker friends, building a pattern of shared ministry.[19] In the earliest years, the itineration was limited to a Saturday, walking out and back home to Kaimosi on the same day. Sometimes a chief would offer a room for the night or build a hut for the visitors. Sometimes Arthur took his own tent.

45

Early Church Planting

On Sundays, the industrial work was laid aside and large numbers of Africans, both men and women, began attending the Sunday worship programs at Kaimosi.[20] Attendance varied according to weather conditions, but people were listening and considering the message. Understanding often seemed limited, however: "It is such a privilege to tell the people of the Lord but so hard to get them to understand."[21] While the *shauri* might have had moderate attendance, the Sunday gatherings at Kaimosi were larger, and sometimes included a great many non-Christians. On the occasion of a big dance, Arthur spoke to several thousand. "It was a blessed privilege. Now I must soak the message in prayer."[22]

At one weekday morning service, one of the workers spoke up and said he wanted to go to heaven. "O how it thrilled my soul." Wrote Arthur, "If I could only tell him the story in his own language."[23] On weekends and on shortened workdays, he would gather his gear and travel to a village and talk especially with women and children.[24] On other occasions, the relationship-building took place by attending funerals—and there were many. Within a few years, a seekers' class was developed and held on Sunday afternoons, and this later turned into a probationers' class. A two-year probationary membership became standard among Friends throughout Kenya and was the pattern for the new work in Burundi decades later.

While so many mission histories recount the work of the expatriates, a Kenya Friends mission-council meeting of 1911 is instructive in its attention to the African church itself. Of the seven points of discussion, six deal with the emerging infant African church. How should the church be organized? How should African marriages be regularized? How should teachers be trained? How should offerings "in kind" (like eggs, meat, and corn) be used? How could congregations support their teachers financially? How could various congregations be networked?[25] In that same year, the gathering of African Christians came together with representatives from Kaimosi, Vihiga, and Lirhanda—the beginning of a quarterly meeting regional church structure.[26] Rather than merely maintaining and

46

promoting the institutions controlled by the mission, the heart concern was for the church!

Levinus Painter noted a significant breakthrough in conversion evangelism that took place about 1916 or 1917 that assumed "the proportions of a mass movement under the effective preaching of Arthur Chilson and his associates."[27] Prior to this, the number of converts had been modest, but now hundreds and at times a thousand attended services at Kaimosi and Maragoli. The consistent pattern, however, was the requirement of careful instruction for two or three years before full membership was achieved.

Emory Reese and Edgar Hole wanted to concentrate activities in a few centers, but Arthur Chilson and Jefferson Ford argued for rapid expansion into new communities. By 1917 there were more than fifty village congregations with schools at most of the same locations. The pressure of Roman Catholic advances may have contributed to the desire for more rapid expansion.[28]

Ane Marie Rasmussen, a Danish sociologist writing in the 1980s, portrays Arthur Chilson as a leader in evangelism, pressing forward into new regions of western Kenya, zealously calling for new missionaries to counteract Muslim and Roman Catholic incursions nearby.[29] For Arthur to accomplish this, African involvement was essential. In his diaries, Arthur records and affirms the great value of Kenyan preachers and teachers, but in a letter to the mission board in 1923, he encouraged "a wise, firm, loving control" by the mission to guide such teachers and preachers.[30] Thus Rasmussen saw a turning in Arthur's mind in the early 1920s toward "the preservation of what had already been won."[31] In twenty-first-century terms, this might suggest more concern for leadership training, for church development, and for church discipline. Modern church-growth advocates would press for both vigorous evangelism and "perfecting ministries" simultaneously, encouraging national initiative in outreach wherever there was receptivity, but standing with the Africans in intense theological and practical instruction. In other words, discipleship and evangelism go together. Rasmussen is undoubtedly right that Arthur Chilson was pressing for ministries to perfect the existing church, but he hardly advocated an end to new evangelism. If he is to be criticized, it may be for his paternalistic control, not for his desire to see a holy church with believers well discipled.

By keeping the boundaries of ministry continuously expanding, Arthur Chilson likely contributed to less cultural overhang and to more indigenous cultural elements within the churches. Donald McGavran declares that rapid expansion with relatively few missionaries tends to affirm indigenous cultural forms. There is some evidence Arthur was concerned to develop such African forms. For example, he built a permanent brick building in a modified African design, perhaps attempting to use African architecture, says Painter.[32] Nevertheless, by the time of the writing of the 1920 field report, their stated objectives were still both to evangelize Africans and to Christianize the social order.[33] Decades later, we might wonder if "Christianizing" of the social order was not actually "*Westernizing*" the social order, as was happening broadly throughout East Africa.

Church Discipline

As already alluded, another example of mission control lay in missionary involvement in church discipline. By most accounts, including that of Ane Marie Rasmussen, Friends adhered to a stricter moral teaching and standard than the neighboring Roman Catholics or Anglicans.[34] "Heathen customs and homemade beer" were the most common vices, especially among the elderly.[35] "Heathen customs" were likely the practices of witchcraft, polygamy, smoking tobacco, lying, and stealing. On one occasion, an African elder recommended that faithful African Christians always be present when seekers were being counseled by the missionary in order to avoid deception.[36]

On another occasion when church discipline was being considered, Maragoli Monthly Meeting posed the question to the missionaries: "If a black Christian makes a mistake, will the white people alone judge his words, or will they judge him together with a few black people?"[37] We don't know how the missionaries responded, but the force of the question seems to ask that blacks be included among the elders who disciplined new Christians. It seems they were asking for a change. Perhaps African Christians were more eager to be involved in discipline than the missionaries thought. We don't have an authoritative list of discipline issues, but teaching Christian marriage relationships and tithing were among the most serious topics in the church.

How much did the missionaries allow their Western culture to unnecessarily color their judgment, and how much did they build sensitive relationships, allowing Africans to form their own judgments? We may never know. But we can safely assume the foreigners had come to Kenya with a preconceived liking for Africans and that the Africans were likely predisposed to imitate the love they experienced.[38] Arthur Chilson's diaries confirm his deep love and affection for his African colleagues.

Vernacular Language

In some ways, the Americans were ahead of their day. The British "strongly advised against" teaching English to Africans, and evidently felt few Africans would ever need to speak English. Language superiority helped secure a sense of permanent control over the African protectorate. Church of England missionaries urged the use of Kiswahili as the basic language of education for all of East Africa.[39] In contrast, Friends felt they could get closer to the people by using Luragoli, the major tribal language of the area. Vernacular language study was approved and time allotted for the missionaries to do so.[40] In 1921, the Missionary Alliance of British East Africa discussed the adoption of a common Bantu dialect to be used in translations. Friends had already settled upon Luragoli in their schools fourteen years earlier, and the translation of the New Testament into Luragoli was well under way.[41] Friends were well ahead of the curve on the use of the vernacular.

Vernacular language learning aided not only verbal communications but gave insight into culture and traditions. The gospel presented in Luragoli seemed less foreign and more a part of Kenyan culture than it would have if presented in Kiswahili.[42] Local language informants collaborated with the mission from the very earliest days. Ahonya, one of the first converts and Arthur Chilson's personal helper, was especially useful as an interpreter for the Reeses and assisted in their mastery of Luragoli.[43] While Emory Reese is credited with the greatest impact on vernacular study, Arthur Chilson, Jefferson Ford, and others collaborated fully in the project and their families became fluent in Luragoli. Under the linguistic leadership of the Reeses, the Luragoli New Testaments arrived in western Kenya in 1927, while the Chilsons were still present. Arthur's close African colleague, the local pastor Joseph Ngaira, directed the unloading of the packages and led the celebration,[44] suggesting Arthur was closely involved also.

The Emerging Friends Churches of Western Kenya

By 1928, Friends in Kenya practiced a number of significant distinctives, which stayed prominent for years to come. Arthur Chilson had taken leadership in organizing and establishing the first congregation in Kaimosi in 1907, and Friends built their organization around the local congregations rather than around bishops or a hierarchy outside the local meetings. The absence of outward ordinances stressed the simplicity of Christian faith, which they generally viewed as a help rather than a hindrance to understanding basic Christianity.[45] Africans lived in an integrated world where faith, health, education, and culture blended into one mosaic. Friends' industrial-mission practice may well have tended to affirm a unity in the culture rather than a separation between the spiritual and the material.[46] The Quaker concept of male and female equality argued against plural marriage and brought a Christian influence upon family life.[47] The vernacular language had become uniformly used in music, preaching, and church business meetings. Friends conducted business without formal votes but rather by group discussion and decision making, "not too different from the procedure in conducting tribal affairs."[48]

The emerging Friends church formed largely by Arthur Chilson and other American Friends faced the awkward challenge of British white settlers establishing farms in some of the most productive of Kenya's highlands, at exactly the same time the Friends mission was rapidly developing. On the one hand, the white farmers offered employment for some of the better-trained workers from Kaimosi and from other Friends stations. Some of the workers who became Christians and received basic education among the missionaries rose to managerial positions, and some new Christians even helped establish churches and schools for Africans on white settler farms. On the other hand, however, the white settlers often treated their workers poorly and were resented by Africans. The American mission was sometimes caught in the middle and accused of arrogance against the Africans. The Mau Mau Rebellion of the mid-twentieth century grew partially out of this simmering anger. The Mau Maus classified white missionaries with white settlers.

How do we evaluate the role of the missionaries? Were these American Friends arrogant colonialists demanding conformity to their patterns and plans? Or were they gentle and loving listeners and helpers following the cues of those they had come to love and help? Neither description is totally accurate. The missionaries were indeed aggressive and demanding, sometimes to the point of coercion. Sometimes the missionaries punished their mission station employees, even with beatings or fines, but at least Arthur Chilson cringed at some of the grosser activities of fellow white people and declared whatever he did was "out of love for them." It is not recorded that public beatings were used in Kenya as a form of church discipline for seekers, probationers, or members, but the Chilsons *did* use it on women in Burundi in later years, suggesting it was a pattern they brought with them from Kenya. Public beatings were undoubtedly a custom used within African culture for foolish and unruly behavior. This would certainly be acceptable within the American church, and even in the 1940s was soundly rejected by fellow Friends missionaries in Burundi as being inappropriate and humiliating.[49]

What was the cultural influence of the mission's industrial activities? Levinus Painter maintained that "these Quakers were aware that the Christian message cannot be proclaimed effectively in a social and economic vacuum," suggesting that the sawmill and gristmill and other industrial efforts were necessary to "fill a vacuum."[50] But does such a thing as a "cultural vacuum" exist? European and Western perspectives answer "yes," yet the Africans undoubtedly held a different view. We do get the picture of Western Province Kenyans being quite receptive to European ways, open to change, and alert enough to sense the direction of the political winds. The least we can say is that Kenyans willingly embraced the cultural changes the missionaries brought and that they came under the hearing of the Christian gospel at the same time.

Arthur Chilson, Edgar Hole, and their colleagues may have been father figures to the Africans and may not have understood the limitations that role placed on their African friends. But neither were they dandies served hand-and-foot by Kenyans. The missionaries worked hard alongside equally hardworking Kenyans. After one long day spent preparing the mill pond, Arthur wrote,

> All day I have been working with one of our men cutting the trees down in our mill pond before the water gets too high. I have been in water nearly to my hips all day. I am asking the Lord to keep me from getting sick for it is work I must do, for it is dangerous for one of these natives to be out there alone, for they can't swim and some places the water is nearly ten feet deep.[51]

The Missionary Family in Evangelism

Through Arthur's second term of service (1907–1912), Arthur and Edna busied themselves with several new missionaries, new mission stations to the north of Kaimosi, and the birth of daughters Esther (1908) and Rachel (1910). Arthur now had the family for which he had desperately longed, and the four of them traveled, camped, ate, and preached together. With time, he taught his daughters to ride the motorcycle, to drive cars, to shoot guns, and dispense medicines. The parent-child connectedness was strong first with Esther and later with Rachel.[52] Father and daughter traveled and consulted incessantly while Edna maintained house and home. Yet Edna shared broadly in preaching and teaching responsibilities throughout their marriage. The esteem of these three strong and independent women—Edna, Esther, and Rachel—was extremely important to Arthur. And he felt it essential to live a consistent life of holiness before his family. Their love and respect of him was more important than that of others, and when on one occasion Edna and Rachel teamed up to correct Arthur on an issue, he felt it deeply.[53] In later years, daughter Esther spoke of her father only in the highest terms of honor. The influence of "Father's" teaching and influence upon her was without measure.[54]

Mission Station Evangelism

The typical approach to church planting in the late nineteenth and early twentieth century was the establishment of quasi-colonial enclaves in the midst of African populations. The so-called "mission station" became mission-owned property that offered a number of community services: medical, educational, industrial, and spiritual. Mission employees often lived at the mission station in close proximity to the missionaries in charge. Buildings were constructed at mission expense using Western architecture. Two or three decades later men like Donald McGavran of India began decrying this approach to evangelism as separating converts from their culture and creating an unhealthy dependency upon missionary leadership. From 1907 through 1928, however, Arthur and others thought primarily in terms of extending evangelism by planting new mission stations. As McGavran would have predicted, the first Kenya Friends converts were the male employees, although chiefs and headmen were often sympathetic and encouraged Sunday worship attendance.[55]

Initially the "out-schools" that sprang up—and doubled as places of worship—were very simple affairs, teaching reading and writing so people could read the Swahili Bible. With time missionary Emory Reese created a written form of Luragoli that became the medium of education among Friends for many years.[56] Fortunately, the out-school movement seemed to carry the momentum of evangelism far beyond the first male employee converts at the mission stations, to the point that perhaps something of a dual system developed—one system Europe-centered and the other African-centered. The total management of the mission stations and their institutions remained in missionary hands while schoolteacher/pastors were encouraged to be self-supporting and focused on developing local congregations.

In 1914, as storm clouds of war descended over Europe, a great opportunity seemed to be opening for a new mission station to the north of Kaimosi. In that year the Chilsons returned from their first furlough, touring Palestine on the way to Kenya. Despite the 1885 Berlin Conference that had essentially divided most of Africa among European powers, the balance of power between German East Africa and British East Africa was untried and uneasy. Tanganyika, Urundi (later Burundi), and Rwanda were held by the Germans, Kenya and Uganda by the British. Upon arrival, the Chilsons began working intently with Chief Shivaiki north of Kaimosi, and continued to do so for months and eventually years in a region that came to be known by the station name of Malava. But the British colonial government prohibited Friends from establishing a full-blown mission station, largely because of the war and fears of German occupation. The ban against a new station came in February 1915 and was not lifted until after the close of the war in 1919. In the meantime, the government encouraged road building and did not object to evangelism, so by the end of the war, significant progress had been made opening the region to Christian witness, even without a new mission station at Malava. In retrospect, the Chilsons themselves could see they had made significant progress in evangelism and schools despite the absence of an official mission station.[57] Perhaps the government prohibition allowed for a more culturally sensitive presence to be developed around Malava than standard mission policy would have promoted.

The War Years

Life was hard from 1914 through to the middle of 1920—an overextended term of service for the Chilsons due mostly to World War I and its aftermath. The Chilson children suffered from colds; Rachel fell across Esther's arm, fracturing it, and Edna sprained an ankle all while Arthur was away in evangelism. Commodities were scarce, especially flour; at times of famine the government sent corn to the mission for distribution to the Africans.[58] The witch doctor rainmakers failed to produce rain, prompting the Chilsons to pray that the people might turn to God instead of to the ancestral spirits for help.[59] Arthur had to mediate over a cow stolen by the Nandi;[60] he would also hunt wild game for distribution to the hungry.[61] Toward the end of 1918, many people became ill with the worldwide pandemic of the Spanish influenza, resulting in a thousand deaths in the region.

The Evangelistic Message

Prior to 1928, the East African world was a pastoral world and an animistic world populated by unseen spirits and ancestors that, by tradition, required appeasement through animal sacrifice. Arthur Chilson believed and taught that Jesus' blood was superior to the blood of animals.[62] The traditional emphasis on the sacrifice of Jesus took a different form in Africa than in the West, but Arthur saw a clearly universal message. He wrote that Jesus' blood "was shed as much for the beastly African as for the polished American."[63] To be more politically correct or culturally sensitive, we might want to switch the wording: "Jesus' blood brings forgiveness for either the beastly American or the polished African." The point is clear, however, that Arthur believed the message of Jesus' sacrifice had direct relevance to the African and that it made sense within their culture.

Responding to a Strange Culture

By 1920, Edna lamented in her journal that the girls badly needed to return to the United States for education,[64] and in the fall of 1920 the family began a furlough that continued through 1922. In the United Sates their missionary message drew a dark picture of Africa. A newspaper reported Arthur as saying:

> Every thought of the African's heart is evil. There is usually the most degrading and filthy talk among both men and women. They wear no clothing; live in the crudest of huts together with their chickens, goats,

sheep and cattle. Life is so cheap that a man may be killed for something very small. Out there, only God values life. They are always haunted by evil spirits. Unless they get the message of God, they will live in fear of these evil spirits until their bodies are crowded down into their little Christless graves.[65]

Sacrifice to the spirits, especially ancestral spirits, was an expected part of Kenyan animism.[66] The Chilsons enjoyed the help of Africans Joseph Ngaira and his wife, Mwaidza with whom they worked for many years at Malava.[67] Ngaira was cook for the Chilsons and had earlier played an important role in a village council that approved of Friends entering Kaimosi.[68] Together they faced the challenges of how to hold together African family values without communion with the ancestral spirits. In the non-Christian African mind, the dead and alive dwelt together, and depended upon each other, requiring trances, omens, and offerings. Some believed the dead ancestors reincarnated themselves in other human bodies or in animal form.[69]

The simple outstation schools were often founded just prior to the establishment of a worshiping community. Helen Kersey Ford declared that when a boy came to school, it was often a way of declaring his readiness to become a Christian and a willingness to break with the witch doctor. Those who were unwilling to continue as Christians soon would drop out of school.[70]

The role of the shaman and the role of the herbalist were sometimes intertwined, meaning that illness and medicine and the unseen spiritual world were not easily separated. Arthur and preaching colleague Jefferson Ford quickly became aware of amulets as the focal point of power for the witch doctor. The amulets were publicly repudiated and declared powerless over a follower of Jesus.[71] It was believed that the power of the witch doctor was maintained largely by trickery and deceit.[72] Arthur and Jefferson believed it necessary to break the fear of the witch doctors' taboos in the process of leading people to Christ.[73]

Sometimes Africans believed the shaman to protect the clan against the ancestors, yet in reality people were often tempted to hypocrisy and deceit. The shaman was thus both respected for his power and hated for being a villain within the clan.[74] Right or wrong was usually determined by clan loyalty, so that theft or murder within the family was wrong, but not necessarily unethical if committed against outsiders.[75] People who broke taboos were considered worthy of supernatural punishment. The ancestor cult was one of the primary integrating forces of rural West Kenya, so to challenge the ancestor cult held the threat of disintegrating the entire leadership pattern and ethics of the culture.[76] How well Arthur and his preaching colleague Jefferson Ford dealt with the ancestor cult on a theological level is unclear. But during the 1920s they preached against the ancestor cult and presented Christ as the integrator of a new society.

Levinus Painter, in his history of Friends in East Africa, acknowledges that the Friends pioneers did not really understand Kenyan culture, but he assumes that the basics of medicine, education, and industry were foundational human needs. We, on the other hand, might correctly assume that the industrial-mission approach brought the trappings of European culture in inextricable ways— ways hard for the Africans to accept without their turning away from some of the positive values within their own culture. Might the pioneers have been more sensitive to culture? Probably so, but they did some things right.

One of those "right things" was Arthur's single-minded focus on the goal of evangelism. Yet industrial development remained a strategy that opened doors for evangelism. Some supporters back in America objected to missionaries building milldams when, they felt, they should be preaching. Arthur, however, saw no conflict in these activities, and took a new water turbine back to Kenya with him, while maintaining a clear commitment to verbal preaching, conversation evangelism, and church planting.[77] In 1915, a few years later, he wrote, "We are tempted to feel that we are not doing missionary work [when we build roads]. Yet our stay among these people is beginning to bear fruit."[78] Arthur worked alongside people, got acquainted, made friendships, and then preached and taught; he came to be an expert in lifestyle and friendship evangelism.

Levinus Painter accounts for a relative openness to the Christian gospel because there were fewer basic antagonisms toward outsiders in Western Kenya than elsewhere, except in areas where Islam had already been formally accepted. Tribes in Western Kenya were less affected by the slave trade, and the practice of electing chiefs allowed a relatively democratic process to prevail. Local headmen settled most social issues; these headmen gathered their people into village assemblies to listen to preaching and to receive basic educational instruction from the missionaries.[79]

Some functional substitutes to non-Christian practices began appearing among Kenyan Friends by 1920, often at the suggestion of missionaries. The practice of circumcision was one of the clearest. Village boys ages twelve through fourteen traditionally joined a cohort to live the rigorous forest life for three months under the tutelage of elders or witch doctors in a program considered partially harmless and partially hideous by the missionaries. Many positive values were instilled: Self-reliance, respect for elders, honesty, and hard work. In some places in Africa, a month-long period of Christian training was instituted and circumcision was done at a mission hospital by doctors at parental request.[80] At times, Arthur personally accepted the request to perform the circumcision.[81] Boy Scout founder Lord Baden Powell of South Africa evidently picked up from the African circumcision training some patterns and positive values he felt should be carried forward by Christian boys everywhere. Fred and Alta Hoyt, colleagues in Kenya with the Chilsons, recognized that Boys Scouts in Africa quickly began taking on more Western characteristics, but "tried for years to urge them to keep up their original Bugoosi [good conduct] movement intact."[82]

Once stationed back in Malava (Lirhanda) in early 1923, after the Chilsons' two-year furlough, Arthur resumed travel and evangelism. At times, Arthur kept close to the culture, on occasion sleeping in native housing on safari, although this was not an experience he relished: "It is not a pleasant experience to sleep among natives, chickens, goats, sheep and cattle—to say nothing of smaller things that inhabit the homes of most Africans."[83]

MISSIONS BY THE SPIRIT

Revival Fire in Western Kenya

While there had been hints of larger movements toward Christ during the isolation years of World War I, it wasn't until after 1920 that the greatest changes began to take shape. Five mission stations were in full operation at Kaimosi, Maragoli, Malava, Lirhanda, and Kitosh (also known as Lugulu). A plan for tithing was reintroduced, and in the fall of 1921, board secretary Willis Beede became the first American official to make an extended visit for long-range planning.[84] Strong revival expressions broke out first in Lugulu (Kitosh) in 1924 with confessions, weeping, and solemn decisions for a deeper spiritual life. Arthur Chilson and Jefferson Ford actively encouraged people to make decisions to receive salvation and sanctification and to respond first in silence by raising their hands and then to kneel in prayer.[85] Similar "native prayer conferences" were held in Malava (where the Chilsons now lived), in Kaimosi, and elsewhere.[86]

A 1926 report from the field makes an interesting turn of attention. After the standard recounting of institutional work related to industrial development, schools, medicine, and publishing, the report author turns to the African church. Emory Reese stresses that African self-assertion was clearly growing and that the church was "the hope of the future for East Africa. It must increase while the Mission decreases."[87]

Further revival preaching in 1927 brought large numbers of attenders, many seeking and receiving "the baptism of the Holy Spirit," with Arthur Chilson evidently the central preacher, although Jefferson Ford was very active in a similar ministry. Wrote Edna Chilson, "We have prayed for years for this thing we are seeing and rejoice that we are permitted to see the beginning of such a movement among these people—both young and old; to see the natives weep over their sins, not able to sleep because of the burden."[88]

In public services, people expressed sorrow "for their sins, making things right even though it may mean jail, asking forgiveness of others for harsh, unkind things that have been said, and others praying for and receiving the baptism of the Holy Spirit."[89] But Arthur was concerned it might turn into "wildfire" and that there was a need for wise supervision. He fretted over how things might develop as he and Edna prepared for furlough in the United States, when the Fords were already there.[90] The Chilsons nonetheless were heartened by the repentant spirits and by changes in Christian living. Malava Monthly Meeting, for example, recorded a suggestion to its members that Christian men and their wives eat together at a table, instead of the husband eating at the table alone while his wife and children ate seated on the floor. Additionally, others suggested that men should walk alongside their wives, not ahead of them.[91]

Ane Marie Rasmussen raises an interesting controversy she discovered from Kenyan independent church sources—the degree to which Arthur Chilson participated in and encouraged Pentecostalist-style manifestations. The independent "Holy Spirit churches" point back to 1927 as the decisive year when the native prayer conference was held in Kaimosi. Holy Spirit Church leaders interviewed by Rasmussen in the 1980s recalled Arthur Chilson preaching to Kaimosi school students who received the Spirit in October 1927 and "began to shout and speak in tongues."[92] Something similar happened throughout Maragoli. According to an interview Rasmussen held with Kefa Ayub Mavuru, high priest of the African Church of Holy Spirit in 1975, Arthur himself read Acts 2:1-4, pointing out that "when they shook and spoke in tongues they were influenced by the same power of the Holy Spirit which had seized the disciples of Jesus on the day of Pentecost."[93]

True as it is that the Holy Spirit churches point to Arthur Chilson as their founder, to paint him as a Pentecostalist is simply incorrect. When asked about that possibility, granddaughter Anne Fuqua totally dismissed that as a possibility. She quoted her mother Esther Chilson Choate as specifically stating she knew it was possible to experience the baptism of the Holy Spirit *without speaking in tongues,* because her father's Christian life was singularly marked by holiness but *he never spoke in tongues.*[94] Arthur's diaries certainly affirm he was open to emotional expression and expressed himself emotionally on occasion, as one sees in *Ambassador of the King,* written by his wife, and in letters, which frequently refer to "the baptism of the Holy Spirit." It is highly unlikely, however, that this ever meant the same to him as it had come to mean to the Pentecostal Movement.

Helen Kersey Ford mentions Jefferson Ford's strenuous efforts against "the fanatical movement" when he returned to Kenya in 1929, efforts that continued for several years. Some Africans returned to the Friends movement, others were trapped in "excesses that sometimes led to immorality" and others gave evidence of demonic possession, writes Helen.[95] This was almost certainly related to the same Holy Spirit church movement written about by Rasmussen. In the early 1930s, a large number left Friends permanently for the newly formed Holy Spirit Church, despite Jefferson Ford's successful efforts to reclaim many.[96]

Ezekiel Kasiera, an African writing his doctoral thesis in Scotland, asserted that Arthur Chilson's theological language was more similar to that of Pentecostals, while Jefferson Ford's was more along the lines of holiness revival language.[97] It is likely that Rasmussen correctly identifies four major traits among revivalist American Friends that are embedded within the writings and thought of Arthur Chilson: conversion, sanctification, faith healing, and expectation of Christ's second coming. And, says Rasmussen, it was Ohio Yearly Meeting (and the Malones of Cleveland) that adopted the fourfold gospel most fully.[98] The same is evident in Arthur's earliest diaries and references to the teachings of Walter and Emma Malone. Kathleen Staudt, Rasmussen's friend and colleague, takes the next step and assumes Arthur Chilson himself approved of any and all Pentecostal manifestations of the Spirit, and because of the revival was recalled to America and not sent back.[99] This is highly unlikely, however, and a serious historic misunderstanding by Staudt.

What Kasiera, Rasmussen, and Staudt may have missed as they studied Arthur Chilson was the existence of a somewhat different and broader theological controversy brewing among Friends at the time—a breach between evangelical and liberal theology. Rasmussen, apparently basing her opinion on correspondence from board members Willis Beede and Errol Elliott, came to believe Arthur's "evangelical theology too revivalistic and intolerant of other ways of thinking."[100] Arthur is called "the most uncompromisingly revivalist missionary."[101] The full truth may be impossible to reconstruct, but from Arthur's perspective, the tension between himself and the American Friends Board of Foreign Missions (Five Years Meeting) was not so much revivalism per se, but the authority of Scripture and the holiness message so dear to his heart.

Certainly several new missionaries were assigned to Kenya with whom the Chilsons heartily disagreed. They included Lewis and Ruthanna Moon who stayed for less than one year, Margaret Parker, Elizabeth Haviland, and Edith and Bryan Michener. In 1927 Arthur Chilson and others tried to question Parker and Haviland about their stance on the inspiration of Scripture, but they refused to answer, and General Secretary Willis Beede approved of their non-response. Jefferson Ford in 1930 likewise objected to the Micheners, who he believed did not support the full inspiration of the Bible.[102] Both events clearly upset Arthur and likely contributed to his permanent disillusionment with Five Years Meeting. Diaries from later years in Burundi record communications from the Fords and the Hoyts about those they considered non-evangelical among the new arrivals appointed by Five Years Meeting.[103] At the very least, history would seem to record that the home mission board failed to take into consideration the theological compatibility of some of their new recruits with the evangelically oriented Chilsons, Fords, and Hoyts. At worst, the home board wandered from its evangelical moorings.

Continual evangelism was a theme in Arthur Chilson's ministry, and the development of churches, church discipline, the use of the vernacular language, and a holistic view of culture were intended to complement evangelism. Despite the mission-station approach generally practiced, evangelism spread beyond the stations, carrying a message couched in terms understood by animists. Arthur and his colleagues were serious in presenting a contextualized message, and were ardently committed to revival, the deity of Christ, and the authority of Scripture.

Other events joined in setting the stage for the Chilsons to separate from Five Years Meeting and the mission work of Friends in Kenya. The family accepted a preaching invitation from fellow Cleveland Bible Institute graduate Esther Baird, a missionary in the Bundelkhand province of north central India. The Chilsons left Kenya in early 1928, and traveled to India for this preaching assignment. They then left by way of Arabia, and through the Suez Canal and to Palestine a second time. While in Palestine, Arthur received an official invitation to serve as general superintendent of Kansas Yearly Meeting of Friends.[104] He finally accepted that invitation in the fall of 1929, after a year of promoting missions in England and across the United States.[105] In later years the Chilsons returned to visit Kenya several times. They maintained strong friendship ties with the Fords, Hoyts, and probably others, and received Kenyan visitors in the new field they pioneered in Urundi. But it was their return to the United States in 1928 that marked the beginning of a new life chapter: Arthur's last eleven years of life, spent in the United States and Urundi, Africa.

Reflections:

The growth of the Friends Church in Kenya began early and continued for decades. Why do you think it was so successful? What of that success can be duplicated in our day?

Which of the Friends distinctives displayed in Kenya seem especially important in the planting of new churches today?

How well did the Chilsons and others respond to the new cultural forms they met in Kenya?

chapter 4

A New People to Be Gathered:
The Latter Years

The Kansas Years

FRIENDSHIP AND FAMILY TIES between the Chilsons and Quakers in Kansas grew during the years the Chilsons were in Kenya. In 1928, Arthur, Edna, Esther, and Rachel left Kenya permanently and returned to the United States. Edna's parents had lived in the Wichita area and Arthur and Edna had maintained church membership at University Friends Church. Esther and Rachel, now ages twenty and eighteen, enrolled at Friends University in Wichita and enjoyed playing basketball together, shouting secret instructions to one another in Luragoli. After a speaking tour spanning much of a year, Arthur accepted the invitation to serve as general superintendent of Kansas Yearly Meeting of Friends.

As superintendent, Arthur distinguished himself with constant travel (the railroad lines gave him free clergy passes!), a program of "year round soul-winning," counseling of pastors, and aggressive evangelistic and revival preaching of sanctification as a "second work of grace." He preached in California, Oregon, and Idaho, and was well-positioned for a new round of missionary fund-raising.[1] Arthur maintained the superintendent position in Kansas for roughly four years (1930–1933) before accepting the challenge to find a new "untouched field" upon which Kansas Friends could focus its missions energy.[2]

Funds for an exploratory trip were raised, a serious undertaking in the early depths of the Great Depression. Some funds came from Kansas and some from faraway Oregon.[3] The Chilsons also preached in Ohio before boarding ship for Africa, thus promoting a nationwide awareness of a new field-to-be, someplace in Africa.[4]

There is no official mention of reasons for not returning to Kenya, other than that Kansas Friends wanted an outlet for missionary work. But the Chilson diaries paint a picture of burden and disillusionment with a non-evangelical trend in Five Years Meeting Board of Missions and some of the new staff they assigned to Kenya. The Chilson estrangement from Five Years Meeting was permanent even though warm friendships continued with many of their former colleagues. Rachel Chilson, for example, had a close friendship with Wendell Hoyt, son of Kenya Friends missionaries, and they may have talked of marriage before his tragic death in a motorcycle accident in February 1937 in the United States. Arthur Chilson made one last visit to Kenya in May 1937, greeting the Fords and Hoyts before gathering personal belongings left there nine years earlier.[5] Jefferson Ford had quite clearly picked up much of the spiritual oversight of Kenyan Friends churches, including evangelistic and revival preaching, a continuation of the work Arthur Chilson had done years earlier.[6]

God's Guidance to Urundi

As her husband's biographer, Edna Chilson records a strong sense of spiritual guidance during the exploratory trip. On Arthur's first exploratory in 1902, he had been one of three men. On this second exploratory trip, he was accompanied by his wife, Edna, and daughter Rachel (now out of college). After arriving at the coastal city of Mombasa on the Indian Ocean, they traveled west to Nairobi where they bought a used "box body" vehicle for their journey. They struck out from Nairobi southwest through the Serengeti plains to Mwanza located on the southeast corner of Lake Victoria in the British-held colony of Tanganyika, (now Tanzania), carrying personal supplies and camping in tents as they went. They considered a number of locations in the area before being impeded by muddy roads, sleeping sickness, and tsetse flies to the south. So instead of heading around the south end of Lake Victoria toward the Belgian Congo and the League-of-Nations-mandated territories of Urundi and Rwanda, the Chilsons loaded the car on a lake steamer at Mwanza and sailed north on Lake Victoria to Uganda. They felt it important to visit areas further west before making a decision.[7] Wrote Edna, "We were on a mission for The King; the whole matter was in His hands: He had been in it from the beginning; He would see us through."[8]

Just as Willis Hotchkiss and the 1902 team looked to Africa Inland Mission as a sponsor for Friends in Kenya, Unevangelized Africa Mission helped "sponsor" the Chilsons in Urundi and promised to help secure Belgian approval for their new work.[9] The group proceeded by land around Lake Victoria through Uganda and south into Belgian-held territory, some expatriates receiving them gladly while others—not wanting them to settle anywhere near for fear they might some day want to develop that area themselves—had a "dog in the manger" attitude, said Arthur.[10]

Finding Kibimba

By January 30, 1934 they found their way to the Danish Baptist mission at Musema, Urundi, where they presented letters of introduction from a Belgian Protestant leader and from former president Herbert Hoover (a Quaker), no less, who was remembered in Belgium for his World War I relief work.[11] They were quickly and enthusiastically received and were offered one of five sites vacated by German Lutherans at the beginning of World War I—a site technically designated to the Danish Baptists, but never occupied by them. This began a mutually helpful relationship between the Danes and Friends that lasted for decades.[12]

After identifying the new site (Kibimba), the Chilsons retraced their steps through Congo and Uganda back to Nairobi, Kenya, where they collected their belongings and wired Denmark for Danish Baptist approval of the transfer of a station to Friends. And waited! In the meantime, in Kenya they renewed friendships with Clara Ford and with Fred and Alma Hoyt, commiserated with them over modernist Friends, and waited some more. Rachel began having doubts about her role in a new work, something Arthur attributed to her attachment to Kenya. "The Lord told me last night that Rachel had not died out to the old work. When she does, she will be contented and happy."[13]

Finally, the cable came from Denmark and the guiding cloud seemed ready to move. "We know a little how Moses must have felt at times," wrote Arthur.[14] The family spent a month securing a truck, installing a charcoal-burning gas producer[15] and readying their gear. After another month of retracing their steps from the earlier trip, they arrived back in Urundi at Kibimba (or Kivimba) Station on April 21, 1934.[16] The truck that ran on charcoal made it! The Chilsons delighted in the beauty of the green, forested hills and deep valleys that spread out before and below them on three sides from Kibimba. "This is far and away the most beautiful mission site we have ever lived on,"[17] declared Arthur, who was also deeply pleased by the Urundi African workers the Danes sent to help them turn Kibimba into a European-style center for living.[18]

The Second Time Around

In many ways, pioneering in upcountry Urundi was similar to pioneering in Kaimosi, Kenya. As in Kenya, there were colonial officials nearby, this time in Gitega where the powerless king of Urundi also lived under the watchful eye of the Belgians. As in Kenya, the work was physically demanding—always Arthur Chilson's delight. He willingly lived close to the people and shared life with them in many ways, although he was always the *bwana* (lord) who hired and fired workers. As in Kenya, these employer-employee relationships were the first meaningful contacts with the people who spoke the national language of Urundi—in this case Kirundi. Within days of the Chilsons' arrival, more than five hundred people showed up, wanting work. The Chilsons signed on twenty men.[19] Arthur prayed for God's help in winning the confidence of the people, just as he did in Kenya. Years later Edna observed, "They did not know us nor our people in America. Were we good people? What did we want? Would we leave, after a time, as the other missionaries [the German Lutherans 20 years earlier] had done?"[20] And as in Kenya, says Edna, some of the best friendships began in the very first days, "when men would quietly sit and watch, sometimes talking with [Arthur] or again saying not a word."[21] At this stage of life, however, Arthur had a new tool to attract attention and disarm suspicion: He could perform the oddity of removing his false teeth and did so to the surprise and gales of laughter of the Africans.[22] His was a "cheerful disposition and an optimistic spirit."[23]

Likewise there was a new language to learn, Kirundi, this one also of Bantu origins with some similarities to Luragoli learned in Kenya. For the most part, however, Arthur and Edna continued to use Kiswahili, their first African language, during their remaining years in Urundi. Kiswahili was a less-used trade language in Urundi and the need for the Kirundi vernacular became swiftly apparent. Rachel Chilson, by all accounts, including those of her parents and later fellow workers, was unusually gifted in language learning and began using some Kirundi immediately. Within months she was preaching publicly in Kirundi, and as early as November 1934 she was translating for her father who continued to preach in Kiswahili.[24] Her command of the language only grew with the years, giving her entrance into the homes of sub-chiefs, chiefs, and even the king of Urundi and his family.

Rachel Chilson

Rachel Chilson has a story within this story. Assertive, the life of the party, gregarious, and attractive, she stepped into the role of her father's companion that her older sister, Esther, had with Arthur before Esther's marriage to Ralph Choate. In the early Urundi years, Arthur and Rachel traveled and preached together continually. Arthur labored spiritually over his younger daughter at times, praying for spiritual victory, praying for healing from her frequent headaches, loving her as a precious daughter but fearful over apparent temptations she was suffering. He took pride in her translation work[25] and her fluency in Kirundi,[26] which was better than his own. "How I wish I could speak Kirundi. I can get along with Kiswahili but [O] to be able to give them the Gospel in their own language."[27]

Rachel, however, was distressed over being "an old maid," wrote Arthur. Rachel's friendship with Wendell Hoyt might have been headed toward marriage, but the diaries hint at Rachel cutting off the relationship with Wendell by mail in early 1935.[28] Yet when news of Wendell's sudden, accidental death back in the United States came as much as two years later, Rachel was devastated with grief.[29]

The king of Urundi, Mwambutsa IV, was reported to have had various extramarital affairs, including some with European women.

The exact nature of his relationship with Rachel is uncertain, but it, too, came to be clouded with hints of scandal.

The diaries recount repeated visits the Chilson family paid the king in nearby Gitega. King Mwambutsa IV dressed as a European gentleman, owned a car, and associated with Belgian officials as an equal, but apparently had little real power except that of influence among village headmen and the indigenous hierarchy of officialdom. As a Tutsi he was a part of the ruling class in a complex social network that maintained control over the majority Hutus and the small groups of Twas (pygmies) of the Urundi highlands. In general, the Tutsis were favored by the colonial forces, and received priority in education and in economic opportunities. Arthur repaired the king's vehicle, and along with Rachel bought a used car from him on one occasion. Arthur did other large and small favors for the king, seeking to win his approval and cooperation.

It was not long before Rachel's sister, Esther, and Esther's husband, Ralph Choate, left their home in Greenleaf, Idaho and joined the Urundi Friends team. Rachel's brother-in-law, Ralph, saw Rachel's friendship with the king as a part of a strategy to make friends in high places, among both Africans and Belgian colonialists.[30] This friendship with the king, his brother, and their wives continued on with Ralph and Esther (Chilson) Choate. Arthur's granddaughter, Anne Choate Fuqua, remembers sitting in the lap of the queen in the royal palace in Gitega as a young child. The royals would visit Kibimba for tea or coffee, and the Friends missionaries would likewise visit Gitega.[31]

Within a few years, Rachel became a somewhat self-appointed defender of human rights for neighboring Africans, especially for the new converts; she pled their cases before chiefs and colonial officials alike.[32] Her active negotiating with Urundi villagers included talking schoolboys back into school after a defection.[33] With freedom to drive vehicles and make contacts at the highest level, the ugly rumors began to swirl—at least in African circles—of Rachel's late-night visits with the king. Whether there was substance to the rumors, the king likely had other mistresses and the adding of one more would have been expected in that cultural milieu. Neither the Chilsons nor the Choates ever spoke openly of this suspicion, but some in later years came to believe the rumors may have had some basis in fact. One thing is historically certain: When Rachel Chilson returned to Urundi in 1944 with her mother and with new missionaries George and Dorothy Thomas, she was refused a residency visa while her mother and the Thomases were granted visas. The assumption of some was that because of her relationship with the king, Rachel had become a political liability, a *persona non grata* in the region either with too much power with the king or a potential embarrassment to him. So Rachel moved to Kenya and lived out her life there. She maintained some relationship with Friends, but for part of the time she worked with World Gospel Mission and at other times she worked independently. She continued to be highly revered as a holiness preacher and teacher on her occasional visits to Friends in Kansas Yearly Meeting.

Before her death in Kenya in 1996 at age eighty-six, Rachel had endeared herself to many loyal Kenyan Friends but alienated herself from others. Elisha Wakube, a Kenyan Friend writing a doctoral dissertation in the United States in 1990, gives a most unusual account of Rachel Chilson's objection to having her name read into the minutes of a Friends gathering a year or two earlier. She objected because she did not want to be associated with Friends United Meeting. "I am Shiganga's daughter," she declared publicly and then stalked out of the meeting, Wakube wrote.[34] To Rachel, "I am Shiganga's daughter" would likely have meant, "I am the daughter of the founder, the broad-shouldered man who was a faithful protector of Africans, the protector of Christian orthodoxy, and the man we should remember as a faithful example of servant leadership." She is known to have objected strenuously to Africans jockeying for power and prestige.[35] Earlier, she had asked Wakube, "Will you preach the gospel which our fathers proclaimed in the past? I mean: Chilson, Hole, Hotchkiss, Hoyt and Ford?"[36]

Wakube follows this account with a withering critique of Rachel Chilson's action. He called her behavior unchristian in tone, and he claims she vulgarly used a nickname for her father; he took "Shiganga" to be an insult to her father, not a loving memorial. Wakube labeled her egocentric, setting herself aside from fellowship with other Christians, and "extremely controversial."[37] Exactly why Wakube chose to attack Rachel so vehemently is hard to know for certain. Perhaps he was trying to establish Kenyan Friends' identity with Friends United Meeting and totally separate from Evangelical Friends International, who by the time of his writing (1990) had claimed Arthur Chilson as one of their founding fathers in Africa, specifically in Urundi. There is no real proof others agreed with Elisha Wakube's attitude toward Rachel Chilson, but the incident is important because it reminds us of the close relationship between father and daughter and of the Chilson family history of separation from Friends United Meeting.

Medical and "Industrial" Work in Urundi

As in Kenya, medical needs in Urundi were overwhelming. Within weeks of the Chilsons' arrival, a typhus epidemic prompted Belgian colonial officials to respond with a quarantine and prohibit travel across the region.[38] Within a few months as many as two hundred patients queued up for medicine and simple attention at the dispensary[39] and with time the numbers only grew. On a daily basis, teeth were pulled, wounds bandaged, and ulcers lanced and cleaned. Other emergencies arose during the first years, including a famine and yet another epidemic. When the Choates opened the Mutaho station to the north of Kibimba shortly before Arthur's death, the established pattern of medical dispensaries continued to draw hundreds daily.

Arthur consistently believed that the technological advances white people could bring to Kibimba—bricks, tiles, roads, bridges, and a hydraulic ram to draw water from the valley to the hilltop— would make people favorably disposed toward the missionaries.[40] He spoke of "interrupted days," however, when manual labor was laid aside for a wedding, funeral, baby dedication, or some other responsibility.[41] It is left to later analysts to judge whether the technological advances tended to produce unhealthy dependency or to create a basis for self-support for the national church. Arthur's desire was the latter; the reality included some of the former.

School Work

The out-school pattern from Kenya was also adopted in Urundi, with schools being as much an entry wedge into new communities as preaching. Within a few years, even before Arthur's death, African teachers began serving not only as teachers but also as preachers. Initially, Rachel ran the schools and taught reading to children, but during 1935 adult men and women became students in the classes as well.[42]

Relations with Roman Catholics

A significant difference from Kenya was the somewhat entrenched opposition by Roman Catholic priests and workers in Urundi toward Protestants. Sometimes the opposition came from the Roman Catholic Belgians, although Belgian district commissioners could at times be as open and friendly as some non-evangelical British officials in Kenya had been. The Chilsons' arrival in Urundi coincided with a fairly rapid turning toward Catholicism by the African population of Urundi and Rwanda; perhaps if nothing else, this was a cultural move toward the symbols of colonial power and prestige. Arthur wrote that he thought "the Roman Catholic bondage [was] worse than the pagan bondage they were in."[43] On one occasion a Roman Catholic headman refused to let boys attend the literacy school set up by the Chilsons, but he eventually became more reasonable and was convinced to recommend the Chilsons to the Africans as good people.[44] But in general, headmen, evidently at the behest of priests, ordered people to stay away from the Friends school and services.[45] Arthur received an insulting name from one priest,[46] and on other occasions African priests would drive by Kibimba on their motorcycles, even onto the station grounds, to intimidate Africans from associating with the Protestants.[47]

In Arthur's eyes, the Roman Catholics seemed to place little value on African family life, probably because of the culture's plural marriages, low status given to women, and lack of care for the children. "Unless the home life is changed they will remain in heathen squalor," said Arthur.[48] Certainly instruction in Christian marriage was one of the first major challenges. The patriarch Arthur performed weddings regularly in hope that the institution of marriage would be elevated to "something more than the purchase of a household slave."[49] The Chilsons created a strong example by respecting women as equals in family and ministry. Edna, Esther, and Rachel regularly shared morning devotions with workers and took part in Sunday preaching responsibilities, along with the two men. In later years, one female Urundi pastor would point proudly to her marriage having been consecrated by a woman—Esther Chilson Choate.[50]

In February 1936, there was a confrontation between one of the Roman Catholic "White Fathers" missionaries and the Chilsons. The White Fathers, a large Catholic missionary order founded in the late nineteenth century, placed its primary focus upon Africa and was noted for the white robes its priests wore. Ralph Choate rather gleefully recounted the Chilsons sternly rebuking a priest, attempting to show the Africans they had nothing to fear from the Catholic priests or their pressure.[51] Later, one of the priests threatened to bring a crowd to attack the Kibimba station, but it did not materialize.[52]

Cultural Sensitivity (or Lack Thereof)

Arthur Chilson's first diaries in Urundi contain significantly fewer entries about the wretchedness of African culture and the paganism that was so startling to him in Kenya. He had, obviously, experienced African culture for thirty years and had likely developed different attitudes. They were interested in the unique elements of Urundi society and the uneasy balance between the regal and empowered Tutsis and the working class Hutus. They attended drummings and dances in Gitega, watching the "inherent dignity and grace of these tall Watussi [Tutsi] rulers. The missionaries were respectful and interested.[53] The Chilsons and Choates believed that Roman Catholicism had prohibited wailing at funerals and furthermore were against respect and reverence to the native king, something at least Ralph

Choate thought might be good to revive. Ralph felt the reverence had been unwisely switched from the king to the Roman Catholic priests.[54] In general, the vast majority of the population around Kibimba was Hutu, and it was the Hutu population with which the missionaries naturally tended to identify.

In many ways, the Chilsons carried Kenya missionary customs with them to Urundi. They regularly consulted with headmen; took part in *shauris* (councils) to meet personal needs, including arranging marriage partners for workers;[55] and curried favor with people of influence. Many times a favor to a chief was repaid to them with farm produce. "We don't *give* them anything but the Gospel," Arthur wrote.[56] There may have been somewhat less itineration in Arthur's work than there was in his earliest days in Kenya. Only once in the early months in Urundi did Arthur mention random evangelism in his diary.[57] Probably more people than they could quickly disciple were flocking to services in Kibimba from the heavily populated hills. The missionaries gave a great deal of time and attention to tree planting, carpentry, brick making, and construction work, most of which opened up close contacts with Africans, although these were usually one-way rather than reciprocal relationships. Being an employer was demanding, not only in keeping workers on task, but in dealing with the boss-servant relationships that developed. These workers requested higher wages, sometimes the work did not please the white bosses, and orders were sometimes misunderstood. In the work of the station (hospital, buildings, and school), the missionary ruled supreme. Thus, the approach in Urundi was amazingly similar to that taken in Kenya.

In the work of the church, Africans were drawn into teaching, evangelism, and discipline, although not as rapidly as some missionaries might have desired. The issue of discipline was a thorny one, especially with no established eldership, and with the offenders many times employees rather than new converts. One head worker who had shown interest in Christ was caught stealing firewood. Should he be discharged or should he be given another chance?[58] Two days after being caught, he left on his own accord.[59] Later, two were caught in adultery and dismissed from their jobs.[60] Wrote Arthur, "May He help us to make a clean church."[61] Rachel expelled a student for smoking. Later, in the name of keeping out "the Catholic influence," she would expel a student for leading some of his fellow students down to the road to talk with a White Father passing by on his motorcycle.[62] This suggests the high level of tension at the time and the assumption that the priest was a spy. Rachel went so far as to refuse medicine to Catholics who came to the dispensary but would not stay for Sunday services. The Africans frequently reported Catholic opposition and were tense about it.[63]

Mild physical punishment was meted out by the Chilsons to the Africans at various times, either to workers, school children, or later to Christian adults who had strayed in some way. While such punishment was a missionary practice in Kenya, it is not clear whether this was culturally acceptable to Africans in either place. It may have been an indigenous pattern employed by the missionaries, or it may have been deeply offensive to Africans. At any rate, on one occasion two young female students who were prospective wives for one of the workers were ordered to stay away for a month, evidently to avoid fornication. But they showed up in line for school the next day anyway. Ralph Choate restrained them and Arthur whipped them with a switch.[64] Was this culturally appropriate? What long-range paternal relationships were being formed that might be hard to break in the future? After Arthur's death, missionary Clayton Brown was invited by Edna to wield the stick, but he stoutly refused.[65] At any rate, with the passing of the Chilsons and the raising up of African elders, the practice of corporal punishment as church discipline by missionaries quickly disappeared. Fairly early, however, as in Kenya, African Christians were called upon to help in the discernment process to screen applicants for probationary church membership and for full membership.[66] This surely aided in developing a more Africanized process of discipline.

Responsiveness to the Gospel

Clearly the level of response in Urundi in the first three years was larger than at first in Kenya. Why? Perhaps the Roman Catholic presence was an opening wedge and leaven, even though the Chilsons and Choates saw it as primarily negative. Perhaps the quicker use of the vernacular and Kiswahili helped. Perhaps the gospel seed sown by the Danes or Germans finally sprouted. (Some of the Danish Baptist converts preached and taught at Kibimba by invitation.) Or was it the denser population with easier dissemination of the message? Even though Western Kenya was thickly populated, the central highlands of Urundi were even more so—it was the most densely settled area held by the Belgian colonialists. There is no clear answer to why the initial response was so great, but all visitors, even some from Kenya, remarked on the rapid progress and advancement of the work, although part of that was in praise of Arthur Chilson's and Ralph Choate's abilities to build up a European-style mission station, rather than praise for the developing church.

Edna Chilson remembered the earliest preaching in Urundi to be simple, and something easily understood. There were word pictures about a bird being caught by a small thread or string, or childhood stories of their growing-up years in America. Little children would press around Arthur and slip their hands into his.[67] A seekers' meeting was established April 1935, just a year after the Chilsons' arrival. Fifty came to that first seekers' gathering—cause for great rejoicing among the missionaries.[68] With greater understanding the missionaries began moving toward the empowerment of new Christians and encouraged them to speak publicly of their conversions. A year after the seekers' meeting began, a probationers' meeting was started, and probationers—converts who were being prepared for full church membership—began giving their testimonies before the larger congregation.[69]

The Banana Beer Issue

Perhaps the first and greatest controversy the Chilsons faced in Urundi was over the drinking of sweet banana beer. This apparently was an issue of little or no importance among Roman Catholics, and drunkenness was not uncommon. The Danish Baptists preached against drunkenness, however, and urged Christians not to drink the fully fermented banana beer, but since the line between sweet beer and the full-blown alcoholic drink was so hard to identify, drunkenness occurred frequently. Of the Baptists, Arthur wrote, "I am afraid the standards for Christians has been pretty low as to beer and tobacco."[70] To the Chilsons and Choates this was "a chief downfall" of the Baptists. Ralph Choate felt they would have to come to grips with the difference of opinion between Friends and Baptists, as there was talk among the Africans.[71] Arthur took a strong stand against any consumption of the banana brew, and in his pursuit of "a clean church" he was willing to be thought "too particular."[72]

Thus, Arthur and Edna established a new pattern among Protestants in Urundi: Avoid the sweet beer altogether and no one will be caught in drunkenness. The Chilsons accepted and encouraged confession and restoration, however, when someone expressed repentance for drinking and desired to return to church.[73] Public confession was required and grace was extended.[74] Across the years, this conservative demand was frequently criticized by other Protestants, while at times they spoke approvingly of it.[75] A full-blown "Kibimba Rebellion" took place in May 1959 and one of the issues was the missionaries' unrelenting opposition to the consumption of sweet beer.[76]

Arthur Chilson: The Closing Years and Aftermath

Even though the last two years of Arthur Chilson's life were marked by chronic sciatica pain, physical weariness, and eventually a series of cerebral hemorrhages that took his life, he continued to be an active and aggressive leader in many ways. The diaries record contacts with officials and trips to the capital city, to Gitega, or to neighboring missions for routine business and fellowship. He met with the Protestant Council of Rwanda-Urundi in March 1938, and made an exploratory trip into the eastern portion of Friends comity territory in May.[77] He counted over 2,500 enrolled in schools—a number, he said, that could be much larger were there only more African teachers and missionary supervisors. He lived long enough to comprehend that central Africa was responsive to the gospel and that the church was being well built.[78]

On the day before Christmas, 1938, Arthur went to bed after an apparent stroke, slipped into a coma by January 12, 1939, following a probable second stroke, and died January 14. His burial was the next day, Sunday evening, January 15, in the presence of the highest government officials of Gitega, Free Methodist and Danish Baptist missionaries, and the young king of Urundi. A short service, mostly limited to white people and officials, was conducted in the Chilson home followed by a graveside service with a large number of Africans present. A Free Methodist missionary gave a short message, Esther Choate prayed, Rachel read Scripture and gave a short message, and "Mushingantahe" (seer, or perhaps the "wise one") was laid to rest at dusk.[79]

American observers remembered Arthur and Edna Chilson as a "strikingly handsome couple" singing duets together, and Edna was declared "far too beautiful to be sent out to Africa." Other remarks were similar: Arthur had "keenness of insight and quickness of action." He had the power to make lasting friends, held to firm conviction, and maintained a warm devotional life and an unswerving loyalty to the Lord.[80] His eulogizers recognized his urgency and aggressiveness of action,[81] and his willingness at age sixty to undertake a strenuous new challenge in central Africa.[82] A pastor from Iowa alluded to controversies and theological stances taken by Arthur, and to misunderstandings and criticism by some Arthur counted as close friends, but said that Arthur stood by his convictions. When Arthur felt it was a question of right or wrong, he was willing to submit to others when it was of minor importance, but on what he considered core issues, he was firm. He felt great sorrow over some changes among American Friends.[83]

Whatever some Africans may have felt about harsh discipline or strict standards, there is every indication of genuine affection by many Africans for Arthur Chilson. "He took time to talk with us and be friendly; he was our friend," said one. He was considered "happy, kind and considerate."[84] Until his death Arthur retained a vision of the equality of all cultures at the foot of the cross of Jesus, said Byron Osborne. His was no ordinary courage, but one based deeply on moral convictions and a sense of God's personal call upon his life.[85]

A Final Word

The Chilsons were pioneers in spirit, yet they relied on a number of people who had preceded them on their epic truck journey into Urundi looking for "the place." Among their predecessors were David Livingstone and Henry Stanley who had crossed the same area, as had Anglicans who entered Uganda and Rwanda ahead of them. Although hostile in many ways, the Roman Catholic White Fathers had advanced into the Belgian territories simultaneously with secular administrators. And then there were the German Lutherans who ceded locations to the Danish Baptists, who in turn did the same for Friends. Africa Inland Mission and Unevangelized Africa Mission also served as mentors in Kenya and Urundi. Yet as far as American Friends were concerned, Arthur became something of a David Livingstone, calling Friends' attention to Africa and its spiritual needs.[86]

Arthur Chilson went looking for God's specific will for a new mission, much in the way he pursued the mission in Kenya three decades earlier. He did that by looking not just for a location, but also by studying "untouched peoples" and languages, and by considering feasibility and practical barriers. His family of Edna, Esther, and Rachel joined him in active leadership in a medical, industrial, and educational ministry in Urundi reminiscent of Kenya. As in Kenya, the family did not let muddy roads, biting insects, or rustic shelter slow them down much. Perhaps their greatest resource in Urundi was the family's ease in facing the cultures and geography of Africa. Instead of facing hostile Nandi tribesmen, they dealt with hostile Roman Catholic priests and headmen. Yet their journals and memoirs reveal their happiness in living in Africa, and depict a family that took quiet walks in the evening, enjoyed friends, played tennis, and liked to laugh! They created sporting events for students and encouraged games and dramas. They served tea and coffee to Europeans and shared meals under the trees with Africans. And perhaps more than all else, Arthur Chilson created relationships as he worked hard with his friends to build roads, houses, and furniture, to repair cars and to plant trees.

Through it all, Arthur Chilson had a passion for converts and disciples. His focus was upon the church. His first evangelistic contacts were with mission employees, followed quickly by schools, medical dispensaries, and public worship services. He established a routine of prayer, singing, preaching, and testimony. Seeker services and instruction for probationers came next, followed by the probationers' incorporation into the community as full members. Elders were named and some basic procedures for church discipline and order were established, but in at least the major congregation of Kibimba, missionaries tended to overshadow African leadership longer than might have been expected. Furthermore, the pattern for "new work" was to establish schools and dispensaries—programs that depended upon mission funds and supervision, creating a system of dependency and a notable lack of African-led initiative into new areas. Missionary supervision and funding tended to limit the growth of what could be accomplished by and through the mission, and did not produce a full-blown indigenous effort. Nevertheless, within two decades after Arthur Chilson's death, a number of large congregations were built up with their respective out-schools, congregations and leaders. A large amount of expatriate missionary effort went toward a hospital, formal academic teacher training, and industrial and vocational training, in many ways following the patterns established by the Chilsons in the founding years of the 1930s.

Whatever the shortcomings of Arthur Chilson, his family, and his other missionary colleagues, it is hard to fault Arthur's impulse for evangelism and the building of the church as the body of Christ. His successors established many new patterns, some significantly different than those of Arthur Chilson. Yet Arthur sincerely sought a pure church, holy and honoring to Christ. He believed in the transforming power of the gospel and he loved Africans, even if his cultural responses may not have always been appropriate. Had evangelistic Friends never entered Africa in the fields pioneered by Arthur Chilson, the Friends movement would be less than half the size it is today. Roughly 400,000 Quakers of East and Central Africa look back to Arthur Chilson as one of their primary founders.

Reflections:

What were Arthur Chilson's greatest successes in developing cultural sensitivity? In what ways was he culturally insensitive?

What strikes you as great evidences of Arthur Chilson's bravery and persistence in Kenya and Urundi?

Living conditions for pioneer missionaries have changed dramatically since the early 1900s, but a pioneering spirit is still required 100 years later. What do we learn about a "pioneering spirit" from the Chilsons?

We may never know the full story of Rachel Chilson in Urundi. We do not know with certainty that there was any moral failure. But are moral failures or rumors of such among Christian workers worth pursuing or are they best forgotten? Why?

Ruth Esther Smith

chapter 5

The Early Years: Pioneer
in a Hostile Environment

THE CHILSONS OF AFRICA probably never met Ruth Esther Smith of Guatemala, but their missionary careers overlapped closely in time and they undoubtedly knew each other by reputation and through shared friends. The Chilsons and Ruth Esther Smith had ties with Friends churches in California and Kansas. They had fellow workers on their fields from California and Kansas. They knew Jefferson Ford well, and Helen Kersey, who would later become Jefferson Ford's wife, worked with Ruth Esther Smith (known as Esther) in Guatemala. Both the Chilsons and Esther, impacted by the Holiness Movement, shared a deep commitment to a personal experience of purification and to reaching out to the poor and oppressed. They steeled themselves to expect opposition to the gospel. In Kenya, animism and spirit worship posed the greatest threats to the gospel. In Guatemala, a hostile Roman Catholic hierarchy promoted and encouraged what many observers have called Cristo-paganism built around ritual form, little Bible knowledge, and a great deal of priestly control.

Childhood and Early Adulthood

Ruth Esther Smith was born in Selma, Ohio—south of Springfield and west of Columbus—on August 11, 1870. She was converted at age seven while riding home from a revival meeting in the family carriage,[1] and she experienced a rather sheltered Christian childhood in Ohio and later in Kansas. After her parents resettled in Kansas, she studied in Emporia[2] at what was then the largest "normal school" for teacher training in the United States.[3] Esther taught school in Kansas for a while, but before 1895 her family had migrated west to Long Beach, California, and she came in contact with what became known as the Huntington Park Training School for Christian Workers.[4]

The Training School for Christian Workers

Founded in 1899 mostly by Quakers, the school underwent a number of mergers and relocations and is now known as Azusa Pacific University. The similarities between the educational environment Arthur and Edna Chilson experienced at Cleveland Bible Institute (later Malone University) and Esther Smith experienced at the Training School were profound. Female leaders were prominent in both. Both schools faced corrupted urban culture, carried concerns for women, practiced relief of the poor, and offered practical service as an expression of God's love.[5] Walter Malone advised that ministry in the cities begin "at the bottom and go up."[6] These schools welcomed people who some believed hopeless and derelict. John Oliver points out that such schools could be legalistic, but had a sort of tough spiritual discipline combined with rigorous social service, rather than a "holier-than-thou" aloof legalism. They were not afraid to mix with what might have been considered the dregs of society, and did so with grace.[7] This holiness spirituality, combined with a concern for the oppressed, tended to become a casualty of the twentieth century in North America, but Friends missionaries carried it forward in Kenya, Guatemala, and—as we shall see later—in India and Bolivia.

The Training School produced the majority of pastors and missionaries serving California Yearly Meeting of Friends in the first half of the century.[8] At its beginning it represented Friends orthodoxy in California in conscious opposition to a liberal interpretation of Scripture that seemed to stress social and peace issues at the expense of personal faith in Christ. Whittier College, while claiming to be Christian and orthodox, became the rallying point for less evangelistic interests and gradually the two educational institutions grew apart ideologically.[9] The Training School was zealously religious in nature with a focus on Wesleyan holiness, and it offered practical subjects appropriate for missionary training.[10] The Training School for Christian Workers went on to become a model for Esther, for her colleagues in the mission, and for the training school they created in Central America.

The Training School offered a missionary conference in July 1901, and Esther attended. A fellow student, Cecil Troxell, one of the founders and future statesmen for the National Holiness Missionary Society (now World Gospel Mission) also attended. He became a missionary to China,[11] but the ties between the Holiness Movement as a missionary enterprise and Friends missions continued in Central America, South America, and Kenya for the following fifty years. William Abel, a Native American converted in a Friends church in nearby San Diego, was also among the first students, and organized gospel teams. After ten years distributing Bibles and related literature in the Philippines, Abel spent eight months in Bolivia preaching, singing, and playing his guitar, later to die there of smallpox.[12] Decades later, the connection with William Abel eventually led R. Esther Smith to travel to Bolivia to visit Abel's grave and to encourage the beginning of a Friends mission in South America. Esther was equipped with vision, managerial skills, and a mature understanding of Scripture.

Within the first year of opening the Training School for Christian Workers, a seven-member "Guatemala Band" of missionaries was formed. Two of the members—Quakers Thomas J. Kelly and Clark J. Buckley—left for missionary service in Guatemala at the end of 1901. In late 1902, Kelly returned to California for other recruits, leaving Buckley alone in Central America. Buckley died in neighboring Honduras later in 1903. Kelly, while away, got married and also successfully recruited four other team members for the Guatemala band: Charles and Gertrude Bodwell, Esther Bond, and Alice Zimmer. Kelly himself was too sick, however, to accompany the expanded Friends band back to Guatemala when they left the Training School in December 1903, and he died in California in January 1904.[13]

Esther Smith joined a remnant of this band in late 1906, settling in Chiquimula and following up some of the same contacts made by Kelly, Buckley, and the others. Before leaving for Guatemala, however, Esther Smith not only spent study time at the Training School for Christian Workers, but for several years wrote a missionary-department column in the *Christian Workman,* a publication of California Yearly Meeting. From the first she was a mobilizer and a participant in missions.

Sunshine Mission

Before her call to Guatemala, Esther joined the California Yearly Meeting-sponsored Sunshine Mission in San Francisco, and served as its superintendent for urban missions for several years. The Sunshine Mission—housed in a former saloon[14] well-stocked with gospel tracts—conducted children's and mothers' clubs, distributed clothing and food, offered prayer and preaching services, and ran a program of "continuous Bible teaching." It also sheltered abandoned wives, children, and other homeless people. Esther Smith's responsibilities included visiting jails, hospitals, and brothels. While she served, Esther used her writing in *The Christian Workman* to promote the exploits of her friends and classmates from the Training School who had gone ahead of her to Guatemala.

April 18, 1906, brought Sunshine Mission work to a screeching halt for Esther, when one of the world's great earthquakes shook San Francisco, and a ravenous fire killed 3,000 people, destroyed 514 downtown city blocks, and drove more than 200,000 people out of the city as refugees. The mission building and all its contents were totally destroyed, leaving only the "imperishable word sown in the hearts" of men, women, and children.[15]

On June 8, less than two months after the earthquake and fire, Esther—while walking down a street in Oakland—felt she heard God's word to her: *Guatemala.* Joy filled her heart at the thought of joining her friends there. Guatemala missionary J. G. Butler of Atlanta, Georgia—one of the leaders of what became the Nazarene mission in Guatemala—reported Esther's call to a Yearly Meeting gathering later that month in Southern California.[16] Initially, it was thought Esther would continue her mission work as a ministry to children, being supported by the Christian Endeavor youth society of the yearly meeting, but within a short time, the entire mission staff in Guatemala came under the direct support and administration of

California Yearly Meeting, a relationship Esther had been advocating for some time before her own call.

After having also served as the pastor of Long Beach Friends for a few months, Esther, now a recorded Friends minister with teacher training and urban mission experience, arrived in Guatemala on November 20, 1906, along with friend and companion Cora Wildman. Esther and Cora joined Esther Bond and Alice Zimmer, but Bond and Zimmer were both gone within one year, essentially allowing Esther Smith and Cora to start over in the task of learning the language and building relationships.[17] Esther's partnership with Cora lasted until 1921, when tragedy struck.

Chiquimula Mission

When Esther Smith and Cora Wildman arrived in Chiquimula in the last days of 1906, the mission counted a mere eight converts in that city and four in neighboring Zacapa. Everything Esther and Cora owned could fit into one oxcart, Esther would say later, and they lived together in a rented house with the aid of one Guatemalan believer and her ten-year-old son. They began Spanish language study by immersion, exchanging English lessons for Spanish, depending upon a few trusted friends to explain culture and local news events as they happened. Esther spent weeks and even months speaking Spanish almost exclusively, mostly with the native children and women. Within a year Esther and Cora were practicing at speaking Spanish among themselves and preaching and teaching more fluently, although Esther was conscious of her own "poor use of the language."[18]

By June 1907 rumors of war and soldiers on the move around Chiquimula reached the mission. A more real danger, however, was a local Catholic priest who came to the windows of the house to listen to singing and preaching, and to look for ways to counter attack. The missionary band recognized "a large class of people" who did not believe the priest and who had never had their children baptized. The missionaries sensed receptivity to their message,[19] and bravely set up a literature table in the city square during the Virgin festival in August, believing their prayers needed to be matched by actions.[20] One would guess that gender actually served to protect them. On the one hand, they were considered harmless, and on the other, it would have been unseemly to physically attack a woman. Male Guatemalan believers were not as well treated as the women and were regularly "cruelly assaulted by the priest and beaten by policemen!"[21]

Protestantism in Central America at the time arose against the backdrop of a raging and ruthless Roman Catholic Spanish conquest, tempered by sacrificial mendicant friars who at times heroically protested some of the worst Spanish policies. The native Mayan population had accepted Catholic baptism in mass numbers from 1550 through 1850, while still retaining many animistic beliefs and practices.[22] By the arrival of Friends, however, a *ladino* (mestizo) class had arisen, created through the unions of Spanish conquistadores and their Indian mistresses, many who eventually became legal wives.[23] In the nineteenth century the ruling Spanish populations and ladinos become restless under what appeared to be an antiquated Roman Catholic provincialism, and they began looking for a more secularized approach to government and economics. This opened the door for evangelical Protestant ministries in the 1880s. Ladino influence had grown out of proportion to its first numbers as the Indian population became decimated through heavy labor, war, disease, and low birthrates. Indian population may have declined by as much as 90 percent by 1600.[24] While in the last four hundred years Mayan populations have grown sizeable again in the mountains and highlands of Guatemala, the culture of many cities, villages, and rural areas took a decidedly ladino direction with the loss of Mayan culture and languages. In the Chiquimula area where Friends began their work, for example, ladino culture reigned, although nearby Jocotán and some other mountain villages retained Mayan language, dress, and customs. Comity arrangements designated the western highlands and their resurgent Mayan populations for evangelization by other evangelical bodies.

Guatemalan Justo Rufino Barrios (president from 1873 to 1885) is considered the founder of Guatemalan liberal politics and an early friend to Protestant missions. He helped open the nation to economic development, restricted state Roman Catholicism, and looked to Protestantism as a counter balance to Catholic hegemony.[25] Entrenched oligarchies continued to hold political and economic control over landless Indian peasants for most of the twentieth century, however, leaving the poor without many secure human rights in an economy dependent upon fickle outside markets for its raw resources and agricultural products.[26] Over all of this hovered the jealous Roman Catholic priests whose power was only partially blunted by Barrios's liberalizing policies.[27]

Near Chiquimula is Esquipulas, a major pilgrimage site to a Black Christ statue that served to bolster Roman Catholic identification with the ladinos and Indian masses in what many continue to call a "Cristo-pagan" blend officially sanctioned by the Church. Hordes swarmed to Esquipulas from throughout Latin America. In the first decade of the twentieth century, Esther Smith and others found Esquipulas unusually resistant, but they quickly began making evangelistic inroads into Chiquimula and other neighboring towns and villages.

In general, the ladino population was probably freer from the control of local governments than the village Indians, and more in control of their own decisions—a benefit to the Chiquimula missionaries that they may not have realized. Between 1898 and 1944, (Esther Smith lived in Guatemala from 1906 and onward), Central American dictatorships grew increasingly oppressive, but in Guatemala there was a government position of favoring foreign influence to counter the conservative Roman Catholic hierarchy.[28] There was a heady mixture of some improvements in health and public services, and hopes for foreign investment retarded by political corruption[29] and little improvement in education.[30] It was not coincidental that Esther and other Friends in Chiquimula felt a need for education, and began various primary and secondary programs; this was a specific social need that had largely gone unmet.

First Steps in Evangelism and Discipleship, 1906-1918

The Bible colporteurs Buckley and Clark helped set the pattern of evangelism with itinerant travels to sell Bibles and literature. Charles Bodwell followed suit, as did Esther Bond and Alice Zimmer. In 1907, R. Esther recorded her first contacts with the native people: attending a funeral for a child; teaching a Bible class at the missionaries' home; making application to start a school; sending a meal to a sick man they met in the market; inviting friends for an evening meeting followed by cake and coffee. They threw a party for thirty-five children. Hospitality with food and food and food! They attended graduations, school parades and ate tamales with the landlady. In contrast to Kenya, Chiquimala was a resistant and hostile location with only a small number of inquires about the gospel—mostly children who came to services[31]—but the missionaries were building up friendships and learning the culture. Many times the table guests were married couples and their families who came to listen and ask questions.

But before she completed her first full year of ministry, Esther fell gravely ill with malarial fevers on a visit to the Butlers, Nazarene missionaries in Coban. She remained with them there through October and November 1907, and did not return to Chiquimula until February 7, 1908. On the day Esther returned, Cora Wildman wrote, "Esther Smith's life has been spared and she is again able to work for God in Guatemala."[32] When Esther returned to her room after an absence of more than four months, she was shocked to see her room unchanged. Resuming the task of journal writing for the group, she wrote: "All seemed so natural. My unanswered letters were on my desk and my aprons hanging behind my door as I left them. In a sense it seemed like coming from the dead. The old duck was in the back...and the gray cat sat in the kitchen window as before."[33]

Nothing more is mentioned of the illness, and her work resumed. The report at the end of 1908 declared that her work and Cora Wildman's work was "almost wholly evangelistic" as they served as preachers, teachers, pastors, Bible-sellers, tract distributors, Bible school superintendents, visitors, organists, choir leaders, and janitors![34] Imbedded in the program of evangelism, six major concerns emerged and served to carry the missionary band forward during the early years.

The first concern in evangelism was children's and women's work. In many ways this was indeed an extension of Sunshine Mission of San Francisco, with poor and ill-kept children flocking around Esther and Cora for love and attention. But the women seemed conscious of the need to establish adult relationships, which they did with the children's fathers, mothers, and grandparents. It was important to the missionaries to observe, learn, and at times simply be a faithful presence.[35] In the earliest years, Esther is said to have displayed a phenomenal memory, knowing the names of every one of the believers, their spouses, and their children, as well as their kinship links.[36]

A second great concern in evangelism and discipleship was the defining of a clear message of salvation. Esther Smith called for spiritual transformation as the essence of the gospel, "not mere moral reform." "Civilization is not Christianity," she wrote, "and neither is reformation regeneration."[37] This was often a polemical message cast in contrast to what Friends believed were empty Catholic rituals without biblical content. Esther believed that the true Easter celebration, for example, was not about the nailing of a dead Christ to a cross, but the hope of new life.[38] She viewed priests as alien parasites, morally corrupt and contributing to "domestic anarchy, to religious bacchanals, to the worship of grotesque images."[39]

A third concern was holiness preaching, which became an integral part of discipleship from the mission's very early years, urging new converts to surrender to the fullness of the Holy Spirit. The earliest holiness messages focused upon a surrender of the will that, it was believed, would allow the Spirit to purify—to alter the inner moral nature of the believer—and create a fervent love for God and power for witness. Local conferences featured visiting nationals and missionaries from the Nazarenes, and others who invited prayer for the baptism of the Holy Spirit as a second definite work of sanctifying grace.

A fourth concern in evangelism and discipleship was the evangelistic mule trips that began almost immediately and extended mission attention broadly over the whole southeastern segment of Guatemala; the trips extended across the border into Honduras and El Salvador within just a few years. The mule trips became legendary and journals recount beginning the day at 3:00 a.m., eating breakfast at 8:00 a.m., attending a preaching gathering and having lunch at noontime, and then going on to another village. The missionaries were left "tired but happy."[40] In a 1908 end-of-year report, Esther Smith said she had traveled 650 miles by mule, 400 miles by train, and 30 miles by river.[41] Sometimes they faced harsh priestly opposition to their work, but sometimes they found surprising openness, encouraging them to look for "evangelists with no headquarters nor pastoral cares" who could keep extending the witness to new locations.[42]

Esther Smith valiantly promoted circuit riding and the development of a whole pack of mules for missionary and national itineration as early as 1909, a pattern that continued well through the 1930s and beyond. It was no small task to feed and care for the mules! "These are pioneer days in Central America and there is no substitute for consecrated flesh and blood on mule back," she wrote.[43] They entered a town, secured a room from the municipality near the plaza for meetings, tried to distribute gospel tracts they printed at a mission press in Coban, and set up a folding organ and the "magic lantern" for a slide-like presentation.[44] They greeted fellow travelers, prayed for the sick, gathered a village flock for singing and reading, and watched carefully for interested people for future follow-up.

One of the most memorable mule-trip stories comes from the fall of 1910 when Esther and Cora headed toward the Honduran border to search out a man who had recently bought a Bible. They carried with them a new shipment of green-bound Bibles. Unbeknownst to them, Pedro Leiva, an assistant to a Catholic priest at Esquipulas and the brother of the man Esther and Cora hoped to find, had a vision twenty-five years earlier of foreign women, dressed in white, coming toward him and giving him a green book that told

94

him about God. Esther and Cora found Pedro's brother, who seemed disinterested. But seated nearby was Pedro himself, tired, sad, and covered with mud. His head was wrapped in a towel as a sign of mourning. A beloved daughter had just been buried. He approached the women and asked if they had a book about God. When the green book was handed to him, it seemed to burn in his hands as a fulfillment of the vision. He listened hungrily and responded quickly. He became an outstanding church planter and pastor in the border region until his death in 1935.[45]

A fifth abiding concern was leadership training. Missionaries taught lay training classes and held revival conferences in local congregations. An informal Bible school started in 1910, followed by a correspondence course prepared and sent out in 1911; two weeks of Bible classes for workers were offered annually for several years. The curriculum consisted of studies on the New Testament, prayer, holiness, music, and John Wesley's sermons,[46] duplicating that of the Training School for Christian Workers from Huntington Park, California. Esther Smith dreamed of the workers from the training classes and the boys' and girls' schools fanning out across Central America.[47] Undoubtedly Esther's greatest work as an evangelist was by proxy through students. However paternalistic she may have been in the control of workers even in the very earliest years, she respected and encouraged national leaders to fulfill their callings. The missionaries' concern for training culminated with the founding of a three-year Bible-institute program in 1920.[48]

A sixth concern was the creation of schools in Chiquimula for girls and boys. The girls' school opened in 1908 and was believed to be the only school for girls anywhere in Central America at the time; a boys' school opened in 1912. As early as 1910 girls came from fifteen cities and towns and the missionaries hoped to widely scatter the gospel teaching through these students. The girls received not only basic education, but also training in manual arts and in giving their Christian testimonies. They were viewed to be little missionaries and sometimes came in from a village for instruction in singing and reading.[49] Children of Christian families were often boarded in Chiquimula. Perhaps it is of little surprise that a group of female missionaries would give priority first to a girls' school in a culture where education for girls was sharply undervalued. Esther Smith viewed the schools as a direct ministry to children as well as a way to break down Roman Catholic prejudice.[50]

Undoubtedly the school strategy worked to some degree, perhaps especially in the earliest years, but decades later Friends missionary Paul Enyart faulted the schools for consuming a disproportionate share of resources during the 1930s and 1940s without contributing significantly to church growth.[51] Nevertheless, the valiant role of children in the first ten years of the mission grew to almost mythic proportions; this was especially true of the children's role in revival (seen in the next chapter). Esther Smith declared "One constant purpose is to make the schools an evangelistic agency."[52] The Friends vision was to transform society through "Evangel and School" expecting to bring "a Christian civilization, a moral regeneration, peace and prosperity" to the Central American republics.[53] This was not unlike the expectations of Quakers in Kenya at exactly the same time. Esther Smith believed schools were the logical complement to itineration, a "form of evangelism and more faithful in its results than passing through a town and shouting out John 3:16."[54] Schools, she wrote, were to provide systematic and continuous work, guarding the seed of the gospel.[55]

The Role of the Field Superintendent

Esther Smith quickly became identified as field superintendent by the supporting board in California, and wrote reports annually until her death in 1947. Information was channeled from the board through her to the field missionaries. She took the lead in determining with the missionaries the type and location of service they were to render, whether at the headquarters in Chiquimula or at an outstation. She served as editor of *The Harvester,* a newsletter and fundraising tool published and mailed from Guatemala to constituency in the United States. She was the one to call for a new missionary for a specific ministry, and on furloughs she frequently made contact with recruits. She was also the one commissioned to complain about unanswered letters from the board, scolding them that "we trust it not continue so."[56]

It was Esther Smith who reported in frustration the 1910 resignation of Casper Wistar, a young medical recruit from Philadelphia Yearly Meeting who had surgical experience. His resignation came, she felt, due to conflicts caused by a lack of "the divine glow of a spiritual experience" and a deficiency in Bible knowledge. Esther gives a withering critique of Casper that helps to capture the expectation that she and others had for their staff. Although deficient in Spanish and unable even to correctly pronounce *evangelio*, the Spanish word for "gospel," he refused to study and showed little interest in exactness in writing and speaking Spanish. Casper, Esther said, denied the vicarious atonement of Jesus and took issue with the prohibition against alcohol. As superintendent she had forbidden Casper from preaching sermons, although he was encouraged to participate in prayer, witnessing, and personal sharing. Casper embarrassed the missionaries by talking to nationals of "the sacrifice the missionaries made to be [in Guatemala], of which we do not speak." He seemed to refuse menial tasks arrogantly, and he was preparing to marry a young Guatemalan woman in the capital city—against mission policy. Esther granted that Casper was "young, self-supporting, well equipped materially, neat in appearance, reasonably well and strong, in some things unselfish," but objected that he had nothing to replace the necessary "spiritual life, victory and conquest....He has no sympathy whatever with the doctrine of Holiness and repudiates it."[57]

Another policy promoted by Esther was to create a headquarters in Chiquimula that would serve as a lighthouse and a spiritual center, and then go occasionally to other large cities and rent quarters and hold meetings. This was at the heart of her vision for combining pastoral care with evangelism, providing for the lambs "food warm and often." The work of the colporteur had quickly come to include the work of evangelist and pastor.[58] In the early days the mission paid the workers, a practice that continued for decades. It is likely the mission unilaterally chose such workers. Some support came from local churches, but other support came from churches in the United States.[59]

How dictatorial or conciliatory Esther Smith was in the early years is impossible to determine from the record. In writing, she stoutly declared major decisions were done "in unity," which she probably intended to mean as unity within the mission staff; there is no indication nationals were drawn meaningfully into the decision-making process. She became famous for calling the staff at headquarters to prayer, to labor in prayer over many decisions, and to delay decisions until much prayer had gone up.[60] Esther was usually the one to provide the written vision, goals, and objectives that became the basis for mission expansion. She held tenaciously to itinerant evangelism and pastoral care, training programs for pastors, education for children, annual local church conferences, and holiness revival preaching. It worked and the churches grew, although not without great difficulties.

The years 1907 to 1918 under the direction of Esther Smith were marked by painful hardships and problems. Roman Catholic priests were believed to have circulated horrific stories of evangelicals worshiping the devil, of signing away their souls with their own blood as ink, of making soap out of children and shipping others to the United States as slaves. Priests accused the missionaries of paying for converts and of being spies for a United States government plan to imperialistically take over Central America. Some said that the missionaries were actually men masquerading as women! The schools were chronically understaffed and insecure in locations. The girls' school moved from one rented property to another eleven times. Priests often thwarted attempts to buy property. Transportation was slow and painful; the nearest railroad was twenty miles from Chiquimula, making mule-back, oxcart, and foot traffic the only modes of travel during this decade. The nearest hospital was seventy miles away. And in the later days of World War I, Central America's supply of food and other items from the United States was cut off.[61]

Despite the hostility, growth was solid. In 1910 there were seven American and five Guatemalan workers, and eighty-nine church members spread across six towns and cities. By 1911 there were 187 members, and the workers were making visits into Honduras. In 1912 there were twenty small congregations and a membership of 287, and a permanent boys' school was opened. In 1913, thirty-two national workers attended midsummer Bible classes, and one woman, Magdalena Hernandez, served as a pastor over a district of eight to ten congregations.[62] In 1914 missionaries Irvin H. and Dorothy Cammack left Chiquimula and opened a work in the Tegucigalpa region of Honduras, a work that eventually became a separate ministry decades later. By 1916 there were eight missionaries and twenty-two native workers, and the Cammacks began reporting independently from Tegucigalpa, Honduras. The strong emphasis on church-planting evangelism and founding of congregations brought about local churches (monthly meetings) that were then grouped into districts (quarterly meetings).

What contributed to this early success? Was the ladino population disillusioned with Catholicism and seeking something more from God? Did a dogged persistence in church planting and leadership training began to pay off? Was success the result of the leadership of an intelligent and aggressive superintendent? Was the work better suited to women? Or did the spiritual factors of prayer, holiness revival, and surrender to God's will bring growth? Likely all these factors contributed to some extent, but we must give further attention to the spiritual dynamic of holiness revival.

Reflections:

What are you learning about how God guides the church through "networks" in establishing new mission fields?

Does anything strike you as especially important about Esther Smith's preparation before she went to Guatemala and her Spanish-language study when she first arrived?

How was pioneering in Guatemala different from pioneering in Kenya? How was it similar?

As you read this chapter, what specifically stands out as the most likely reason for success in the early hard days in Chiquimula?

chapter 6

Turning Point: The Chiquimula Revival of 1918–1919 and Church Growth

THE GLOBAL POLITICAL TURMOIL that surrounded World War I was seldom mentioned in Central America, where local politics and Roman Catholic opposition to evangelical ministry eclipsed other concerns. The Chiquimula missionary staff placed great emphasis upon the spiritual nature of God's work. Esther Smith and her staff maintained a "Friends Mission Journal" of the group's daily activities from 1907 through 1914, trying to chart the spiritual vitality of the churches and schools. Their ardent desire for heart religion played out across the years before 1918 in phrases like "signs of some revival," "much spiritual interest," "many confessing and praying," "a real hunger to receive the Holy Ghost," "a long altar service," "souls weeping, seeking God," or "a revival spirit in the school."[1]

Esther Smith had dreamed of a "pentecost" as early as February 1910 and they occasionally saw "precious tokens" of revival. Annual camp meetings in the districts and the yearly conference in Chiquimula conditioned people to seek spiritual blessing and renewal. The annual conference in January 1918 was marked by confessing, weeping, praying, and seeking. Armando Peralta spoke at the conference that year, calling for workers to enter the whitened harvest fields. "A revival did not burst upon us, but revival was among the people," wrote Esther in March.[2] What happened in workers' classes beginning in July 1918 was different, however; a more compelling and sweeping emotional power brought many more to the altars for prayer.[3] The full force of revival broke out in September 1918.

On September 16 in the boys' school, the regular 2:00 p.m. prayer meeting was prolonged and no further class work was done that day. Several of the missionary staff and perhaps some nationals spent that night in prayer.[4] Then the next day—September 17— revival services began in the boys' school, and these included singing, testimony, and prayer. Many of the intermediate-level boys prayed for conversion, and one of the rebellious older boys was "brought out of the tomb." He and a group of younger boys entered the dining room together, and instead of eating their suppers they began praying and shouting. They then formed a line and marched from school to the Chiquimula Tabernacle several blocks away with seven older boys leading another prayer service that attracted a small storm of attention.

In the girls' school on September 20, the students were called from classes for special meetings of prayer, which were followed by several days of singing and exhortation. At one point, girls spontaneously clustered in corners of the room for prayer. Crying and shouting continued through Saturday both at the girls' school and at another location where older girls were housed. Sunday services at the tabernacle were given over to testimonies by the girls who, with tears streaming down their faces, preached to non-Christians and urged Christians to full commitment.[5]

Years later, Josephine Still remembered Helen Kersey's impressions of those days of prayer and revival:

> The intense joy...was so great and so prolonged she [Helen Kersey] had to look at the bricks on the floor and convince herself that she was still on this earth and not in heaven. The inanimate things around also seemed to have voices that praised God—the noise of the broom as the girl swept the corridor said "hallelujah, hallelujah"—the rain as it splashed in the *pila* [sink] sounded like *'Gloria a Dios'* [Glory to God]. More than once several people heard the same sound and went to investigate the source of the praise and glory about them. The very [greatest] of the revival lasted three months, but the effects of it set the tone, the expectations, and standards of the people for the next 50 years.[6]

Both boys and girls seem to have soon traveled to their home villages or to other towns with testimony and song, carrying revival enthusiasm with them. The mission recorded conversions and formed eight evangelistic teams to visit neighboring congregations and villages. As school was closed down for the year (at the traditional time of year-end vacation in Guatemala), missionaries were assigned to accompany each group of students and workers, forming a rich multigenerational and multicultural mix of North Americans, ladinos, and Indians.[7]

Manifestations of the Revival

"Arise, shine, for your light has come," declares Isaiah 60:1, and Esther Smith believed this was fulfilled in the 1918–1919 revival.[8] As the teams fanned out around Chiquimula, word of the enthusiasm went before them and created great expectations before they even arrived. Missionary Matilda Haworth reported many were "mown down by the spirit of prayer. They seek God. They stay on their faces." The missionaries counted twenty people "taken in vision, two school boys, eight school girls, eight believers in four different places and two girls in San Jose."[9] Awakening from visions, some told of things to come, some brought messages for individuals, and some spoke of spiritual conditions in the churches.[10]

It was probably Matilda Haworth who, along with Esther Smith, witnessed the trances and visions of Adolfo Marroquín on the night of September 24, 1918. The eighteen-year-old student went limp during intercessory prayer, and the two women positioned themselves next to the boy for several hours; they placed a pillow under his head, checked his pulse, and noted his breathing was normal. He occasionally raised his hands, spoke a hallelujah or smiled, but for the most part remained quiet with his eyes closed. As the night unfolded and as others in the room continued to pray, people focused their attention on one girl in the back of the room who was struggling in prayer. Matilda Haworth came to believe Adolfo, in his trance-like state, was praying for the girl. Adolfo continued in his trance until about 8:30 the next morning, breaking out of it shortly after the girl gave testimony of spiritual victory.[11]

Upon awakening he lay back down and began speaking, and Matilda Haworth asked for a paper and pencil and recorded his words for the next three hours. Six of Adolfo's male classmates were present for much of the time, along with several of the girls, their matron, and a nurse. Many times his eyes seemed to focus upon the boys with a few words of exhortation to them, a few bites of food, and frequent expressions of ecstatic joy. At noon, Haworth sent the students from the room and someone brought Adolfo his noon meal, which he ate eagerly. He reclined again and spoke of a spiritual, unseen experience. He had sensed God was bringing purity to his classmates, and that while no physical healings were shown to him, he believed there would be spiritual healings. He believed the families of the boys and girls were to be converted. He eventually fell asleep and at 5:30 p.m., Matilda left him there on the platform. An hour and a half later, some of the older boys returned and awakened him. A deep burden of prayer for non-believers in the schools then came upon Adolfo and he once again fell into a trance.

A similar pattern was repeated that second evening with Adolfo alternating between what appeared to be painful intercession and joyful praise. The physical changes to his face and voice were striking to all present, so much so that one awestruck woman cried out, "It is a second Christ!" Matilda rebuked her soundly: "He is just one of our boys honored by God for Jesus' sake" she declared. Meanwhile, some of the boys and girls in an outer corridor continued in prayer and personal soul-searching, sometimes with screams and despair over the exhortations Adolfo had given to some of them. He later told Matilda he was not much aware of what he had said, but he spoke of heaven, of seeing Jesus all glorious seated at the top of a series of stairs. The Lord told him to "carry the burden" of prayer for his classmates. He also saw two of his Guatemalan instructors strolling the streets of heaven, returning from worshiping the King. He saw wonderful mansions and a revival spreading from Central America to South America and then to North America.[12]

Despite the revivalist tradition of all the North American missionary staff, it seems this was a bit more than any had ever experienced and they were not sure what to make of it! Helen Kersey had to check her eyes and Matilda Haworth insisted on writing down events as they unfolded. These were clearly out-of-the-ordinary, intense activities. Even "holy laughter" is recorded but nothing is mentioned of speaking in tongues. Strangely enough, for these conservative Friends missionaries the events were not particularly controversial and they did not publish greatly detailed accounts, although some from other denominations in Guatemala heard the reports and questioned what the Friends missionaries in Chiquimula were allowing to happen![13]

The general response among the Chiquimula missionaries, however, was that it was of God. One even said, "If you have a problem with this, talk to God about it!"[14] The mission superintendent in California counseled Esther Smith to maintain balance with an emphasis on moral discipleship, but he did not try to order an end to the revival. He expressed confidence that she and others would be able to guide the movement away from self-centered emotionalism and theological tangents.[15] By every account that is what happened. Paul Enyart makes the strong claim that the 1918–1919 revival issued forth a period of significant church growth, especially in Honduras, which lasted for at least a decade.

The Spanish Flu

About a year after the revival, the influenza pandemic that struck elsewhere around the world hit eastern Guatemala. The mission promised to secure the help of two Christian nurses, but instead they found sixteen who gave their time to help the sick and dying in and around Chiquimula. Esther Smith reported the mission was assigned two parts of the city where the epidemic was most severe and where the people were the poorest. Mission mules were saddled daily for workers with medicines and supplies, many of them from families and merchants of the city. Some of the missionary women canvassed their section of the city, seeking the sick. A makeshift hospital was created out of a donated house. Esther said they were invited to the homes of all classes as people called from windows and streets for help. It now seemed difficult, wrote Esther, for the people to remember that the missionaries were the dreaded Protestant "enemies." The gratitude of the convalescents was the missionaries' reward. Songbooks, organs, and chapels were closed because of the plague, she observed, but the hearts and homes of many were opened to them instead. "God is with us."[16]

So it was that revival was described in terms of ecstatic experience, but was played out in moral change, discipleship, and social compassion. And perhaps even more importantly, the church grew.

Revival and Church Growth

If mission historian Paul Enyart is right, this may have been one of only a few emotional revivals that directly advanced church growth. Personal introspection did not stall the revival. The introspection happened and personal repentance was a major issue, but the revival moved out into fresh evangelism in a startling fashion, and included new work across the border into western Honduras. In this case, some of the most striking manifestations focused on intercessory prayer. Fairly quickly the energies of many of the leading participants became channeled into itinerant evangelism—joyful, upbeat, and outward-looking. And, as has been charted in many revivals, the revival moved from urban to rural, from a center of education to areas without education, and from the economic-market area to the service area.

In looking at statistics, one might come to the conclusion that the entire period from 1910 to 1922 was one of growth, and the 1918 events merely prolonged the growth pattern that brought the church from 89 to 1,858 members.[17] Mission workers had developed a fairly efficient organizational structure and area conferences gave a sense of belonging to insiders, but churches remained open to attract new people. It was a lay movement that involved a wide array of leaders, but Esther Smith as "a woman of great faith and vision" is credited with doing the most to solidify the movement.[18] As Helen Kersey Ford noted, the key contributing factor of the revival may have been the expectations for moral purity and active and joyful evangelism that guided much of the overall tenor for decades to come. This, combined with the empowerment of national leaders, extended church growth.

In 1919, as the effects of revival continued, there were twenty-four national workers with an average age of only thirty. In 1924 there were forty-five men and women on the list, and in 1929 there were sixty-six names. Across the years, the missionaries declared these Central American men and women to be of outstanding ability.[19] Josephine Still, in a speech at a Guatemala Friends Centennial celebration of 2000, cleverly and graciously shifted the attention away from missionaries toward national leaders. To paraphrase, she said: "We missionaries were everyday, common people. God called out people of great abilities who now lead the work forward far better than anything we could do."[20] Perhaps the greatest strength of Esther Smith and the others—mostly female missionaries prior to 1920—was their success at empowering national leaders.

Controversies

Some believe the single greatest blow to the Chiquimula mission in its first thirty years was the defection of pioneer missionary Cora Wildman. "Corie," as her mother Rachel called her, arrived in Chiquimula with Esther Smith in December 1906 and was the only person to share with Esther the entire span of years from 1906 to 1921. They shared living quarters and mule trips together. From 1919 to 1920, Wildman was the district superintendent over the work in Ocotepeque, Honduras.[21] Then in June 1921, she went on furlough in Long Beach, the home congregation for the two women.[22] The scandalous details are not recorded, but sometime in the last half of 1921, Cora Wildman returned to Central America and eloped with a married pastor, the father of several children. Esther Smith went to Wildman and tried to reason with her, but gave up and wrote a letter of explanation to Wildman's family in Long Beach.[23]

Esther Smith made no mention of Cora Wildman in the 1922 report she read personally to the Yearly Meeting in California, but admitted to "new provings and deep sorrows. . . . pressed in spirit and tried in faith."[24] Surely she was referring to Wildman. Helen Kersey was named the new district superintendent in Ocotepeque, Honduras,[25] and Wildman lived with the former pastor as his wife for the following decade, probably spending much time in Guatemala City. Wildman's husband eventually left her and returned to his first wife, abandoning Wildman and informing her that he had never really been divorced from his first wife. Josephine Still, when asked what influence the Cora Wildman scandal had upon the mission, gave a short answer: "deadly." However much Cora may have been a victim of deceit, her bad testimony was notorious in Honduras and elsewhere for years to come.[26]

Despite its relative isolation, the Chiquimula mission found itself caught up in other controversies, including one among Friends in the United States. In 1919, there was a strong move to place the Chiquimula mission under the direction of the American Friends Board of Foreign Missions, a move the Chiquimula staff ardently opposed. "It is a thing we cannot, do not desire, and we beg you not to require it of us," Esther wrote to the board in California. "We are not in unity with said board in doctrine nor policy. Its organ, *The American Friend* does not present the blessed doctrines of the Holy Ghost nor refer to Pentecostal possession. Its theme is reconstruction in France and not regeneration in the heart of man." To emphasize their unity, each member of the mission staff, with the exception of Cora Wildman who lived at a distance in Honduras, personally signed his or her name.[27]

The concern of the missionaries was heard, and the work of Friends in Central America stayed under the administration of California Yearly Meeting. The issue never died entirely, however, as California Yearly Meeting remained within Five Years Meeting until its withdrawal in the 1990s. The same controversy caused Oregon Yearly meeting to withdraw from Five Years Meeting in 1928, sparking interest among some Friends in California in withdrawing from California Yearly Meeting to join Oregon so that the Guatemala mission might come under the direction of Oregon Yearly Meeting.[28]

Such an idea never gained much steam, however, but Esther Smith, on furlough in California from late 1929 and into early 1930, found herself drawn into a controversy. She does not state the nature of this controversy, but perhaps it had to do with the administration of the Chiquimula mission. Esther was accused of siding with some who were causing disunity within the Yearly Meeting. But the mission board came stoutly to Esther's defense and the issue, whatever it was, was laid to rest, her good reputation in the yearly meeting preserved.[29]

Founding of Berea Bible Institute

In the aftermath of revival, the necessary elements came together in 1921 to form a more permanent training institute for Friends leaders in Central America. The capable Mae Burk became principal and a call went out for young people to come train for ministry as pastors and evangelists. Mae Burk (who later married Lester Stanton), had been on the field since 1909 (Stanton arrived in 1913) and in later years she formed a strong partnership with Esther Smith. While Esther steered the rudder of the mission by the vision, articulating the goals, and raising the funds, it was, according to Josephine Still, Mae Burk Stanton who got the jobs done and dealt with many of the details.[30] Mae Stanton created the three-year curriculum and established the discipline for study that inspired pastoral leadership for more than thirty years.

It was left to Esther, however, to raise the funds for the Bible institute through *The Harvester,* and she began writing immediately upon receiving authorization from the California Mission Board. The plan of study and practical work was patterned after the holiness training schools in the United States—schools like those in Huntington Park; Cleveland, Ohio; and Portland, Oregon.[31]

Juan Ayllon and the Bolivia Mission

One story about the founding of Berea Bible Institute concerned one of its first students, a young Bolivian named Juan Ayllon. Juan was the illegitimate son of a Catholic priest by an Aymara Indian woman. Juan heard of the plans for Berea, probably through Emma Morrow of the Central Friends Mission in Bolivia.[32] It is believed Juan had had contacts in Bolivia with William Abel, a classmate and friend of Esther Smith at the Training School for Christian Workers in California. William Abel played his accordion and preached on the streets of La Paz briefly before succumbing to smallpox. In November 1920 Juan Ayllon struck out for Guatemala from Bolivia, traveling over the Andes to the Pacific Coast, working his way north on a steamship by shoveling coal. He traveled through the Panama Canal and ended up, not in Guatemala, but in New York City where Quakers in Brooklyn took him in and bankrolled his passage back to Puerto Barrios, Guatemala, and on to Chiquimula.[33]

To Esther Smith, Juan's arrival at Berea was a fulfillment of an earlier scriptural promise to her from Isaiah 60:4, which reads, "All assemble and come to you; your sons come from afar."[34] Juan completed his three years of theological studies at Berea, married a Honduran student named Tomasa, and returned to Bolivia where he and Tomasa opened their first preaching point in 1924. For a number of years the churches of Central America, led by the tabernacle congregation of Chiquimula, supported the Ayllons, until the new work was accepted by Oregon Yearly Meeting (now Northwest Yearly Meeting).

It was Esther Smith who encouraged and championed the work in Bolivia, and almost single-handedly urged Friends in Oregon to accept the challenge of a field in Bolivia. She corresponded with the Ayllons regularly and finally mounted the longest of her missionary journeys, a boat trip through the Caribbean to the Panama Canal, through the canal to the Pacific, and down the west coast of South America to Colombia, Ecuador, and to Lima, Peru. From the southern Peruvian port city of Mollendo, she traveled by train through the sand dunes near Arequipa and over the western range of the Andes populated by llamas, alpacas, and vicuñas at a 14,000-foot elevation. She was appalled at what she felt was gross Catholic ignorance, superstition, and oppression. She passed over Lake Titicaca by steamer and then resumed her train trip on Bolivian soil, passing by the ancient pre-Inca ruins of Tiahuanaco, at the time the oldest known ruins in the Americas.[35]

Somewhere in the process she visited the Inca capital of Cuzco, but her real destination was Sopocachi, a suburb of La Paz, Bolivia, where Juan and Tomasa Ayllon lived. Her account, recorded in a booklet entitled *In Aymaraland*, displays a mature awareness of geography, history, pre-conquest animism, and a vision for missions as a non-materialistic conquest for God, which leads to human liberation. Her goals were in sharp contrast to the exploits of the Spanish conquistadores, she said, who traversed the same roads four hundred years earlier in search of gold, not God.[36]

In La Paz, Esther met the Aymaras, a large indigenous people group, and wrote compassionately of their role as social outcasts. Her practiced eye as a missionary in the urban ghetto of San Francisco, California, helped her see the urban homeless and the rural feudal peons held hostage by an oppressive upper class and an oppressive Roman Catholic priesthood.[37]

Like a whole generation of expatriates after her, Esther Smith seems to have read the ugly cultural case studies that described Aymaras as surly and hostile people who rejected strangers. So she was surprised by a warm reception by fellow Christians: "They received a woman from far away, one they had never seen, and greeted me with tears and gladness."[38] While she clearly delighted in the unique historic archeological sites and the extreme altitudes, it was the people she wrote about most—the Aymaras: "None of these things were so interesting and so grand as the rare privilege of getting near to the heart of the Aymara, a race forgotten, oppressed and despised. What a great joy to have met and ministered unto them."[39]

In Bolivia, she spoke through an interpreter into the Aymara language, wept, and prayed with young Christian Aymaras. Although her primary purpose was to encourage the Ayllons, she methodically surveyed the work of other missions, including the work of Central Yearly Meeting Friends missionaries from Westfield, Indiana, in Sorata, and the work of the Canadian Baptists and Southern Methodists in La Paz. Before leaving La Paz, she visited the grave of her classmate William Abel, placed a green wreath at his tomb in the public cemetery, and prayed, thanking God that "the mantle of this His servant had fallen to...Juan Ayllon."[40]

Esther Smith's interest in William Abel and Juan Ayllon is noteworthy and helps us understand how Oregon Yearly Meeting became drawn into missionary activity in South America. She mobilized Oregon Yearly Meeting on behalf of Bolivia. Earlier she had discussed the possibility of Juan Ayllon working with Central Friends as an established Friends mission in Bolivia. But the Ayllon ministry may have been caught in the crossfire of conflict as the biblical seminary of Westfield, Indiana, and Central Yearly Meeting of Friends broke relations with Five Years Meeting (Friends United Meeting) and Central Friends struggled with their own internal disagreements. Who would support the Ayllons—Central Friends? The seminary? The Sorata group of holiness Friends? Had Juan Ayllon been contaminated by contact with California Friends who were members of Five Years Meeting?

At one point, it seems Esther Smith was waiting for Westfield Seminary to take the next move, but no satisfactory answer came. Superintendent Charles S. White of California urged against "desertion of the work by the Ayllons."[41] Upon her return to Central America, she wrote a lengthy letter to Friends in Oregon urging them to undertake a new field of service in Bolivia on a permanent basis and to care for the Ayllons in ways Central American Friends could not. That historic letter was received in 1929 and officially accepted by Oregon Yearly Meeting sessions in 1930.

On June 18, 1930, the minutes of the board of missions of California Yearly Meeting recorded that the Chiquimula mission "has turned its mission work in Bolivia over to the Oregon Yearly Meeting Mission Board, relinquishing all authority and responsibility therefor [e]. This move was made believing Oregon Yearly Meeting was in a position to meet the needs of and expand the work in that field better than was possible by the native church of Chiquimula Mission.[42] That same year Guatemalan Friends missionaries Carroll and Doris Tamplin began the process of transferring to Bolivia under Oregon Yearly Meeting. Thus, in a real sense Esther Smith was a parent figure not only to Central American Friends but also to South American Friends. A second couple, Howard and Julia Pearson, left Guatemala in 1935 to join the effort in Bolivia, once again strengthening the historic ties between the two fields. Both the Tamplins and the Pearsons already had strong links with Oregon Friends.

Reflections:

Does anything about the history recorded in this chapter surprise you?

What is the role of emotion in the work of spiritual ministry? How should emotional balance be maintained?

What do you think were the most important "fruits" of the Chiquimula revival of 1918–1919?

Why do you think the moral failure of Cora Wildman seemed especially damaging?

If you had to choose between "social reformer" or "conversion revivalist," which term would you use to describe Esther Smith, and why?

What traits of a social reformer do you see Esther Smith display in her visit to Bolivia?

chapter 7

The Middle Years of Plateau and Advance, 1922–1935

AS WE HAVE NOTED, the Guatemalan Friends Mission was composed mostly of women for its first forty years. The Quaker conviction of women's inherent right to participate in ministry was carried out more in Guatemala than in perhaps any other Friends field in the early twentieth century. Esther Smith and Cora Wildman picked up from Alice Zimmer and Esther Bond in 1906, and Esther continued the pattern of women in primary leadership throughout the 1920s and 1930s. No one remembers when "R. Esther" became "Miss Ruth," but the tendency was for North Americans to refer to her as "Esther" or "R. Esther," while Guatemalans thought of her affectionately as "Miss Ruth." She was the one in charge.

In the mid-1930s, missionary statesman Kenneth G. Grubb visited Chiquimula on a tour through Central America. Perhaps he needs to be forgiven for the male chauvinism latent in his report: "[Chiquimula Friends] is an interesting mission, mostly manned by women missionaries: it is rare in Latin America to see stable work built up with such a high proportion of women to men."[1] Various men did serve briefly, but only B. B. Williams and Lester Stanton served long term. Meanwhile, Esther Smith, Mae Burk Stanton, Matilda Haworth, Clara Howland, Helen Kersey, Helen Oakley, and Lenora Cammack each served ten years or more during the same period. Of those who severed shorter terms of service, fifteen were women and eight were men. Grubb was right: The total ratio was about two female Quaker missionaries for every one male[2] and the most prominent leaders were women.

Despite the dominance of women on the mission staff, the leading Guatemalan national preachers were mostly men, although ladino women were frequently given preaching and pastoral assignments. Esther Smith and others shepherded men like Bernardino Ramirez, a hard-drinking army officer imprisoned for stealing, who escaped but was returned to jail where he accepted Christ. He became a well-known evangelist and respected advisor. Another favorite of Esther Smith was Pilar Alvarez, a confirmed alcoholic by age fifteen who had grown up torturing his body as penance and carrying images through the streets. As a youth he was recruited as a mercenary into a Honduran revolutionary group; he survived (while many died), attempted suicide, was hit by a train, and was led to Christ by Bernardino Ramirez in a hospital in Quiriguá. He went on to be an itinerant evangelist in Guatemala and a pastor in several locations in Honduras.[3] Clearly the stereotype of female leaders attracting only other women to Christ was not based on reality.

Paul Enyart marked the years of 1922–1930 as a nine-year period of relative plateau in growth for the entire Friends field in Central America. Yet when Enyart looked more carefully at the statistics, he decided there was actually decline in Guatemala but rapid increase in Honduras.[4] War and revolution hampered work in Honduras at the beginning but evangelism went forward anyway, and the church grew well there. The Guatemala churches, on the other hand, suffered several blows among their leaders. There was the married pastor who left his family for Cora Wildman. Then another well-known and powerful preacher fell into sin, and still other workers did not remain faithful. Paul Enyart believes the image of the church was damaged, forming an obstruction to growth.[5]

Despite all, Esther Smith gained attention as a capable organizer and an efficient administrator, "a woman of great faith and vision" who often worked against great obstacles.[6] A leader of the mostly female team, her particular gifts and administrative policies were formative in carrying the work forward. Her gift of compassion, her gift of "mothering," her gift of administration, and her example of prayerfully waiting on the Spirit for guidance gave structure and stability to the work.

A Gift of Compassion

Miss Ruth became known through the middle years for small gestures of helpfulness to national Christians. Sometimes she might mend a shirt. Many times she offered a glass of cold water to a traveler.[7]

In the beginning of the missions work in Guatemala, a missionary administered medicine from the medicine cabinet. Then there were missionary nurses, followed by Guatemalan student nurses who received training in the capital. The care given during the 1918–1919 influenza epidemic was particularly noteworthy. This thread of compassionate care was especially fleshed out as Esther strenuously advocated for a Friends hospital in Chiquimula, administered and staffed by Christian doctors and nurses. She went so far as to equate medical work with evangelism. While it isn't certain she wrote the following words, she surely approved: "True medical work is evangelical. Our Lord never separated the two but preached and healed as he went, and so should we. If we do not combine the two we cannot succeed. The true method is the Bible in one hand and the lancet in the other."[8]

For a decade or more, Esther promoted the cause of Angel Castro, a bright young boy who grew up in the center of the Chiquimula church family, and who had the intellectual and personal gifts to become a doctor. Miss Ruth monitored his education one step at a time for years, until he eventually completed an M.D. degree in the United States, married Mildred, and returned to Guatemala. As it turned out, Angel Castro served a mere two years with the mission before financial and organizational difficulties forced him to move to a government hospital where he continued to serve for many years.[9] The dream of a Friends hospital never came to be, but it wasn't for lack of concern by Esther Smith.

In retrospect, Paul Enyart came to believe the concern for a doctor and a hospital actually siphoned off resources of personnel, time, and money that could have been better spent planting new churches. He pointed to the years 1931–1935 as a period of positive growth, sparked by revivals in Desmontes, Chiquimula, and across the fields, but followed by plateau again when attention became focused mostly upon mission institutions like the hospital.[10] Could a witness to Christian compassion have been more effective by Christians working under government administration? The government was extending and improving health care to some degree, and perhaps quality workers serving within the government framework was more effective than the dreams for an institution under the mission's direction. But the failure to create a self-sustaining Christian hospital in Chiquimula was probably one of Esther Smith's great disappointments.

Yet her personal spirit of caring for others in crisis—including fellow missionaries in crisis—was strong. When the quiet bachelor farmer B. B. Williams came down with a painful and serious urinary-tract infection at age eighty, Miss Ruth and Helen Oakley oversaw his transport to a hospital. Berea students carried him on an iron cot, and he traveled by train to Zacapa. In Zacapa he was transferred to another train bound for the hospital in Quiriguá, down the Motagua River toward the Caribbean coast. Although B. B.'s prostate was removed, kidney function did not resume normally, and his heart was affected and he died. Over the next days Esther found herself weeping repeatedly, and she and Matilda Haworth and Helen Oakley were deeply touched by the believers who met them at various train stations as they returned to Chiquimula with the body. She was deeply touched by the many expressions of appreciation and condolences that came to the missionary staff and by the hundreds who attended the funeral. She had his body laid to rest in a tomb built near the grave of Paul Pearson, the ten-year-old-son of Howard and Julia Pearson, who had died a few years earlier—another funeral over which she had presided.[11]

A Gift of Mothering

It may be hard to prove scripturally that a gift of "spiritual parenting" actually exists among the gifts of the Holy Spirit, but Esther Smith repeatedly stated she felt it was one of her callings, especially in relationship to pastoral workers. Paul called Timothy "my true son in the faith" (1 Timothy 1:2), and his emotional tie with the Philippians sounds like a father's heartfelt affection (Philippians 1:3-11). We don't know the age difference between Priscilla and Apollos in Acts 18, but Priscilla may have "parented" him as she "explained the way of God more adequately" (verse 26). For many years Miss Ruth knew by name every one of the earliest believers, their spouses, their children, and their kinship links. She maintained a constant contact with many of them. Across the years she wrote daily messages to many, and later, daily messages to outlying groups of Christians. It is said that if there was no news to send, she sent a message anyway, saying "no news today," just to keep contact. In return, she was loved like a mother. The return telegrams were so regular on Mondays that one telegraph operator questioned if workers were paid for each convert reported.[12]

Esther Smith not only parented the pastors, she also loved the babies, taking them in her arms and playing with them. She often carried small gifts for toddlers, and she asked about the schooling opportunities for the older children. Young people—not just the "good ones, but the erring too"—received prayers and letters. Briefly before her death, for example, three young workers appeared early one morning for a final good-bye, saying they could not bear to return to their assignments without seeing her once more. When one young man named Agustin entered, she asked about his family and then about the work, and she urged the other two to tell her about their work and to write to her to keep her informed.[13] Down to the time of her death she tracked the traveling teams going out from Chiquimula and even the welfare of the mules.[14]

A Gift of Administration

Part of Esther Smith's administrative ability was writing comprehensive reports and maintaining a lively correspondence with the mission board and with supporters in California. She was listed as editor of *The Harvester* and as "founder of the Mission" for most of her forty-one years in Guatemala. Her task within the evangelical community was to evangelize a section of eastern and southeastern Guatemala in obedience to a comity agreement established in the early 1900s. Presbyterians, Nazarenes, Primitive Methodists, and Central American Mission took other segments of the country, while Friends worked the departments of Chiquimula, Zacapa, and Izabal. Thus, early evangelization was done without undue competition from other groups and aided in relationships with the government.[15]

While the national church was growing and developing, it was the mission, through Esther Smith, that controlled most of the church activity.[16] Although she was a leader, Esther lived her middle years not as the sole Quaker leader, however, but as a part of a community. She was involved in all major decisions, but individual missionaries were released to develop their specific gifts, talents, and calling.[17]

One great contribution Esther made was the recruitment of new mission staff. Lester Stanton wrote that everyone who came to serve in Central America during those years did so at least partly through the influence of the life or words of Miss Ruth.[18] Some of her letters and reports repeated the call for additional workers and the need for specific skills. Other letters were laced with the scheduling of furloughs and missionary health concerns. She had a staff to place, to care for, and occasionally to replace.

Another of her primary concerns was the administration of buildings and properties. She reported regularly on the numbers of chapels and meetinghouses built, the condition of the Chiquimula properties and the care of property titles. In early years a holding society was created with both American and Central American trustees listed, since it was illegal to issue a title in the name of a religious organization. The majority of the board of directors had to be nationals; only a national, not a missionary, could not serve as president—an important empowerment to the national church. As complicated as the process seemed—and as fraught with possible fraud—it worked reasonably well and no properties were lost or deadlocked in debate over ownership, even though this was common elsewhere in Latin America.[19] Superintendent Esther Smith was diligent in her watchful care. In her last year of life, after returning from a lengthy hospitalization, Esther's first request was to be wheeled through the Chiquimula properties to see what repairs were needed.

As noted earlier, R. Esther was not pleased with Five Years Meeting and took various occasions to distance the work of Friends in Central America from what she viewed as theological liberalism and a decline of missionary zeal within the parent group to which California Yearly Meeting belonged. She read *The American Friend*, the Five Years Meeting publication, and on one occasion lamented its lack of doctrinal references and little appreciation of the work of her good friend Jefferson Ford, Arthur Chilson's colleague in Kenya; she felt he was being slighted.[20] She was committed, she said, to "old-fashioned repentance and conversion of the sinner, to holiness of heart for the believer, to entire consecration in service and to that power that prevails in prayer." Those invited to minister in Central America included not only Friends like Jefferson Ford from Kenya, but holiness Methodists, Nazarenes, and Pilgrims (later the Wesleyan Church). The interdenominational holiness bent could not have been clearer.[21]

Esther Smith's annual reports of the Chiquimula Mission to California Yearly meeting were *tours de force* of statistics and details. They form her most concrete written legacy over her forty-one years of service, and included demographic surveys, records on giving, numbers of believers, monthly meetings, quarterly meetings, local camp meetings, pieces of property, bookstore sales, and the various departments of ministry: Bible schools, printing press, publications, farms, and industries! Annually she listed the staff and their locations and one year even counted all the livestock—ten kinds of animals including eighteen mules, six horses, ten oxen, thirty-five goats, assorted cows, one deer, plus uncounted chickens, turkeys, ducks, and rabbits.[22]

A major part of Chiquimula mission headquarters was the oversight of the mission institutions: schools, clinic, the print shop, the bookstore, and farms. The mission sold some products, but most of the farm products went to sustain missionaries, students, and teachers. For a few years a commissary bought lumber and manufactured goods wholesale for the convenience of the missionaries and some others in the community.[23]

Even though at times there may have been a shadow behind her optimism, Esther Smith's enthusiasm became legendary: "A day of blessing is here" (1923). "We unite in praising the Lord for the 'greater things'" (1924). "We enter the new year with glad and expectant hearts" (1925). "The Mission has no debt and is occupied with the conversion of sinners and the sanctification of believers" (1929). "In spite of financial strain, we have seen encouraging advances" (1931). "We have had a good year although we have sorely...felt the loss of funds" (1932). "We are persuaded that the missionary passion does not come of knowing the field, but [knowing] the Father; not the sins of the multitude, but [knowing] the Savior" (1934). "In these days of...widely separated standards of belief...we place emphasis on regeneration of the heart..." (1935). "We offer multitudinous proof of...truth and glory...of lives... transformed" (1936).

Yet deep struggle marked these years. Geography was not gentle and neither was society. In 1925, Esther wrote that, "In Guatemala the work calls us to labor in the mountain heights, among the difficulties of the frontiers, in fanatical centers, in the humid climates of the banana land, and in the Sodoms along the railroad."[24]

Political revolutions shook Guatemala and Honduras; the staff suffered severe malaria, typhoid, and dysentery; the entire mission deeply grieved the deaths of an elder missionary and a young missionary child. Growth itself also caused strain. New churches needed new pastors, buildings, and camp meetings. The Gualán district, where United Fruit Company workers were especially responsive, grew by leaps and bounds, as did the work in Honduras. But a revolution forced Honduran believers from their homes into the mountains. A massive earthquake and mudslide in Ocotepeque, Honduras, took not only a major portion of that city but also the lives of some Friends Christians. Revolutionary fighters stole an offering for the Bolivian field. A fire destroyed equipment at headquarters, and that same year a trained nurse drowned. The Great Depression years of the 1930s created empty accounts for mission programs.

Waiting on the Spirit

Esther Smith taught everyone that prayer was the most important part of his or her ministry. By all accounts, Esther's calls to prayer were her greatest contribution to the ministry. The headquarters staff, under her direction, formed a tight family as they shared meals around one table and enjoyed a great deal of interaction and collaboration. Josephine Still says, "Everything was dealt with by prayer"; this included personal conflict, financial support, and decision making. This was a pattern from very early times[25] and continued into the 1960s, twenty years after Esther's death. When a letters or messages related concerns, or when a problem arose, Esther Smith sent out from headquarters a call to prayer. Prayer included soul-searching, and waiting for solutions, but frequently also involved reconciliation and people "getting right" with God.[26] Mae Burk Stanton wrote that her dear friend's source of strength and zeal came through prayer. Esther prayed alone at times but always urged others to join her in intercession.[27] Matilda Haworth praised "her love, her burning zeal, her intense prayer, and call for more laborers."[28]

Disagreements seem to arise in every arena of Christian work. How did Esther respond when the missionary staff was *not* in unity? When Lily Almquist insisted on taking a twenty-four-year-old orphan with no Guatemala family ties home with her to the United States, Esther tried to put her foot down. The older missionaries counseled against Lily's plan, feeling the intimacy and favoritism would cause problems on the field, and that the expenditure of funds would cause tension between nationals and missionaries remaining on the field. While four of the older missionaries agreed with R. Esther, one missionary seemed to disagree and three remained neutral. "The letter is written. Have I done wrong?" Esther wrote. "My heart is wrung over what I ought to do."[29] Clearly she took seriously the work of "guiding this boat for so many years" as superintendent.

Was Miss Ruth right or wrong in regard to Lily? For a while, the young woman's trip to the United States was delayed because of health issues. There may well have been stress through the process, but the orphan in question, Hortensia Acosta, lived in the United States for a number of years, received a good English education, and eventually returned with missionary support to work in Guatemala and Honduras for more than twenty years.

Esther Smith was certainly strong-willed and maintained entrenched opinions. Perhaps she would not have survived emotionally or physically had she been otherwise. Yet, Helen Kersey (Ford), an early coworker, wrote of a tender side of spiritual discernment when R. Esther often sensed God was speaking to others and not just to her. The group followed a consensus model of decision making, talking out changes and waiting prayerfully so there could be unity of action, a pattern she consciously tried to carry forward from earlier years.[30]

Some time after Jefferson Ford's first visit to Central America, where Helen Kersey had served as Jefferson Ford's interpreter, the widower wrote back and proposed marriage to Kersey. Somewhat shocked and confused, she took the letter to Esther Smith. Esther had become famous for declaring that single women were more effective missionaries than married women, but to Kersey's surprise, she responded heartily, affirming there could be a good place of service for Jefferson Ford in Guatemala alongside Helen Kersey! After Jefferson and Helen married, God's leading went in another direction: the couple went to Kenya instead.[31]

What was the great contribution of Esther Smith's middle years? As much as anything it was her persistence, which allowed for continuity among field, field staff, and home constituency. Her emphasis upon holiness spirituality never wavered, and her joyful enthusiasm for Christ blessed many. Some, however, likely responded to her strength of character by feeling stifled and controlled. While she was appreciated for her parenting skills, there is some evidence that nationals were eager to make more decisions on their own. With time, the strong hand of a comprehensive administrator , however, created an administrative bottleneck.

Reflections:

How do you feel a woman in Christian ministry should respond to bias against women in ministry?

Of Esther Smith's various leadership gifts (compassion, "mothering," administration, and prayer) which is most appealing to you and why?

How important do you think relationship-building was to Esther Smith's spiritual gift of leadership?

What are the positives and negatives of a "strong-willed person" serving in missionary ministry?

chapter 8

The Declining Years: Finishing the Race

BY 1935, R. ESTHER SMITH had reached what would be considered the retirement age of sixty-five, but by no means had she stopped her active work. The California Friends Board had no mandatory retirement age. B.B. Williams, for one, died on the field at age eighty. Miss Ruth had no intention of returning to a homeland where she felt increasingly uneasy, where she had no close living relatives, and where people probably felt she was out-of-touch. Guatemala was her adopted country. Here she was appreciated as a mother, surrounded by work she knew and understood. She left California as a mature young woman of thirty-five, and by 1935 she had lived almost half her life in Central America. The last decade of her life was busy and eventful, but in some ways marked by limitations and decline.

Continued Plateau

In retrospect, we can see a general failure in church growth, according to Paul Enyart, who charts a plateau he believed lasted until the early 1950s. While the ladino church did not grow, neither was there growth among English-speaking Jamaicans, Chorti, or other indigenous Indians. Esther Smith's reports repeatedly called attention to the presence of these minority groups, but records indicate little action and less response. Esther and others had a true missionary awareness of unreached peoples, but they do not appear to have been well-equipped with the cultural tools necessary to discover a unique approach to reach populations other than the ladinos. Jamaicans and Chortis probably felt less welcomed in the schools and at Berea, and few non-ladino workers were ever commissioned. The *Amigos* school as early as 1929 noted that Christian families were moving to Chiquimula to enroll their children as day students rather than as boarding students.[1] Few Jamaicans or Chortis could have afforded to enroll or move. This lack of insight was certainly not Esther Smith's fault alone, but was shared equally with other staff members and the home board.

The Dark Side: "I'm in Charge Here."

Esther Smith's annual reports from 1936 through 1946 leave little doubt of her interest in the continued development of the mission and church, although her level of effectiveness is not as easily determined. She regularly encouraged a stream of American visitors and evangelists for annual church conferences and camp meetings. The numbers of such meetings gradually increased from forty-eight to sixty, although the estimated number of believers seemed to continue to remain close to 4,500. Berea Bible Institute was cleverly organized as a monthly meeting (a local church) to promote and govern their own practical ministries, personal spiritual disciplines, and to practice church governance. Esther Smith frequently extended her love and encouragement to the Ayllons of Bolivia as they spent time back in Chiquimula, returned to Bolivia with the United Bible Society for Aymara translation work, and then became reassigned as workers with Oregon Yearly Meeting in Bolivia.

In her later years, Esther Smith's ties with the Training School for Christian Workers at Huntington Park, California, came full circle, with the visits of officials of Oriental Missionary Society (a holiness mission agency, now OMS International), and of classmate Cecil Troxell and other people from National Holiness Missionary Society (now known as World Gospel Mission). With the rise of war in the Pacific, these two agencies were cut off from ministries first in China and Korea, and later in Japan and elsewhere in Asia, and were casting about for other outlets. A number of Holiness Society missionaries were reassigned to work with Central American Friends for several years. In consultations among the Tegucigalpa field superintendent, the California Friends Mission Board, and World Gospel Mission,[2] the entire work of Friends in the Tegucigalpa, Honduras, area was transferred to the National Holiness Society in 1944.[3] R. Esther Smith may have had little direct involvement, but she certainly knew everyone involved. This was much to the dismay of a core of loyal Honduran Friends workers who felt they were somewhat betrayed, having been left out of the negotiations.[4]

The Chiquimula Mission remained a faithful participant in Guatemalan comity arrangements. In the 1930s, it began sending delegates to the national synod (an organization of Guatemalan Christians that came to be known as the "Evangelical Union"), and the Inter-Mission Conference, a gathering of expatriates. Miss Ruth was well known among evangelicals throughout Guatemala, as evidenced by those who attended her funeral. During her last days, there is no effort to track Friends who moved to the capital city or to other departments that might have spurred new growth there, something that would have been frowned upon by the comity agreements to stay within limited geographic regions. Comity produced coverage and growth, but with time probably stifled the building of natural contacts and urban growth.

Esther's last two reports of 1945 and 1946 included the standard accounts of buildings, revivals, house-to-house saturation evangelism in local communities, and both men and women graduating from Berea.[5] Friends ministry in Chiquimula was centered on a large cluster of institutional buildings of several adjacent compounds, including a workshop to make school and church furniture, and where carpentry and masonry were taught to bi-vocational pastors.[6] She ended her last report stating a lifelong conviction: "Romanism could not spread what it did not have." She firmly believed the Roman Catholic Church had largely lost the essence of the gospel and that the work of missions in Latin America was that of pioneer evangelism, not sectarian "sheep stealing" from Catholicism.[7] She continued with a deep confidence in educational work to "break down prejudice."[8] Paul Enyart critiques this view, saying the prejudice and opposition may have been far less by the 1940s than reflected by a statement like this, and that more aggressive, broad-ranging evangelism and less attention to the education of a small, urban element seeking education was called for.[9] Even though the school children and youth were frequently channeled into evangelism, the usefulness of young evangelists under the tutelage of mission personnel might be questioned. The students were drawn from a narrow band of the population, and because of close ties with missionaries, were often somewhat cut off from national church leaders.

Paul Enyart came to believe that the church had outgrown the limits of Esther Smith's control and that no single person could effectively direct the work as she was attempting to do. He noted her strong, loving desire to maintain personal involvement. "She loved people, took pride in knowing the believers by name, and always maintained a warm and personal relationship with them. Needless to say, the people loved her, and 'Mis Rut' was a very special person to them."[10] But would it have been possible to maintain that loving warmth and yet transfer direct supervision to others? Enyart was doubtful.

Years earlier, Esther noted the churches were largely self-propagating "but less self-nourishing," indicating a lack in what we might today call discipleship.[11] That's the positive side of it. The negative side of her observation could have been a lack of confidence that national Christians could come to full maturity without reliance upon the spiritual nourishment provided by the missionaries. Undoubtedly, the potential for greater independence from the mission was hard for the missionaries to see, given the notorious political instability of the so-called "Banana Republics" through the late 1930s and World War II. The policy of the United States government that treated Central America with a combination of neglect and imperialistic self-interests would have helped set a tone of dependency that the Chiquimula staff may not have been able to resist.

Organic growth of new monthly meetings (local churches) and quarterly meetings (districts) went on apace and regional superintendents continued to be named, but in the later 1930s, when one would have expected more, the action toward field-wide self-governance was slow. The pattern had been established: The pastors and national workers were expected to report to Miss Ruth and she very faithfully encouraged all of them.[12] The first central church government was formed in 1932 with the naming of a general council of nine men and three women. Their rather limited task was to cooperate with the missionaries, arrange programs, and maintain doctrinal purity;[13] the missionaries were still basically in charge. Four years later, a body of representatives was formed of representatives elected from each district to meet annually during the Yearly Meeting in Chiquimula. In addition, all church members present in Chiquimula were eligible to attend a business session.[14] Still the initiative lay with the mission.

A mission council was organized in 1943 with Esther Smith still serving as mission superintendent over the council, and this council gave more formal opportunity to share in the making of some decisions.[15] Unfortunately, the creation of this council also meant creation of a fourth separate body, and there were no clear lines of authority among the four (the general council, the body of representatives, the yearly meeting, and the mission council). R. Esther Smith's decreased physical strength added to the problem and made her significantly less effective due to hospitalizations and increasing limitations to her management ability. Her travel was restricted, but she continued close relationships with missionaries and national workers, assuring them of prayer and maintaining lines of spiritual authority, so to speak. Her personal closeness to God was widely respected, not only by Christians but also by government officials, business people, and professionals of the Chiquimula region. But she could not offer the guidance needed and she found it difficult to delegate responsibility.[16]

In 1944 a committee to study reorganization began its work and it reported in 1946, leading the way for the creation of a "Faith and Practice" document outlining a structure of church government and defining the role of each component body.[17] Other steps were made in following years to perfect and clarify governance issues; in Esther Smith's last years as superintendent, there was a clear need for change but Esther provided little or no leadership for that change.

The Role of the Aging Missionary

The beloved Miss Ruth became well acquainted with illness across the years. Her 1907 bout with malaria left her feeling as if she had risen from the dead. But thirty-five years later at age seventy-two, she had a break of health that was different. It started with intense back pain that left her bedfast for six months, first in the town of

Quiriguá, then later in Chiquimula and in Guatemala City. Esther's ability to function normally was up and down for two years, and then she fell and broke a leg, causing her to spend more time in the hospital in Guatemala City until she was able to walk without crutches or a cane. From that point on, she alternated between bed and office, "down but not out!"

A few of Esther Smith's surviving letters from the last fifteen months of her life indicate an amazing persistence in the work. In December 1945 she wrote to the mission board a lengthy account of the placement of missionaries and the problems some were facing—loneliness, finding a house, repairs on a chapel ruined by an earthquake, pastoral changes, *The Harvester* going to press, and even the joys of the Astleford baby taking her first steps.[18] In July 1946 she continued official correspondence on behalf of the mission council as field superintendent; she acknowledged new staff coming, noted transportation and housing plans for a new young volunteer coming through New Orleans across the Gulf of Mexico, and expressed eagerness to receive the *Minutes* from the yearly meeting in California. Her letter reads like an annual report: conferences finishing, clinic busy, print shop at work, and grasshoppers coming toward Guatemala with rainless clouds adding to the plague.[19] Two weeks later she wrote of arrangements for two short-term workers.[20] Two months after that, she was negotiating with the Lutheran mission over church conflicts in Zacapa and Puerto Barrios, as comity arrangements had begun to break down and a pastor tried to lead two groups away from Friends.[21] Her serious, visible physical limitations seem invisible in the written record.

In November the new recruit planning to pass through New Orleans abruptly cancelled her journey and no longer considered herself a candidate. Esther ventured it was probably for the best, if the young woman was not living in spiritual victory. Esther looked forward to a visit by the board executive R. Ernest Lamb,[22] which happened during the first two months of 1947 just prior to her death.[23]

Esther was almost entirely bedfast for the last three months of her life, although she sometimes came to meals in a wheelchair. She was weak and susceptible to infections, and in the final weeks, her hearing was almost entirely gone. Her pulse raced to 130, 150, or 180 beats per minute and pneumonia set in. She talked very little during the last ten days, and her death was quiet—"just a cessation of breathing and she was gone."[24] Her death came almost five years after the initial severe back pain that hospitalized her in 1942.

With none of Esther's relatives present, the missionaries acted as Esther's family, greeting "spiritual children" who came to express their sadness. Her missionary family decided that Esther really belonged to the native people and they should be allowed to honor her in their own way, although the missionaries retained control over her public memorial service and the location of burial. Many of the activities in the few days following Esther's death were thoroughly Guatemalan. Sixty telegrams were transmitted around the country, three telegrams went to the United States, and three couriers were sent throughout Chiquimula the following day. An all-night wake was held the night following her death, and hundreds of people appeared for coffee and cake. The standard evangelical practice was followed and the wake became a worship service with preaching and an altar call. The accounts of the wake, while sentimental, indicate something unusual in Esther's bond with the people: "She was our mother." "How can we live without her?" "I loved her." The Presbyterian mission sent 150 Easter lilies, other English-speaking friends sent huge bouquets, and a large number of other floral arrangements arrived anonymously.[25] More than one hundred telegrams of condolences came in during the next two days. It was an outpouring of genuine respect and appreciation.

The funeral service proper was held the following afternoon on the mission property with approximately one thousand people in attendance—the largest funeral the city of Chiquimula had ever seen. Fellow missionary Matilda Haworth directed the service, Mae Burk Stanton read the obituary, Guatemalan friends sang, and Lester Stanton preached a sermon about being "a flaming torch for God" and spreading the light of the gospel. Eighty-eight-year-old missionary Dr. Edward Haymaker represented the Presbyterian mission, and there was a representative from Central American Mission (both were pioneer agencies that entered Guatemala just ahead of Friends). A long procession of Guatemalan Friends traveled all night by train, by car, on mule-back, and on foot to attend the service, and several of their leaders spoke and prayed.[26] Those who spoke shared memories of Esther's whole-hearted devotion, intercessory prayer, and a determination to "preach the Gospel to every creature."[27] Guatemalan men took turns, six or eight at a time, carrying Esther's body from mission headquarters to the nearby cemetery just down the hill.

Lester Stanton, her successor as chair of the mission council, later observed that the death certificate recorded she "died with no will and left no property." Instead, she left a rich legacy of memories. One Guatemalan submitted a lengthy and florid letter in Spanish about mourning in the schools, in the dining room, and in the garden, and with raised hands in the Tabernacle, and that people recalled "that motherly smile." The letter read, "I greet you no longer in the name of the Lord, but in the presence of the Lord. You are not dead, Miss Ruth. Your memory is more living in our hearts than ever before." The writer noted that Esther's questions about "how the work is going" would be missed, and puzzled over "what impelled you to come to die in a place like this?"[28]

Esther Smith's Legacy

Helen Kersey Ford wrote publicly from Kenya with appreciation that the board had allowed Esther Smith to live out her last days in Guatemala, surrounded by the people and culture she knew and loved best. It was a compassionate thing to do, she said.[29] Yet one of the immediate results of Esther Smith's death was the establishment of a mandatory retirement age by the California Friends Mission Board. They hoped to avoid administrative bottlenecks such as that created by Esther's last five years of illness and subsequent death.

Despite the problems, none can deny the example of a deep faithfulness and commitment to the Great Commission lived and breathed by "Miss Ruth of Chiquimula." An account of weaknesses and failures should not obscure her stature and greatness. She was correctly hailed as a pioneer who gave faithful and fruitful service. Her prolonged, scripturally-based leadership and her seeking the guidance of the Holy Spirit through godly men and women firmly cast a vision for a growing church.[30] A theological refrain from her 1938 report is typical: "Our position concerning what we call vital, has not modified; our sails are still set to the breeze of a full salvation; the compass ever points that way."[31]

To summarize, we note the following major contributions to Friends missionary theory and practice from the life and work of R. Esther Smith:

She believed in prayer and practiced it consistently. People always commented about her life of prayer.

She reveled in the gospel's power to change drunkards into preachers and wife abusers into gentle pastors. She frequently wrote conversion stories in *The Harvester* and believed in purity of heart and actions.

In her own way, she worked to empower workers. She wrote repeatedly that, "Our wealth [is] our native preachers and the sanctified members who are our continual delight."[32] She meant it deeply, even when she failed to release those workers to the supervision of others.

She established and promoted equality of women with men in ministry. Her reports frequently pointed out the effectiveness of single female national workers and also married couples who formed pastoral teams—a strong pattern that has continued among Central American Friends well into the twenty-first century.

She believed in the social uplift of the gospel, and believed schools and medicine were compatible with a holiness gospel, even if some later analysts came to believe this was not always strategically linked to church growth. "We climb upward toward the goal," she wrote, describing the educational program of the mission.[33]

She rallied support for the Bolivian mission and outreach beyond Central America. From Juan Ayllon's arrival in 1922 until the early 1940s, she promoted Juan's ministry and a concern for the Bolivian Aymara Indians. Esther Smith would be delighted beyond measure to know of the autonomous yearly meetings now existing in Bolivia and Peru, and of Central American Friends missionaries now serving in Nicaragua, North Africa, and Southeast Asia.

Reflections:

Had you been present during Esther Smith's last five years, how would you have reorganized the mission for more effective leadership, if it were within your power to do so?

What is your response to God's chosen workers who have passed their prime but still have much to offer in spirit and wisdom?

Review Esther Smith's six major contributions to the theory and practice of Christian missions. Which of these are most commonly omitted in missions of the twenty-first century?

Which of the six contributions do you feel may have represented Esther Smith at her very best?

In what ways do you believe Esther Smith may have contributed to the creation of a missionary-sending church?

Everett L. Cattell

chapter 9

Childhood, Education, and Marriage

EVERETT LEWIS CATTELL, the third of the twentieth-century Quaker missionaries in our study, was the best known, most influential, and most articulate of the four.[1] Yet Everett's twenty-one years in India were haunted by an abject failure to produce a growing, vibrant community of faith, by personal tragedies and severe illness, and by complex criminal court proceedings against him. How was it that from the ashes of failed goals and betrayals there arose a widely admired statesman, an advocate of evangelical holiness, and a proponent of world mission? The story of Everett Cattell is a story of Ohio holiness Friends, of world vision, of India, and of a man uniquely called and equipped for a stunningly difficult job.

Childhood

Everett Cattell was born to Herman C. Cattell and Gertrude Frances Hole Cattell on September 16, 1905, in Kensington, Ohio, about forty miles southeast of Alliance where the family later made its home. Columbiana County was dotted by Quaker settlements in the late eighteenth and early nineteenth centuries, creating the beginnings of Ohio Yearly Meeting. The yearly-meeting headquarters were first at Mt. Pleasant, south of Kensington, and later at Damascus, Ohio, north of Everett's birthplace. Mt. Pleasant was a hotbed of Quaker abolitionist activities in the mid-1800s and the Underground Railroad that harbored escaped slaves that crossed the Ohio River, leaving Virginia for freedom. This was also a region where the nineteenth-century schisms were intense, creating Hicksite, Wilberite, and Orthodox branches of Quakerism.

The Cattell family line identified with the Orthodox and Evangelical wing of Quakerism that was profoundly influenced by the same Friends Holiness Movement that propelled Arthur Chilson and Esther Smith into missionary service. Ohio Quakers like the Cattells carefully followed the exploits of Kenya missionaries Arthur Chilson, Edgar Hole, and Willis Hotchkiss. Esther Smith was born in western

Ohio, and like Edna Chilson, moved to Kansas before beginning her missionary career. Ohio Friends like Dougan Clark and David B. Updegraff were unusually powerful in the Ohio Holiness Movement and placed their stamp upon Walter and Emma Malone and upon the training schools established in Cleveland, Ohio, and Huntington Park, California. At the beginning of his career, Everett Cattell pastored and taught in Cleveland. At the close of his career, he served as president of the Cleveland school shortly after it moved to Canton, Ohio, to become Malone College—its greatest transition.

Both Herman and Gertrude Cattell claimed a lengthy Quaker heritage, one back to the family of Margaret Fell Fox, the wife of George Fox, founder of the Quaker movement. The Cattell home was devout, with high moral standards and principles. Personal and social integrity were important. Mother Gertrude had a deep interest in missions and for a time served as secretary of the Ohio Yearly Meeting Board of Missions. Herman Cattell later served the same board as treasurer.[2] One family story tells of young Everett holding his head out of the open touring car to face the cold Ohio wind, to better condition himself for missionary service.[3]

As a teenager, Everett was a gifted public speaker, entering oratorical contests during high school. He spent one year at Methodist-related Mt. Union College in Alliance, Ohio, and three years at holiness-oriented Marion College in Indiana. He began assisting with revival meeting preaching at age nineteen.[4]

Catherine DeVol

For understanding many of the details and the emotional tone of Everett Cattell's life, we depend a great deal upon the woman who became his wife. Through her own story, Catherine DeVol Cattell has contributed greatly to understanding Everett Cattell's place as a missionary statesman, without really focusing upon Everett himself. Catherine influenced her husband through her own missionary background, her emotional sensitivity, and her openness to people around them, enough so that Catherine's story becomes a major part of Everett's story.

Catherine DeVol's parents met in New York a few weeks before her mother, Dr. Isabella French, left for China in 1897. Romance sparked between the two medical doctors and carried forward to engagement by letters for two years while Catherine's father, Dr. George Fox DeVol, worked to pay off medical-school debts back in the United States. They married in Nanjing, China, in 1900 where they established a medical service in neighboring Luho. There they remained until George F. DeVol's death in 1917, the first of several tragedies and hardships in Catherine DeVol Cattell's life. Strong-willed and yet vulnerable, she struggled with the high expectations placed upon her and her brothers after the death of her mother in the United States three years later in 1920. The pathos and drama of their situation was lost on no one.

Catherine and her two brothers came under the guardianship of Elbert and Martha Benedict of Alum Creek Friends Meeting in central Ohio, but Catherine felt the eyes of all the Yearly Meeting riveted upon her and older brother Charles. Catherine and Charles enrolled at Marion College in Indiana, a school within the Wesleyan Holiness Movement that provided liberal arts education and even pre-medical courses. Educational guardians appointed by Ohio Yearly Meeting fully expected the two older DeVol children to follow their deceased parents into medical missions in China. But neither Catherine nor Charles became medical doctors, it was their younger brother, Ezra, who entered medicine.[5] All three, however, eventually became distinguished missionaries, each with powerfully unique gifts and ministries, beloved and honored by evangelical Friends across the United States.

At Marion College, Catherine DeVol's friendship with Everett Cattell developed as both thoroughly enjoyed college life. And with time, Catherine felt free to be herself and to worry less about what she came to believe was a "phony compulsion to fulfill [her] parents' lifework."[6] Everett *wanted* to be a missionary to China for Catherine's sake, but never felt the inner driving concern or a sense of divine calling to be one. Even though his attraction to Catherine was strong, in all honesty, he never claimed he felt God was calling him to China at this stage. Catherine felt she and Everett were "so right" for each other and that they would eventually go to China just as her brother Charles and his wife were planning to do,[7] so they pursued their romance.

Meanwhile, back in Ohio Quakerdom and the Benedict home, the burden upon the DeVol children grew as people retold the story of their promises to a dying mother that they would return to China as missionaries. As far as Elbert Benedict was concerned, the decision was made and nothing would come between Catherine and her call to China—not even an impertinent young suitor from Marion College named Everett Cattell. So when Everett arrived at the Benedict home in Ohio to ask permission to marry Catherine, he was asked about his call to China. When he maintained his simple integrity that he sensed no call to China, the answer was a resounding "no" to marriage plans.[8]

Over the course of the next few months, Catherine came to peace over the superficial and confusing "call" she had claimed earlier, eventually coming to believe that her call to China was not from God, but from a combination of a childhood nostalgia to return to China, the sense of emotional commitment to her dead parents, and the expectations of Ohio Quakers to follow the family tradition. In addition, her brother Charles and his wife, Leora, were making plans to return to China, which they did in 1926, assuming responsibilities for schools and evangelism in the Luho area near Nanjing. To Catherine everything "human" was calling out to return to her homeland.[9] Wise counselors and Catherine's own ability to sort out her emotions eventually allowed her to believe she could follow Christ and yet make her own God-directed choices. And her first big choice was to marry Everett Cattell.

Marriage

With that settled, plans for the wedding went forward with the acceptance of the Benedicts, although they insisted in Quaker simplicity that the wedding be scaled back considerably and that it not be the "Quaker event" the young couple may have envisioned. The Ohio Friends missionary community Catherine considered her closest friends and family were cut off from the wedding celebration, with at least a shadow of shame for Catherine not appearing to follow God's will.[10]

While prior to their marriage Catherine had found international living at the heart of her identity, Everett was not a stranger to the concept either. His parents both served on the Yearly Meeting Board of Missions and his childhood had included frequent reports from Ohio Friends missionaries in China and India and elsewhere. The concern for missions that swept through Midwest Friends from 1870 to 1905 deeply influenced Ohio Friends, even though they stayed aloof from the Five Years Meeting that became the parent body for the American Friends Board of Foreign Missions. By the turn of the century, Five Years Meeting came to sponsor the majority of Friends missions, including the Friends Industrial Mission of Kenya where Arthur Chilson served, while Ohio Friends instituted and maintained two fields independent from Five Years Meeting— work in central China and in north India. Yet with marriage, Everett and Catherine's thoughts turned to ministry in America, not overseas, as they followed what Everett felt to be his calling and gifting.

The Pastoral Years

The newlyweds Everett and Catherine settled in their first home, a Friends parsonage in Columbus, Ohio, where they lived for three years. Their next charge was a year working with a church plant in Springfield, Ohio, followed by five years at Cleveland First Friends. In Cleveland, Everett taught part time at Cleveland Bible Institute,[11] the school that commissioned Arthur Chilson, Edgar Hole, and Willis Hotchkiss to Kenya, and the holiness tradition that nurtured Esther Smith of Guatemala. In Cleveland during the middle years of the Great Depression of the 1930s, wealthy members became poor overnight and yet Everett oversaw the move of the congregation from what had become the "red-light district" to a more suitable part of town.[12]

In Cleveland, and specifically at Cleveland Bible Institute, Everett Cattell became known for his thoughtful preaching and teaching and his careful reflection upon the deeper spiritual life. He

141

spoke of the Friends' emphasis upon the work of the Holy Spirit and the Wesleyan purity-of-heart emphasis that had so deeply influenced Friends through what came to be known as the National Holiness Association of America. As a young Christian, he had found problems relating the Wesleyan teaching to his own experience, and came to believe the Holiness Movement had stressed some truths to the neglect of others. He began identifying some of those problems: a concern for crisis sanctification at the expense of nurture, a failure to distinguish between a carnality to be eliminated and a purified human nature to be disciplined, and a failure to recognize ongoing temptation in the life of a Christian.[13] He tried to preach with greater clarity, believing the "doctrine of holiness squared better with Scripture when it was kept in balance."[14]

During the pastoral years in the United States he completed a master's degree.[15] As a pastor, he came to believe that the differences between Wesleyan "Holiness" and other "Victorious Life" movements were not profound, and more a matter of definition than reality. Thus, the stage was set for a more wide-ranging evangelical ecumenical ministry yet to come.[16] Everett was strong in intellect, compassion, and integrity. People began admiring him for his selfless concern for others and his rich, personal devotion to Jesus Christ.[17]

Children David and Barbara Anne Cattell were both born during the Cleveland years and Everett and Catherine opened their home to Catherine's brother Ezra who had enrolled at Western Reserve Medical School, helping him with room, board, and personal expenses. Everett's other brother-in-law, Charles, was already in China, and Ezra, too, was preparing for China. Everett and Catherine were enjoying "wonderful years" in a comfortable American pastorate. They could have gone on there forever, they thought. But to their surprise, India abruptly intruded upon their lives.

The Call to India

Catherine as a missionary orphan had depended upon the Ohio Yearly Meeting structure and the Benedicts for years, reinforcing the China missionary family network that included "uncle" Walter R. Williams.

After Williams's return from China, he became missionary superintendent for the yearly meeting with supervision over both China and India. After a visit to India in 1936 to confront a personnel crisis, he immediately issued a call among the churches for new workers to replace several who had just resigned. Without reinforcements, the forty-year-old field would close. Everett, pastor in Cleveland, felt drawn to make a strong public appeal to his congregation on New Years Eve 1935. Although Everett had a strong interest and sympathy for missions, he had never felt a call personally, even though he had prayed for such a call during his college years. His wife, Catherine, later wrote that Everett felt going to India themselves was out of the question, because he believed Catherine would never consider it. If God called them anywhere, it would be to China. Catherine had always felt drawn to China, yet not for what she came to believe were the right reasons.

After Everett made the public appeal to his church for a missionary to India, a burden for India pressed upon both of them separately and without their speaking of it. Here is the conversation that took place three months later as recorded by Catherine in *From Bamboo to Mango*.

"I've been thinking about India a lot lately," said my husband.

"Yes, I know. I have, too."

"You have? Why, I was afraid you would not want to consider it."

"I don't, but I have been doing it anyway."

"I wonder if God wants us to offer to go," he ventured.

"I know. I wonder, too."

Once the subject was open, they could not stop thinking about it.[18] Says Catherine, "India pressed upon us both. The need was urgent. The field was to be closed if someone did not volunteer....Did God want us to consider it? I did some more dying during that time."[19]

One day in their burden and enthusiasm, they started driving from Cleveland south to the yearly-meeting headquarters in Damascus, Ohio, to tell the mission board of their call. Catherine, however, felt somewhat checked and asked Everett, "How can we assume we will do any better than the five [missionaries] who resigned?" In response, Everett turned around and headed home. They decided together to speak no further to anyone and wait for the board to act. "If God wants us to go to India, let Him suggest our names to the Board. That would be a confirmation." When a telephone call came several weeks later in early June, Walter Williams invited them to think it over for a while. Everett responded, "No—we have been thinking it over for months. This was the fleece: that you call *us*."[20] The next morning they drove to yearly-meeting headquarters and were placed under appointment to India in September.[21]

It was a measure of the Cattells' stature among Friends and the decisiveness of their call that the appointment was completed so swiftly. They knew their own minds and hearts and the board trusted them fully. Family concerns were wrapped up quickly, but a replacement pastor for the Cleveland church was a sticking point. The church was in debt and protested the loss of their pastors. All kinds of reasons were given to turn them away. The problem was resolved by Walter R. Williams himself accepting a call to the Cleveland church, thus easing a major stress upon the Cattells and sending them quickly on their way to India.[22] The Cattells left Ohio in September and arrived in India October 1936.[23] Their close relationship with Walter Williams would last for more than two additional decades with frequent letters, sharing of concerns, and seeking answers for the problems and issues of a mission work that had produced very few conversions.

Reflections:

What do we have to learn from Catherine Cattell's call to missionary service?

How do you think Christian communities can best encourage and nurture a missionary call among their young people?

What do we have to learn from Everett Cattell's call to missionary service?

Read again the opening paragraph of this chapter. What irony do you sense in the life of Everett Cattell in the story yet to come?

chapter 10

The India Mission

THE INDIA TO WHICH Everett and Catherine Cattell journeyed was in the throes of the pre-World War II anti-colonial movement. Hindu and Muslim religious elements conspired against one another while Mahatma Ghandi attempted to weld them into one nationalist movement to wrest independence from British control. The Cattells entered a small missionary enclave in north central India that had survived threats, famine, and internal discord; survival may have been its greatest achievement during its first forty years.

The India Friends Mission

Missionary pioneers Esther Baird and Delia Fistler went to India near the end of 1892 after having sensed a call to India in the environment of Cleveland Bible Training School and under the influence of Walter and Emma Malone. The Malones helped the two young women connect with each other and with the Board of Foreign Missions of Ohio Yearly Meeting. Later, the Malones did a similar service for Arthur Chilson and Willis Hotchkiss. Esther Baird and Delia Fistler traveled to India under the sponsorship of the Methodist Mission with the understanding they would study language under the Methodist umbrella until they could start their own ministry in the name of Friends.

After about three years, they settled upon the province of Bundelkhand as a great "untouched district" with no Christian witness. Then a Wesleyan chaplain to British soldiers called their attention to the Bundelkhand city of Nowgong[1] where they arrived in April 1896 in the middle of a famine. Esther Baird was a nurse and she and Delia Fistler immediately began relief work, feeding the starving and caring for orphans. More than five hundred children were placed in orphanages around India, some of them at a great distance. They themselves cared for a few orphans in Nowgong, with the strategy that these would become evangelists and church leaders. They gave them housing, food, training, schooling, and discipline, and arranged marriages for them from the beginning and across decades to come.[2] They were convinced they were winning a hearing for the gospel through their compassion.[3]

The humanitarian and institutional nature of the India Friends Mission became firmly and quickly established: food and medicine for the sick and poor, orphanages for the abandoned, and schools for the orphans. Courageous compassion was recorded by Merrill Coffin in *Friends in Bundelkhand* and by Esther Baird in *Adventuring with God*, but both books obscure the fact that the new Christians strongly tended to separate from their culture, depended almost entirely upon the mission for livelihood and social standing, and took little initiative beyond obeying directions from the missionaries. Despite all, however, social change was pioneered for untouchables, a few women were freed from the cloister of the Indian *zenana* (women held in seclusion), and a few were converted to Christ.

The first Friends Meeting established in 1902 was led exclusively by missionaries and consisted of their close associates. As much as they tried to avoid an "artificial life" in which "natural habits of life" became Americanized and orphans were separated from their culture, it happened anyway.[4] Everett very quickly observed that the orphanages confirmed an impression that the only people willing to become Christians were those who agreed to cut themselves off from all relatives and friends and go "to the compound to live where you will probably get a better salary."[5] Some orphans who left Bundelkhand found employment and acceptance in Christian communities elsewhere.

The mission staff consisted exclusively of single women for the first seventeen years and only four men joined the staff during the next sixteen years. Each of the male missionaries served only a few years, while nineteen women served varying lengths of time, six of them for long periods.[6] Perhaps there was an imbalance in gender and gifts. Official attention and pride was given to building up the mission institutions in Nowgong and Chhatarpur. A Bible training school opened in 1925 with a curriculum similar to that of Cleveland Bible Institute, but with only three students.[7] In contrast with the women of Guatemala, this group of women were unable to raise up strong and independent indigenous leaders.

Chhatarpur was the regional capital of Bundelkhand, and Nowgong was a smaller nearby town where the work started. When permission was later granted to develop a site in Chhatarpur, Chhatarpur gradually became the center of mission activity with out-schools and some small worship groups in neighboring villages. Village evangelists received payment from the mission and joined the mission-employed Indian teachers, administrators, nurses, pharmacists, and medical aides in living on the compounds. Thus the Friends Christian community tended to separate from the Hindu culture and depended almost entirely upon the mission for livelihood and social standing in a culture where social structure was strictly defined and enforced.

Analyzing Pressures Against Evangelism

Opposition to Christian evangelism was real and persistent—from local princes, from local Hindu merchants, from high-caste business people, and from the regional British administrators. None other than Mahatma Gandhi himself called in Methodist bishop Pickett for a personal consultation to stop conversion efforts. Pickett had the view that "evangelism must come first" and Everett immediately agreed with him, recognizing it would be easier to start a new mission that way. But Friends had a school, an orphanage, and hospital on their hands, and a "compound Christian community" to complicate their task![8]

The complication was profound and actually seemed to add to the pressures against evangelism. "Why our missionaries for forty years have allowed the impression to remain with our people [in the United States] that these [institutions] were successful evangelistic agencies in India, I do not fully understand," he wrote.[9] Although Everett was a person of great compassion, with a high sense of justice and concern for equality and a tender heart toward suffering, he quickly became fully convinced that in India institutions of compassion had turned sour and were stifling evangelism. His focus quickly

147

came to be upon the church—upon empowered and spiritual leadership, upon a church free of foreign control and domination, upon a church culturally capable and eager to win relatives, friends, and neighbors to Christ in an ever-expanding circle of love and transformation. Such a church was not possible through mission institutions.

Shortly after arriving, Everett began looking for ways to keep the worship services and functions of the church from being so missionary-dominated. Esther Baird's ideal of church organization was to follow the Quaker method of having no pastor or designated speaker. In Everett's estimation, however, this merely prevented any Indian leader from being empowered, and actually allowed for missionary dominance to continue. Part of Everett's first year of learning included a study of cottage industries (to learn how Christians could achieve better self-support), and a survey of locations elsewhere in India where revivals and church growth were being experienced. He was a great reader. In his first few months in India he read fifteen books on mission problems in India.[10]

He was adamant about the necessity of a Bible school for training and empowering preachers and teachers to build an independent national church. But schools for non-Christian children, he came to believe, actually built further resistance to the gospel because students in such schools were pressured by parents and Hindu pundits to be wary of the religious baggage carried by the Christian school, and to "capture the education" but avoid being evangelized.

What about using medical aid to overcome opposition? "If the mission [develops medical aid] as evangelistic bait," Everett said, "it seems to erect a resistance to the Gospel and at best it is a foreign thing and makes it difficult later for the church to take it over if indeed there ever is a church there. The tendency is to…establish more and more compounds."[11] He was not opposed to medical ministry in principle, but he wanted it to arise from within the church as an expression of their love and to meet the needs of the church rather than it being a foreign compound-building force, which he believed would only harden opposition.[12]

Dealing with Esther Baird

What were the problems with Esther Baird? Who dared criticize this saintly, self-sacrificing veteran of forty years' service in one of the poorest and most oppressed corners of central India? As a cofounder of the mission, she had persisted for forty years. Rather suddenly in the 1930s, five younger missionaries resigned simultaneously after sharp friction with her. With a barrage of letters the five protested against Esther Baird and the mission board, who they felt never gave attention to their grievances.[13] Earlier, other missionaries had chafed under Esther's direction and had felt equally mistreated, but this time around there were several clear charges. Why was there money for medical work but not missionary salaries? Where was the support for new methods? Why was Esther Baird so unsupportive of mission staff when complaints by disgruntled Indians were leveled against them?[14] How were they to conduct evangelization when there seemed to be hints of a written agreement that the mission would not accept converts to Christianity?[15]

The five resigning missionaries circulated a stinging letter with partial and misleading information to pastors and leaders of Ohio Yearly Meeting. They vented their frustrations and further alienated the senior missionaries and the mission board. The door was firmly closed against reinstating them.[16] According to mission colleague Anna Nixon's evaluation, however, the remaining Mission Council members[17] could not fully defend themselves against the complaints. The charges by the resigning missionaries were based on "facts and conditions" that could not be denied. Nevertheless, "it seemed clear," Anna Nixon believed, "that the Board had [also] been at fault for not listening more carefully to the new missionaries."[18]

The mission board responded by appointing Walter R. Williams as mission superintendent for India and China and by having him visit India to resolve the situation left in the hands of the two remaining missionaries: Carrie Wood and Esther Baird (with Alena Calkins gone on furlough).[19] Williams spent more than three months in India and he wrote his report to the Ohio Friends Board on shipboard as he returned and presented the report in Ohio in June 1936. Esther Baird protested that the investigation was stacked against her from the first. She quoted Williams as saying as much—that it was usually the fault of the senior missionary when a younger missionary does not fit in.[20] His report to the board was far more tactful and balanced, however, as he made five pointed recommendations that were to influence the kind of ministry the Cattells were about to face:

1. The Christian community must become more self-supporting.

2. Although Esther Baird had, more than any other person, built up the institutions of the mission and was held in high esteem, her relationships with fellow workers was flawed and she exercised "too great and detailed supervision over the members of her staff."[21]

3. Esther Baird should be retired by 1937.

4. The staff should be increased to no fewer than eight missionaries.

5. The mission board must develop a steadier plan for financial support.[22]

While the report dealt with immediate personnel issues and recognized something systemically wrong with the small Christian community, it did little or nothing to establish a new strategy. The call for volunteers was successful, however. Everett and Catherine Cattell responded and changes began.

Winning Esther Baird

The mission board specified in August 1936 that Everett was to be made chair of the India Mission Council as early as possible.[23] Yet they faced a ticklish situation. How could he win the confidence of the mission staff and Indian Christians while working to ease the revered Esther Baird out of her position? Furthermore, Esther Baird was a member of the Cleveland, Ohio, church where the Cattells pastored, and Everett was painfully aware of the hurtful situation she was facing.[24]

Everett was nothing if not tactful. He actually spent the first year and longer, he said, "working along the old lines...until I can get a hold well enough to be sure of myself in leading out in new methods."[25] His first great accomplishment in India was winning the confidence of Esther Baird and finding a place in the mission for himself and his family, even though he knew the board wanted him in Baird's place of leadership. In letters home, he told of a casual conversation with her, letting her know he came as a learner and he had no criticism of the past. Given some assurances, Esther Baird came up with a suggestion for new evangelism among the Nowgong Chamar people—a depressed outcast group that had shown some responsiveness. She had already done a lot of thinking about the research of Donald McGavran and Methodist bishop J. Waskom Pickett in mass movements and thought a new approach might be possible under the direction of Everett Cattell![26] A younger new-comer with less pastoral experience and a lower self-image than Everett would not likely have been as successful with Esther Baird.

Everett and Catherine Cattell had been sent to India to salvage a Friends mission program in serious jeopardy of being dismantled. Everett's first task was to encourage unhappy people, to avoid criti-cism of the past and of Esther Baird in particular, and to "bide his time" with Esther until she was gone before making many changes. He was kindly and open, and—amazingly—had serious mission policy discussions with her without alienation.

Esther Baird openly stated, however, that she felt she was being treated as a scapegoat for mission-board failures. While Everett acknowledged her suffering, both to her and to the board, he rejected the idea she was being treated as a scapegoat. With Esther, he defended the board. With the board, he stressed Esther's trauma caused by her lifetime's work being criticized, but in his writing to Walter Williams he agreed with the board's concern that the Chris-tian community was "horribly dependant upon the mission for its livelihood," a concern Esther Baird felt defensive about.[27]

It seems Everett Cattell had an amazing ability to separate his feelings and responsibilities from those of others, as is demonstrated first in his dealing with Esther Baird. Even at this point in history he knew it was not his job to "fix" Esther Baird, but rather to encourage her and to bless her on her way. He could suspend judgment of Esther Baird and yet affirm the judgment rendered by the board.[28] In the process, he admitted the strain and confusion of the cross-cultural setting but still struggled to identify which issues to discuss with the board and which to lay aside as irrelevant—always a concern to an administrator. Years later, close to the time of Esther Baird's death in the United States, Everett noted "radical changes" that came with his tenure, but that through the years after Esther's retirement, she had come to support those changes.[29]

First Steps as an Administrator

Everett Cattell sensed the need to eliminate "the controversial from our field" with the constituency back home. For example, one former missionary's proneness to temper tantrums was enough to lead Everett to discourage the board from re-commissioning that person. Yet Everett wrote about the need "to see both sides of the issue," and to get a larger perspective from outside "his own station's past"—the narrow Bundelkhand experience of Friends.[30]

His early letters reveal a broad-ranging intellect. For example, he was eager to learn from a secularized Presbyterian doctor who understood the culture and needs of India and promoted "a ministry of helpfulness." On the other side of the issue, the World Dominion Movement of England argued for direct evangelism as the highest priority, the importance of working through the indigenous church, and the crucial need for empowered indigenous leadership. They promoted the missionary policy of China Anglican missionary Roland Allen. Donald McGavran's theories were congenial to the same movement, although they went beyond the World Dominion Movement in many ways. To Everett, India, especially Bundelkhand, was light-years away from "indigenous-church theory." For example, he lamented the futility of a missionary taking the lead in church discipline. In one case, Esther Baird solved a conflict between a husband and wife by insuring a mission payroll job if the couple would continue living together! "Far from a work of grace," he wrote.[31]

Another administrative concern was the preparation of a written discipline, or constitution for the church. For forty years, nothing of the sort had been done. A British document outlining Quaker procedure had circulated, but nothing had ever been officially discussed or approved. The only "real discipline in our Nowgong Monthly Meeting," wrote Everett, "[is] the missionary."[32] In the same letter to the Ohio board, he suggested some guiding principles for a constitution: 1) creation of superior and subordinate congregations; 2) the naming of local oversight committees to shepherd souls and preserve spiritual life; 3) creation of a quarterly meeting with representatives of congregations coming together for business and worship; 4) a division of powers between monthly meetings (local congregations) and the mission council until such a time as a yearly meeting could be formed; 5) a beginning document to govern "compound Christians" but a document that could be altered significantly as soon as direct converts from Hinduism began to appear, since the document he proposed failed utterly to deal with idolatry, polygamy, and other moral issues that he knew would arise.[33] Amazingly, no such document had ever been proposed for the India Friends Mission and church.

In all of this, mission unity was placed seriously at risk. Everett, however, saw his responsibility as a leader to bring people together in harmony. His approach was to build up personal trust and confidence in each other to the point that there was trust even when there was a sharp difference of opinion. He undertook this first with Esther Baird and Alena Calkins, and repeated the same approach with Carrie Wood and Dr. Hull Bennett when they arrived not long after.[34]

New missionary job assignments quickly became another major issue. Everett wanted to loosen the chains of the past and open windows for new thinking: "Fixed types of work for missionaries are impossible here for a small mission if we are to avoid the experience of settling into ruts that [are] so easy and so killing."[35] He was ever the statesman, looking at the big picture, struggling to discover abiding principles, and always looking for an evangelistic breakthrough.

Finally, his Quaker roots influenced his administration in many ways. As was Quaker founder George Fox, Everett Cattell was a churchman at heart who saw the necessity of organization. While egalitarian ("the door is open for any man to carry out his God-given concern in our Quaker theory out here") he saw the necessity of empowered leaders working together in harmony under the direction of the Holy Spirit.[36] He lamented what he believed to be "a vast amount of nominal Christianity,"[37] as did Fox in his day. Yet a few years later he also restated the Quaker principle of discovering "where and in what way the Holy Spirit is at work in our field and then our chief concern as to method is simply to cooperate with the Holy Spirit."[38]

Winning the Chamar

Even before Esther Baird's departure, Everett Cattell took seriously the task of fostering a movement among the Chamar caste, a group of defiled leatherworkers. In an article written in March 1937, a full year before Esther Baird's retirement, he stressed the profound human worth of this people group—bright, intelligent, good-looking, and clever, but drunkards, eaters of carrion, and sexually promiscuous.[39] Everett studied their history and looked for bridges of witness. He discovered some Chamars were followers of a reformer who had monotheistic tendencies, but that in general the Chamars of Bundelkhand had received little exposure to the gospel. Bundelkhand was ruled by rajahs and maharajas with only nominal British control and influence. The Chamars of Bundelkhand were even more cut off from exterior influences than Chamars in other parts of India.[40]

Everett took the new charge eagerly and wrote home that he hoped mission evangelists could rise above defeatist attitudes that assumed no converts could be made. He, too, had been reading Donald McGavran's revolutionary writings that urged missionaries in India to look for responsive pockets where conversions were possible. The Chamars of Nowgong seemed to fit the profile of such a group. They were a part of about one-third of India's Hindu population that lived in untouchability, and, according to Donald

McGavran and Pickett, were winnable. Everett hoped for more than lackluster seed sowing and promoted a more aggressive evangelism. He hoped for a group movement of Chamars toward Christ, something that had never really happened in all of Bundelkhand's recorded history.[41]

Everett began to get acquainted with the idea of group decision making. In India, this often happened through the *panchayat,* a village or caste council, not unlike the *sauri* councils in east Africa promoted by Arthur Chilson. Everett observed that the prior pattern of evangelism in Bundelkhand had been to separate a new convert physically from his village and to relocate him inside the missionary compound. McGavran and Pickett valiantly opposed that pattern, and encouraged the new converts to stay among their own people.[42]

In an early exhortation to the two graduates from the Nowgong Christian Institute, where the Cattells were stationed, Everett Cattell began preaching the "basic Quakerism" of Scripture and practical living, but directly linked it to the McGavran and Pickett recommendations. He urged the Indian Christian workers to reveal God to people by teaching Scripture and by the "breaking of bread" in everyday living with the people. He publicly disagreed with the great Indian nationalist Mahatma Gandhi who strenuously opposed the Christian conversion of outcastes because he believed "that they have less intelligence than cows and are therefore unable to make an intelligent decision regarding a proper religion." Gandhi believed Christians were taking advantage of the naïveté of the outcastes and in essence were tricking them into Christian faith. Everett's retort to Gandhi was that if religion were a matter of philosophy, then "Gandhi's objection would be well taken. But if religion is a matter of finding new life, then anyone is able to decide." Everett's challenge to the Indian church was one he would repeat for years: "To take the name of Christ here in our sheltered Compound is easy. To live this life in the village, quite alone, is a very different matter."[43]

Anna Nixon records that, in some ways, the first Nowgong evangelism directed toward the Chamars under Everett's leadership was successful—people listened, they seemed to genuinely honor

Christ, and they even prayed in his name. Esther Baird, pleased by the effort, appointed Everett director of all mission evangelism. But the Chamars would not break caste. The preferred to remain within the fold of impure leather workers who made shoes, ate society's rotted leftovers, and endured the stench from the half-tanned leather and cramped quarters of the poor.[44] Even though they enjoyed no privilege or status within Hinduism, to break caste was to face the wrath of Hindu teachers and officials who rigidly upheld the social status quo of the caste system. For Everett, this was his first major venture into evangelism among Hindus and the beginning of twenty years of study and reflection on the issue.

Esther Baird Retires

The retirement process for Esther Baird unfolded through the spring of 1937, starting first with the British colonial government awarding her the Kaiser-i-Hind gold medal for public service in India as a nurse and community builder. Six-year-old David Cattell had already gained the affection of Baird, who insisted he be included in the formal photograph of her with British officials. That fall, she passed the torch of mission council leadership to Everett Cattell. She sailed away into retirement in the United States in March 1938 after a flurry of English teas, missionary picnics, and church programs. She died in Ohio twelve years later at age eighty-nine, still maintaining a vital interest in the work of the mission. Everett was left in charge and eager to move ahead.

The Cattells' first charge was the Nowgong school and compound that housed an orphanage with more than sixty children. Not only did the mission care for, teach, and supervise the orphans, but it arranged for marriage and employment. Everett saw the problems in this system and tried to find overall answers to the knotty issues of church discipline, self-support, cultural isolation, leaders who would take no initiative, and overall dependency upon the mission. The impression was not of a holy, vibrant, and outward-looking Christian community. Everett was a global thinker and not easily satisfied with partial answers,[45] so he began looking for ways to make major changes.

Everett Cattell's rapport with the mission board was high, and Catherine's whole family had networked with the Ohio Friends Mission Board all of her life in China and up to her marriage to Everett. Catherine's sense of family with Walter R. and Myrtle Williams was unusually strong. Together, they enjoyed the total confidence of the board and expressed their opinions about the work in India clearly and directly.[46] It was an unusually positive relationship that produced a voluminous correspondence between Everett Cattell and Walter Williams over the next twenty years.

During the Baird retirement process and after a few months in Bundelkhand in local language study, the Cattells traveled north to Landour in the refreshing foothills of the Himalayas for further Hindi instruction. Much of their time for the following two years was spent in study. They had had a good beginning in their first months, forming friendships with Esther Baird and Indian evangelists and persuading a few Christians in the Chhatarpur compound to return to villages and support themselves. An earlier study had revealed that of 235 persons in the Friends Christian community (men, women, and children), 180 received direct pay or subsidy from the mission.[47] In other words, India Friends Mission was a classic case study of extraction evangelism in which widows, orphans, and the dispossessed came under the direct protection of the foreign missionaries, were cut off from their culture, and became totally dependent upon foreign aid for their survival. As the Cattells studied Hindi in the mountains, they continued reading about and discussing with other expatriates how to address the huge and complex task awaiting them on the steaming plains below.

Considering Change

The Cattells quickly discovered two "diametrically opposed" approaches to the problem. Some evangelicals demanded that evangelism be given priority and after that the emerging indigenous church could provide Christian social services. Others said evangelism must be paired with acts of compassion. The India Friends Mission had followed the compassion approach for forty years. While Methodist bishop Pickett felt no ministry was fully Christian that ignored compassion, he nonetheless stoutly declared that "no ministry to [the depressed classes] in Christ's name arouses their hopes, and commands their faith, unless it presents the Gospel of the love of God making full provision for the needs of the soul."[48]

Such decision preaching, however, was rare or nonexistent in many places of India, including Bundelkhand. Donald McGavran and Bishop Pickett encouraged their colleagues throughout India to engage in fresh evangelism that spoke directly to the spiritual needs of listeners and called for commitment and inclusion into the Body of Christ. With time, after McGavran became world famous among evangelicals for church-growth theory, he tried to work through the complex relationship between social concern and evangelism. But in the 1930s as Everett Cattell came under McGavran's influence, the India Friends Mission considered how it could break out of the institutional walls of school, orphanage, and compound and extend a transforming gospel to the villages of central India.[49] Forty years of institutional compassion had not established a self-reproducing pattern of any kind. Everett and others came to realize that the extraction evangelism that was the focus of the mission's social institutions touched a few with the gospel, but failed miserably to transform a society at its core. So removed from the culture were these new Christians that they had few opportunities to share their faith. Furthermore, there was no autonomous national church to permeate and leaven the culture. After four decades of failure to create an indigenous church, the mission had subconsciously adjusted its goals, it seemed. They had become happy simply to bear witness without calling for a commitment to Christ.

The stage was set for major changes for the Friends India Mission of Ohio Yearly Meeting, and all eyes focused on Everett and Catherine Cattell for recommendations and action. A few months after Esther Baird's departure in March 1938, Everett Cattell contracted the services of Donald McGavran as a field consultant as a first major step in fresh planning and strategizing. Perhaps there was hope for a solution.

Reflections:

How does the early work of Friends India Mission seem different from the Friends ministry in Guatemala?

What about mission institutions such as orphanages, schools, and hospitals? How are they helpful and how can they hinder the gospel?

What can be learned from Everett Cattell's example as a new missionary?

Which do you think is the biblically correct relationship between evangelism and social action: a) that social action/compassion comes first to win a hearing for the gospel; b) that verbal evangelism comes first followed by social action lived out by the new expression of the body of Christ; c) that the two must always be interwoven and always present to be faithful to the biblical mandate; or d) some other relationship between the two?

chapter 11

The McGavran Report, Suffering, and Hope

EVERETT CATTELL CONTINUED looking for responsive people groups and discovered the tribal Gonds and the low-caste group already mentioned, the Chamars. Both groups were within the bounds of Bundelkhand, a region two hundred miles long and one hundred miles wide where only the Friends Mission represented the name of Christ. Mission strategies throughout India were significantly in flux at the time, and Donald McGavran was at the center of much of the discussion. Everett Cattell took the lead in securing his help as a consultant, and McGavran's report shocked some and challenged others with his evaluation and recommendations.[1] While Walter Williams's report of 1936 started the change in personnel, McGavran's report of 1938 began the change of policy.

Dr. Donald McGavran

At age forty-one, Donald McGavran was uniquely qualified to advise Everett Cattell and the Friends India Mission. He had grown up in India of missionary parents and continued his own adult ministry there as a third-generation missionary. McGavran did not become well known worldwide until the mid-1950s, but went on to become arguably the preeminent mission strategist of the twentieth century, and founder of what is now the School of Intercultural Studies at Fuller Theology Seminary. His grasp of cultural anthropology and his vision of the use of social sciences to better understand the biblical task of Christian evangelism became revolutionary. In 1938 at the time of his report to the Friends Mission, he saw Bundelkhand as "part and parcel of the rest of the mid-India set up" which he knew by "first hand experience and study" done over the prior ten years.[2] He began to realize some churches grew dramatically while others remained stagnant. Armed with four academic degrees, one of them a Ph.D. from Columbia University, he asked, "When a church is growing, *why* is it growing?"[3]

The six-page, single-spaced, typed report from McGavran was forwarded to the Ohio mission board by Everett Cattell, who included a few of his own editorial comments. But for the most part, the report seems to be McGavran's words alone. He urged Everett to develop a people consciousness (the untouchable Chamar caste was reachable, he believed), and to become experts in Chamar customs and relationships. He urged the staff to expect each evangelist to learn a minimum of three hundred Chamar names in a region, and move on to one thousand—a simple clue on how to study a people and learn their family networks. His advice was detailed: Attend funerals and weddings; find the Chamars who are literate and write literature for them; create a worship service that stresses brotherhood and forgiveness of sins; send evangelists to other regions for training in people-group movements happening elsewhere in India; and above all else, pray systematically for them.[4, 5]

McGavran knew that it would be necessary to secure Indian non-Chamar evangelists to start with, until there were converts among the Chamar. This would not be easy, as it would demand people willing to degrade themselves in the eyes of society and step across caste lines to the untouchables. Furthermore, the hospital at Chhatarpur needed to seek to serve the Chamar and to avoid discrimination of any kind. The goal, wrote McGavran, was "to preach, teach, expect, and pray for...*group decision*." They must show how Christ affects the whole group, use recent illustrations of group movements, and avoid accepting converts into the body of Christ until a whole family group was ready together.[6, 7]

The Non-Conversion Clause

The shocking aspect of the report to evangelical Friends of Ohio was that McGavran had discovered a written agreement by the mission *not to seek converts*. Years earlier it was included in the land deed for the Chhatarpur hospital, agreeing that there would be no water baptisms, thus giving Hindus the impression that Friends were following a "friendly helping non-conversion policy." "Don't you know, Sahib," McGavran was told, "they [Friends] are instructed not to make converts, but to preach the gospel for a witness."[8, 9] While this placed the mission in "a universally respected position" in Bundelkhand, Donald McGavran told Everett Cattell it was time for a "show down" (a term he used repeatedly in the report) between the mission and the Chhatarpur non-Christian community.[10, 11] Perhaps Friends theology that water baptism was not a requirement for conversion had been grossly misunderstood, but Donald pushed his point that no culturally appropriate substitute to water baptism for incorporation into the church had ever been developed by Friends. The fact was that a broad impression existed among many Hindus and even some of the evangelists that Friends did not seek converts!

Nonetheless, Donald McGavran complimented Everett on the above-average evangelists working with him—they had a spiritual message and proclaimed Jesus, he said, and they called for people to give up idolatry. But the next step after leaving idolatry was left unclear—and public statements of loyalty to Christ alone were not happening! Until this was resolved, wrote Donald, the matter "will haunt your work and neutralize your efforts." Friends had taken pride in their schools, orphanages, and medical work for decades. They believed such acts of compassion were a necessary prelude to win the confidence of people and would lead to the acceptance of Christ, much as Friends in Kenya and Guatemala believed and practiced. One of the Indian Friends evangelists of Chhatarpur, however, told Donald McGavran privately that he personally feared conversions, because they (the evangelists) "would be sacrificed and the Mission would apologize [to the government] and go on as before."[12, 13, 14]

Donald McGavran pleaded with Everett to go the next step and prepare with great care for a "show down" with Hinduism. They needed to investigate their legal standing with the British, consult with others in similar situations, prepare in advance statements to be made to the government when persecution arose, and lay plans for public professions—the element McGavran felt was especially lacking among Friends.[15] The cutting of the *chutiya* (the Hindu hair lock) and the practice of *inter-dining* (Christians and converts graciously feeding one another as a mark of brotherhood and love) were both recommended as marks of incorporation and accepted by the mission council.[16] The bottom line for McGavran was that Friends develop

> a public ceremony before the people of the village whereby our Lord is acknowledged as Savior and Lord, as the sinless incarnation of God, as the only incarnation of God, the Bible is accepted as the only scripture, and the Church as the sacred brotherhood which every believer must join.[17]

Such an induction would be "clear, final and unequivocal." In addition it should include promises to attend worship, to love the Bible and give attention to it daily, to give to the church at harvest, and to give one's children in marriage only to fellow Christians.[18]

The list of McGavran's recommendations goes on: Do more direct preaching and teaching of the gospel, give more actual budgetary attention to evangelism, and raise the percentage of mission budget dedicated to evangelism from ten percent to a healthier twenty-five percent. He recommended that the Harpalpur school be closed, that the Chhatarpur hospital secure self-support, and that alternatives be found to care for the orphans.[19] It was a plan to de-institutionalize the work of the mission in order to focus upon the founding of an Indian church. The McGavran document ended with a description of how Friends might reach the Chamars—tens of thousands who lived within the Friends area. They represented tens of millions of Chamars, the largest of the untouchable groups of India. "Rome was not built in a day," he encouraged. "People will grow into it. You must feel your way. I have been frankly delighted with the way you are going about things."[20]

Illness and Recovery

Before any meaningful response to the McGavran report could be formulated, however, Everett Cattell nearly died. He left Chhatarpur in mid-February for an appendectomy in the nearby Jhansi Hospital, but a simple medical procedure turned into a nightmare—the first of a series of tragic and near-tragic events in his missionary career. He lingered near death for three months with complications and infections in a time prior to the miracle-working antibiotics mass produced during World War II. The story is Catherine's to tell in *From Bamboo to Mango*; Catherine sat day after day with Everett, who was sometimes unconscious, frequently struggling with phlebitis, and often enduring bedsores and an intestinal obstruction.[21] Once the lengthy medical crisis was passed, his illness left him weak and unable to work.

In the middle of a slow recovery, doctors recommended the Cattells leave the heat of the plains but stay away from the higher elevation of the cool mountains. That meant leaving India altogether, and Australia seemed the least expensive alternative. So leaving their son, David, in boarding school (Catherine felt *abandoned* was the more appropriate word for what happened to David), Everett, Catherine, and daughter Barbara sailed off to Australia where they settled in Sydney. After three months, and a most encouraging recovery for Everett, the three Cattells returned to central India and to David, for whom the experience proved to be seriously traumatic.[22] In the early war years, Everett suffered two more serious illnesses, once with a streptococci infection and once with intestinal troubles. He was prone to unusual complications that strained the best efforts of the doctors. Catherine also suffered repeatedly with amoebic dysentery.[23]

Something of a theology of suffering arose out of the Cattell experience, leaving Catherine highly sensitized to the suffering of their own son, David, when he was left alone in boarding school in north India in the community where they had studied Hindi and where they occasionally vacationed. As she pondered her own potential suffering of widowhood and the possibility of her own children being left without a father, it was like a flashback to the widowhood of her mother in China twenty years earlier and the sense of abandonment she felt as a child. Like Everett, her father George Fox DeVol had been struck down at the height of his missionary career. That was in China and her father was forty-six years old. Now it was India and Everett was thirty-eight.[24] Everett's personal suffering cannot be totally understood apart from Catherine's interpretation of their life experiences. She records her insightful reflections in *From Bamboo to Mango*, perhaps the most readable Quaker missionary biography of the twentieth century.

Everett was embarrassed by his seven months of inactivity, but knew he gained much great patience along with the forty pounds of weight during his time in Australia. He was eager to return and implement some of the changes outlined in the McGavran report. He sensed the opposition of the devil and actually thought it a compliment! They might be on the edge of something big!

Everett saw his suffering promoted prayer and a deeper bond of love between himself and Indian Christians. Nevertheless, his first term of service came dangerously close to being a case of a first-term dropout. But he persisted. He returned. At a point of great darkness, his optimistic and resilient spirit brought him back to ministry objectives and to his devotion to God:

> Once again I refuse to be discouraged, because we have a great God. He is never surprised nor taken unawares....This business of the Kingdom is all mixed up with sorrows and patient endurance. May God keep me steady and loyal through every phase of the Kingdom program. It is nice to think of the Kingdom in terms of waving banners and triumphal processions but we are not ready for that. There must be sorrows and patient endurance and a Cross and crosses. I can't forget that I came to India on the 'grain of wheat' text.[25]

Hope for the Chamar

Back in India after being in Australia recovering from that first major illness, Everett soon returned to his place of leadership in aggressive village evangelism. Indeed, a Chamar named Khub Chand, a most hopeful potential convert, was contacted just before Everett's illness, and the evangelists kept visiting some of the villagers during his absence. In 1941, Khub Chand cut his own *chutiya* (sacred lock of hair), symbolizing of his conversion and confirming in the presence of his people group that he wanted to follow Christ. The event was important for several reasons. First, it was done in the presence of two hundred heads of families who talked seriously of converting. Second, many believed this man, Khub Chand, could be God's selection of a leader who would work from within the Chamar culture to win it to Christ.[26, 27]

Here for the first time was someone willing to defy caste and come out as a Christian. Would others follow, as McGavran predicted? Or would it have been better to slow Chand down until several others were ready to commit to Christ at the same time? The event proved important in a third way: By cutting his own hair lock, Chand established the custom of cutting one's own hair, clearing evangelists of accusations of forced conversions.[28] Fourth, Chand built a Christian worship site that had many indigenous features, where contextualized Christian music and a local chanting method were practiced. This was the first time in Bundelkhand for people to see "what Christianity could be like off a mission compound."[29] Fifth, Chand became something of a test case of an evangelist-preacher who did not receive financial aid from the mission. At times he went without pay, but Chand's near starvation and poverty drove Everett to hire him as a mason on the mission compound. He moved his home closer to Chhatarpur and the mission orbit. Across the years to follow, the issue of mission pay became a bigger and bigger temptation and roadblock to an effective ministry for Chand.

A few conversions did follow, and hope for Friends India Mission was renewed, but response was slower than hoped even though plans for church growth following the McGavran model went forward. Everett led in the belief that the work must be two-pronged: First, the existing church must be "revived, cleansed, and inspired with vision." Then it would be ready for the second prong—the reception of the converts to be won through the new people group approach.[30] Much of Everett's efforts continued on these two fronts, yet an inordinate amount of mission council time was spent on institutional concerns: disciplinary actions for workers and church members, hiring and firing, and details regarding orphans ranging from marriage for the young adults to erecting tombstones for the deceased orphans. The mission, led by Everett Cattell, was making a serious attempt at cutting back the number of people dependent upon the mission for care and protection. Still, on one occasion in 1940, concerns about one new convert focused upon how the mission was to protect and employ her.[31] McGavran's ideas were not easy to follow!

Self-Support

The concern to develop a self-sustaining church appeared on fronts other than direct evangelism. Schoolboys were put to work to cover some of their own costs and schoolgirls made clothing for the orphans. They worked gardens for their own diet. Some of the mission's efforts closely paralleled the schemes of Mahatma Gandhi, who one of the mission staff actually met personally. Writes Anna Nixon, "His schemes did not succeed, nor did the Mission's."[32]

In 1943, Everett fretted over Khub Chand's waffling as he lobbied for his share of foreign funds. Everett looked for jobs for converts in various villages and even bought some goats from Khub Chand, hoping to encourage Christian families to find means of earning a living, all in the name of building independent Christians functioning within the culture. The pattern from prior years, however, had been firmly impressed and proved difficult to break. Money received for mission land sold to the local Maharaja went to build independent houses for mission employees, especially those who had been orphans. This had a measure of success and most were eventually settled outside the compounds.[33] The school at Harpalpur had been an unfulfilled dream of winning students to Christ through education and was jettisoned to state control in 1944 (as recommended earlier by McGavran), and four Christian families were moved to self-support. Those reared in the mission as orphans in Harpalpur, however, felt betrayed and Everett reported their disappointment. Still others were gradually sold homes in villages in order to relocate them away from compounds.[34]

Back in 1940, the Cattells had moved to Chhatarpur from Nowgong, rightly recognizing Chhatarpur as more central to the villages of Bundelkhand, perhaps in the hopes of triggering a people movement like the ones McGavran wrote about. Nevertheless, Everett conducted English services for government men and Hindu professors who wanted to improve their English skills.[35] During the early 1940s, as World War II raged in both Europe and the Pacific Rim, the threat of a Japanese invasion of India spurred the mission council to begin creating church structures independent of missionary control. A pastoral system was introduced, but several dissident leaders who felt threatened by new leaders effectively blocked it for a time. The church recorded (ordained) its first pastors in 1941 despite the threat of schism by the dissidents.[36] Evangelists were placed in villages to live year-round in homes either rented or purchased for them by the mission. Some were self-supporting. Others, including some women who had formerly been paid as evangelists and Bible teachers, witnessed only reluctantly if not paid. A circle of six locations around Chhatarpur formed a circuit that the Cattells visited regularly, always finding deep problems.[37] The goal was to maintain the morale of believers and workers, but it was done at great effort and sacrifice and with limited results, although the existence of a group of small congregations was a significant step forward.[38]

Toward an Independent Church

By 1941, there seemed to be some progress with more national Indian leadership.[39] The "war emergency proposals" were a further step in building an independent church. The threat of a Japanese invasion was serious and missions everywhere in India were making plans for it.[40] Mission agencies based in Europe—British, German, Danish, and Scandinavian—were being cut off from their home funds by the war. How close were the Americans to the same crisis? The U.S. consul demanded everyone have valid passports, and map-watchers read of the fall of Singapore and then of Rangoon to the Japanese. Then Indian/British talks over independence broke down, leaving Indian politicians like Gandhi in jail and India in turmoil. India looked ripe for the picking by the Japanese military machine. In an effort to monitor the accounting system and steady the church if an invasion came, Everett stayed on the plains through one summer.[41]

What other steps could be taken? The seven departments of the mission, all led by missionaries, now were to include three Indians on the various committees. Indian treasurers were appointed for each board, but missionaries chaired each one. Nonetheless, this was a huge step forward in organization, as until now the mission had not included Indians to establish policy, budget, or account for funds. Some church members signed pledges to tithe. A plan was created to sustain school and medical work and to place the orphans in private homes if funds were suddenly withdrawn. Schools would focus on children of Christians rather than the broader Hindu constituency and the medical work would be "pay-as-you-go." The mission also studied a plan to turn property titles over to an indigenous church body, but the home board resisted. The channeling of funds through Indian treasurers was a daring step, but the Cattells and others felt it was a necessary right step.[42, 43]

Evaluation of the Early Years

The drive toward self-support for the church from the arrival of the Cattells through the early war years was an "extremely enervating and disappointing work in a land of poverty." It produced a few steps forward and a few steps backward.[44] On balance, some positive steps toward church growth were taken following the McGavran principles, but with limited success. Under Everett Cattell's administration, the India Friends Mission was a little less institutional and Indian leaders were being empowered, but the remaining programs had yet to be channeled toward winning Indians for Christ. A people movement was being pursued but had not yet happened. More gospel preaching and teaching was happening, but old patterns of nonacceptance remained unbroken.

What can be learned from the Cattell experience from 1936 to the middle of the war years? Perhaps as much as anything, it tells us how hard it is to reform a ministry that is dependent upon outside financial and emotional support. What can be done in such a program may be permanently limited, thus offering the lesson that how a mission is begun will forever color its future. In some such cases, the cultural overhang is so strong that a person's becoming a Christian gives every impression that he or she is leaving culture, relationships, and values of the past behind and stepping into a foreign life where all is changed. The McGavran report might at least help us appreciate the power of a negative example. While it is easy to start a program centered on missionary compassion and foreign affluence, it seldom if ever produces a spontaneous movement toward Christ that is capable of reproducing that compassion. The message may be to new missionaries from Africa, Asia, or Latin America: Establish models that can be reproduced independently of foreign control and support. As we shall see in the following chapter, Everett Cattell understood the principles as early as 1938, thanks to the McGavran report. His own suffering deepened his commitment to India, and for the next nineteen years he struggled with hope to put those principles into practice in the gospel wasteland of Bundelkhand.

Reflections:

Donald McGavran was probably the single most influential missionary strategist of the twentieth century. How do you think the founders of the India Friends Mission—Esther Baird and Delia Fistler—would have responded to McGavran's recommendations?

How do you evaluate the changes McGavran recommended to Everett Cattell?

How did the Cattells seem to interpret the meaning and value of their sufferings early in their missionary career?

What were some of the steps the mission took to implement the McGavran report? Why was their success still quite limited?

If you were to start a church planting mission from scratch in India today, how would you do it? Would you incorporate anything you have learned from the history of the India Friends Mission?

chapter 12

Searching for a Remedy

DURING THE MIDDLE YEARS of Everett Cattell's missionary service—from the mid-1940s into the early 1950s—Everett was occupied with a search for a remedy to crippled and unproductive missionary work. The mission never lost the influence of the McGavran report, but profoundly struggled to recreate mission strategies. The World War II years stretched into the post-war convulsions and breakup of British India into a largely Hindu India and a mostly Muslim Pakistan. Minority groups caught in the crossfire frequently suffered massacres and retaliation strikes. An even clearer hostility toward Western Christian presence developed with restrictions on missionary visas by Hindu India. Letters between Everett Cattell, Walter R. Williams, and others on the Ohio Friends Mission Board were long and detailed—each was eight to thirteen single-spaced pages! Business details, budget estimates, personnel reports, spiritual-life reports relating to evangelists and preaching, and the ever-present woes of missionary dominance and national church dependency filled the reports. What was the solution?

Breaking Institutional Dependency

The early 1940s had opened with intensive village work, looking for that "right first convert to stand against persecution within the culture." Over and over, a steady and independent convert was the stated goal. Yet Everett was dogged by his evangelistic team's dependency upon mission payment, supervision, and accountability directly to him.

Likewise, Everett was drained by the dependency of the medical work. Much earlier, he had written that "if the mission [develops medical aid] as evangelistic bait it seems to erect a resistance to the Gospel and at best it is a foreign thing and makes it difficult later for the Church to take it over if indeed there ever is a Church [established] there. The tendency is to...establish more and more compounds"[1] without evangelistic results. Nevertheless, even from the early years in India, he advocated that brother-in-law Ezra DeVol join them in India as an evangelist/doctor, which eventually came about. Everett's hope was for a medical work more tied to the Christian community, more directly evangelistic in nature, and yet eventually more self-sufficient and independent from mission control. Across the coming years, the movement went in that direction. For Ezra and Frances DeVol, it meant a career of medical ministry and witness first in India and later in Nepal. Both assignments helped maintain the American Friends' attention upon India and Nepal. (Fifty years later, that interest and those contacts produced seven new works around the region for Eastern Region Friends and Evangelical Friends Mission, all independent of Bundelkhand and far more productive in church planting.)

Institutional work in Bundelkhand, however, continued at about the same pace for several years. Everett's approach was to expand the team and look for ways to enter into more active evangelism without suspending the institutional work. Limited funds, financial depression and recession in the United States, and then world war hindered that dream. McGavran had frankly told Everett back in 1938 that he thought the Friends mission budget was "badly out of kilter."[2] It was, he said, too heavy on everything except evangelism.

A New Evangelism

Part of the remedy seemed to be to retrain Indian evangelists in a more personal "identification" with fellow Indians so as to share the gospel in personal conversation. The old pattern was to stop in a public place, begin talking, get two or more hearers, and then start singing, teaching, and preaching. On a tour with Dr. McGavran in preparation for the report back in 1938, Friends preacher Stuti Prakash had come back with a new realization—he could minister person-to-person on a more intimate level than by impromptu public singing, teaching, and preaching.[3]

Another part of a remedy for more effective evangelism seemed to be more psychological than strategic. Rather than count the number of villages touched by itineration, evangelists were instructed to report the number and condition of converts. Yet that simple change was a way to emphasize the creation of reproducing units. By June 1941, four outstations had been opened, so some aspects of the McGavran report were being employed, paying off in small measure in a new focus on church planting.

Empowering Leaders

Along with introducing a pastoral system to Bundelkhand Friends, Everett Cattell and the mission began the process of recording of ministers,[4] and not without difficulty. Established leaders opposed the move and jealousy among members and leaders appeared. "Of course there is a place for the paid mission worker," Everett admitted at that time, "but when your entire Christian community is dependent on Mission funds, the situation is most precarious."[5] He encouraged the church to recognize gifted preachers, hoping the church would sense its responsibility to encourage and support such workers and make a step toward more indigenous leadership.

The debate goes on fifty years later. Observers in the twenty-first century might disagree with Everett's concession that "there is a place for the paid mission worker." Some would contend there is no place for a paid mission worker from within the culture, simply because such an arrangement sets precedent. (Certainly Bundelkhand Friends were caught in a high level of dependency upon the mission.) Others believe some strategic payments can be made, but that such payments must be restricted and a plan for total, reproduced self-support must be in place early in the process. The expectation for many to receive payment had proven deadly in India; for Everett, recording ministers helped shift the focus to Indian leadership and away from missionary leadership.

Also in the early war years, Everett Cattell began grooming Indian evangelist Stuti Prakash to work alongside him to supervise workers in the outstations.[6] It was a long and arduous process, but Everett chronicles the man's gifts, the development of his personality, and his ability to deal with educated people and officials, while also capturing and holding the attention of the common people.

At times in the 1940s in private letters to the board, Everett painted his administration in fairly sharp contrast to that of Esther Baird, who did not pursue a pastoral system, had not recorded any ministers, and who held no village revivals—Indians "had always been given to understand that Friends just didn't do that." By 1941, there appeared to be a major cleavage between young and old men— the older men who had been tutored by Esther Baird were disgruntled, resistant, and of poor moral and spiritual testimony, while the young men seemed more teachable and eager to serve sacrificially.[7]

Adjusting to the Emergency Years

During the early war years of 1941 to 1943, communications flowed fairly well between East and West, but the threat of a Japanese invasion of India loomed on the horizon. The mission goal was both to achieve some modicum of self-support among the churches (especially in view of a possible missionary evacuation), and win a body of new converts.[8] Personally strapped for finances and having no easy way to travel during the war, the Cattells cancelled their furlough and replaced it with a long holiday within India.[9]

General care of spiritual life within the churches was revivalist in nature, often with extended prayer and fasting pressing for repentance from sin for those within the church. Everett Cattell was deeply burdened by corruption among members and leaders, and felt that a surge of new converts would never be attracted to broken relationships and poor spiritual motivation within the church. "The idolatry of the Church," he wrote,

> has not been sticks and stones, but it has been a setting up of the Mission and its money in place of God. This is a vicious system and we are clear that it must be broken....The evil is not so much that we have some paid workers as it is a special mentality that has developed in India whereby Christians regard employment and financial aid as a *right* inherent in their having taken the name Christian. This is a frightful evil which must be smashed.[10]

Although Indian Christians were called upon to repent, Everett also recognized the mission was guilty of contributing to "dependency-building" or "lack of ownership" by the church. Putting it into such stark terms of repentance from idolatry, however, placed the foreign missionaries squarely under the light of the Holy Spirit to search their hearts and to seek a better way on their part.

As World War II ground forward into 1944 and as much of Asia was caught in the web of violence in one way or another, a great amount of mission attention was spent on Indian employees, their salaries, and their pensions. Everett resigned himself to a bad situation and tried to move forward:

> We have tried many expedients to try to re-make these old men—but they are made!...It is our duty to care for their old age as best we can and then labor for a new approach to the next generation....As orphans we took them from their old economic environment and assumed responsibility for their lives. Looking backward it is now easy to see that a large percentage of orphans should have been settled into work in the community independent of Mission funds to give backbone to the Church....These men have been trained in the ideal of "being loyal to the Mission," and the expectancy that therefore the Mission will look out for you.[11]

Still, a great amount of attention was spent on discipline issues, placement and supervision of Indian Christian workers and mission employees, supervision of building projects, and individual nurture of new converts, few that there were. By May 1945, the Cattells were still planning for that first furlough back to the United States.

Early in 1945 the mission experienced a long series of moral lapses among Christians—servants and leaders: adultery, theft, family rebellion, and the demonic possession of a worker's spouse believed to be related to secret sin. These lapses produced a significant falling away of the disgruntled and dependent complainers, enough so that Everett came to refer to it as "the cleansing." "The only ones left are those who are positive spiritual forces," he declared. He was not happy about the circumstances of any of the defections, and even found the mission culpable at times, but the net result, he felt, was the exodus of many "liabilities" to the church. While Chamar convert and evangelist Khub Chand did not defect at this time, Everett fretted over him: "He must be cleansed of this mission money consciousness," he prayed.[12]

Continuing to follow the advice of McGavran, the mission periodically sent workers and evangelists off to neighboring areas to observe the ministry of others, small mass movements, or "people movements" as McGavran called them. Everett was ever searching for mission work built around the structure of the churches embedded in the culture, rather than mission structures where converts were extracted from the culture.

Post-War Tensions

In a letter sent to the United States and dated July 30, 1946, Friends leader Pancham Singh openly accused Everett Cattell of failing to facilitate even one conversion and of closing the mission farm, a mission school, and the mission orphanage—the only methods known, Singh said, to win "true and orthodox Christians." "The missionaries who are working in Bundelkhand....are here to give orders and to rule like Indian princes and not to serve....Don't think that you are sending money for the work of our Lord in this dark land," Singh railed, "because it is not used properly and for the service of God. As long as Esther was here the money was spent honestly and properly. The work and fruits which are to be seen here was the hard and honest work done by Esther and her colleagues."[13]

The letter, well translated from Hindi into English, was forwarded to Ohio. With it came a rebuttal in an unsigned letter, which was not from Everett Cattell, who was actually on furlough in the United States at the time. The unknown correspondent wrote that the letter from Singh represented a few disgruntled older people who had not been "pampered by the Mission."[14]

A few months later—in January 1947—the Cattells arrived back in India and became a part of a greatly enlarged post-World

War II missionary staff of ten adults. Yet the strains between mission and older national Christians were evident and periodically cause for great pain.

Of even greater world significance, however, were the political, religious, and ethnic tensions convulsing British India and the entire sub-continent as the Cattells settled back into ministry in Bundelkhand. While Everett faced all the complexities of managing missionary personnel, budgeting with the mission board, and wrangling with the newly independent Indian government and its bureaucratic representatives, much of Everett's attention was riveted on the chaos of independence and partition of India and Pakistan. Everett clearly favored British withdrawal and giving up of imperial designs.[15] Yet in 1947 and 1948, hundreds of thousands died and millions were relocated in a migration east and west, and north and south—in a movement that has been called the greatest quick human migration of refugees in human history.

A September 9, 1947, letter from Everett recounting a train trip home through the Punjab—the most hotly contested area between Muslims on the one side and Hindu/Sikhs on the other—was widely distributed in Ohio. Bloodshed was tremendous. Hundreds of thousands of people were on the move—Muslims in one direction and Hindus in the other. Minority enclave populations in many places were entirely wiped out, and Everett witnessed murders on his train and along the track. European white people and Christians went largely ignored, however, in the spasm of Muslim/Hindu communal killings, mayhem, and retaliation. Bundelkhand, too, remained largely untouched.[16]

Preserving a Ministry

As Bundelkhand itself was relatively isolated from the great Hindu/Muslim migration, Everett and the mission gave great attention to assigning and settling Christian workers in one place and designating another place for witness and church planting, a far cry from the institutional and compound focus of ten years earlier. Had Everett Cattell and others not taken the mission in a dramatic new direction, by 1947 the work would have died entirely and little or no fruit would have remained in Bundelkhand at all. Obedience and faithfulness paid off in small measure, even though the desired mass movement of culturally sensitive new Christians in Bundelkhand has yet to take place.

Everett gave much attention to administrative details, providing supplies to a larger staff and meeting all their housing needs. Huge quantities of Allied war-surplus materials were available from Bombay and elsewhere, including appliances and Jeeps, all at bargain and near giveaway prices. Additionally, the British were leaving behind schools, hospitals, and administrative buildings, and Everett purchased some of the properties and materials at a great savings. Everett's obvious and excellent administrative skills allowed him to maintain the respect of both mission council and mission board as he worked to strengthen the mission's ministry in days of chaos.

On the leadership development front, Everett worked to push forward Stuti Prakash as a supervisor over Khub Chand, the Chamar caste Christian, always eager "not to be too much in evidence myself." He longed for his work to be culturally integrated and tied to Indian appearances and Indian ways.[17] Nonetheless, mission-paid pastorates and mission initiative in selection of pastors continued to be the rule in the post-war years. There remained, for example, a missionary superintendent over Nowgong district.

A new theme, related to evangelism, developed after World War II: "Occupy the field." Bundelkhand encompassed a far greater region than what Friends in the 1930s and 1940s had occupied and no other evangelical ministries were present. With a larger staff, the mission could now consider a better spread of the gospel throughout the region, moving beyond Nowgong and Chhatarpur.[18]

For Everett Cattell himself, horizons also enlarged greatly. Extra-curricular work became increasingly common after World War II: He was invited to preach in Burma, and also to serve for six weeks as pastor of the Kellogg church in Landour (Mussoorie) in the hills during vacation time away from the plains. Other invitations came as well. Despite the provincial and discouraging nature of ministry in Bundelkhand, Everett gained recognition and began moving in much wider circles.[19] He also became active with Woodstock School, negotiating mission-school relationships on behalf of a number of mission agencies.

Dealing with Persecution

A major part of preserving ministry in Bundelkhand involved dealing with persecution. When the Chamars in one location began "getting out of hand and becoming Christians," local merchants and leading men of the ruling caste went to the head tax collector, to the magistrate, and to the feudal lord to complain. They were promised local protection from prosecution if a mob was recruited to beat up the Christians and drive them away. This negative kind of opposition and persecution traditionally arose in caste India, not unlike tactics still practiced in many parts of rural India sixty years later.

The Chamars were not being "docile and obedient as formerly and that...would not do," wrote Everett Catttell to Walter Williams in 1947.[20] The gospel had produced a small but clear social reformation. A few low caste converts felt empowered to resist the elite—a social leveling that upper-caste people opposed strenuously. Everett's great longing was to see the new Chamar converts hold steady, withstand persecution, and show by example what it meant to be a Christian within the cultural milieu. Great prayer went up while the mission discussed ways it might help, but at the same time missionaries knew the help they could offer was minimal.[21]

In some ways, the pattern in India during the 1940s seems strangely similar to the pattern in Hindu Nepal in the 1990s: Men were the first converts, and women were more hesitant. Missionaries and Christian leaders usually resisted the first requests for public incorporation, waiting until they could more likely withstand the barrage of persecution that always seemed to come. Hindu social structure always felt extremely intimidated by conversions, and Hindu calls for "no conversions" were strident. While Everett believed that "the intensity of this opposition indicates that a real work of God is going on,"[22] a movement in Bundelkhand was never quite consummated as happened among Friends and many other evangelicals of Hindu Nepal about fifty years later. Perhaps the social conditions were not quite right in Bundelkhand; perhaps the examples of

EVERETT L. CATTELL

true conversion were still lacking. Yet some of the similarities in dealing with persecution are strong enough to suggest some permanent patterns for Hindu evangelism seen in the 1940s and again in the 1990s.

Expatriates found themselves in a puzzling role in dealing with persecution. For example, Everett and his staff tried to provide active support and encouragement, especially encouraging fellow Indians to step forward to strengthen new believers. They tried to avoid lawsuits; they listened intently to the rumor mills in the villages; they stood ready to make physical moves to avoid death threats. Then, after a cooling off period, they went back and circulated openly in the area once again, visiting police and the leading persecutors, letting everyone see they were back. When the foreign missionaries did this, it seemed as though they used their prestige clout as foreigners to support the new converts undergoing persecution, a strategy likely unwise generations later. Did it help in persecution then? We don't know, but twenty-first-century movements in India that are succeeding seem to be "working from the margins" with little or no support from constitutional and/or legal defense. At the same time, these movements advocate and pray for greater freedom of religious expression, and support political forces that lead in that direction. Indian Christian leaders in the twenty-first century seem equipped to deal with persecution; sixty years ago, they did not. In the Chamar community within which Everett worked, some non-Christian political leaders opposed their efforts and some were willing to be friendly. But the majority seemed unsure what response to make.

Everett's writings from August 3, 1948, reflect that he understood this, at least partially. Contacts with the Ghuara converts of the Chamar caste reported they were holding steady, even without a teacher to disciple them. Cut off by distance and poor roads, and with the threat of persecution, no Indian Christian was forthcoming to go to their aid, "a sad commentary on the Compound-bred Christians," Everett said. He still lamented the converts' tendency not to venture into the Indian culture outside the protective umbrella of the mission.[23]

The move from Hindu to Christian and the potential for persecution was a complex subject. On one occasion, it became clear to Everett that help from fellow Christians in supplying a wife for a widowed Chamar was probably a necessary step. If they did not offer such help, Christians would appear unwilling to provide this "vital evidence of caste fellowship." Thus, to become a Christian, even in a village setting, was to take on the trappings of a new caste.[24] How was one to lead people to Christ and yet keep them embedded in their cultural milieu? This question remains in active debate in twenty-first-century India.

Promoting Missions at Home

Despite the confidence the Ohio Friends Board placed in the Cattells and their stalwart ministry in India, the relationship with home supporters could be difficult at times. The work showed no great gains yet Everett felt it important to encourage not only continued support, but enlarged support, placing more staff on the field for direct evangelism, all in accord with the McGavran report.

In mid-1948, Everett wrote a twelve-page article with the title "Do Friends Have a Faith Mission?" that caused something of a stir with the Ohio Yearly Meeting board of missions and considerable pain for Walter R. Williams. Williams and some on the board felt Everett was being critical of them and was expressing disloyalty. In the paper, Everett undertook an analysis of the concept of faith missions pioneered and popularized sixty to eighty years earlier by Hudson Taylor and George Mueller. Everett wrote critically of so-called "faith missions" and he urged his constituency to be wiser and more discerning in their missionary giving. He declared that a denominational board could indeed function with integrity as a faith mission. But he also argued for more trust and an aggressive movement forward by faith. Scrupulous financial accounting and auditing, discipline in spending, and living without fixed salaries marked the part of the "faith mission" tradition Friends did well. Taylor and Mueller had even refused to publicize financial needs. But Taylor and Mueller had also urged that candidates be sent to the field quickly, as soon as funds for travel became available, trusting God for the future. This last point—sending candidates to the field quickly, as soon as travel funds were available—Everett pushed forward and thus offended the Ohio board.[25]

To some extent, Everett delivered a critique on "faith missions": Some post-World War II ministries failed flagrantly at disciplining their spending and financial accounting. Some promoted great speakers capable of wringing the hearts of an affluent audience, but kept no separation between personal allowances and work funds. Independent missionaries often became "raw-boned individualist(s)" unable to work harmoniously with others. Spectacular projects were often necessary to keep the money rolling in.[26] Everett abhorred these practices, which, in general, Ohio Friends avoided.

Could Friends claim to be a "faith mission"? Yes, Everett responded, because they conducted business in a spirit of worship and trusting prayer and because faith was a recognized necessity in the spiritual struggles always before them. Their faith was focused on ministry, not on "daily bread" which was provided by the budget![27] Yet he felt the true faith mission paradigm of Hudson Taylor and George Mueller held a challenge for Friends. Could they send out the new missionaries as soon as their outfit and passage was available, "fully trusting God for their future support"? The contention seemed to be that, once on the field, their support would come by faith. Everett was desperately looking for a way to better mobilize Ohio Friends to "launch out in faith to undertake larger tasks and larger commitments than are reasonably to be supported by…limited means in sheer faith that God is able to turn resources into our hands beyond the limits of the giving power of [the] membership."[28] This stung Walter Williams as a criticism from his honored friend.

Everett Cattell also addressed the perennial debate over whether an agency is rash or visionary. He observed that if a great movement forward takes place and conditions change dramatically, leaving a work poorly supported, the agency is labeled as rash. If, however, conditions remain positive, it is considered visionary! Missions inevitably face huge questions: possible war, terrorism, economic decline, inflation, and political or legal shifts. Everett

184

responded to these questions by quoting Matthew 6:34 (KJV): "Sufficient unto the day is the evil thereof." It is not scriptural to base a missionary policy on a fear of the future! Moving into present open doors is always a good thing, he declared.[29]

"I am not pleading for recklessness nor for grandiose expansions....But I am pleading that the whole policy be taken off the level of human wisdom." He repeated, then, his specific proposal that candidates be sent more quickly, trusting that sustained funding would be provided. Whether or not any Friends agency sixty years later would feel free to send someone without reasonable promise of sustained income to support that missionary, we can catch several things from Everett Cattell's concern. First, he was trying to look outside the "box" of limitations that had come to afflict the Ohio Friends missionary vision. Second, he believed God could be trusted to direct greater funds toward missionary ministry. And third, he believed there were candidates and potential qualified candidates who should be sent.

Another problem for the mission was that part of the giving was generated by support designated to individual Indian workers. What was to be done when such a worker defected or backslid, like the boy caught stealing? The dilemma of ethics was real. The staff wanted to communicate honestly with donors and yet wanted to keep an upbeat tone to communications and to give the boy, in this case, time to repent and get his Christian life turned around.[30] Contemporary observers have come to believe that this kind of direct personal support always has its problems, and can easily compromise and embarrass both the national staff and the foreign workers, not to mention a built in dependency upon foreign funds.

Everett Cattell and Issues of Justice

Was Everett faithful to the Friends concern for social justice? The direct face-off with the caste system was his answer. "The Chamars in Ghuara are deeply impressed by the fact that we are winning through. They see in us at last someone who can go to bat for them."[31] A report of a conversation between a headman and a defender of Christians had two major points to it—one point theo-logical, and one point political. First, Christians were said to worship only one God, but all of him—not just a part, like worship of the Hindu God Ram. And second, Christians opposed the forced labor required of Chamars. Christians in the area were clearly per-ceived as pro-social justice, whether the headmen were favorable or not.[32]

Everett held out for new missionaries to be placed with village people not only for language and culture acquisition, but also to expose the missionaries to the serious social needs in the villages. He looked for the day when a stream of new village converts would do evangelism and missionaries would work in leadership and pastoral training. The goals were lofty but clear, and there were a few con-verts here and there through the late 1940s and early 1950s.[33] All the while, however, government restrictions upon evangelism and evan-gelistic missions became increasingly tight.[34]

Living with the Past

Many times the mission was directly involved with firing an Indian employee, placing someone under work probation, or working through other personnel issues. Such responsibilities required a great deal of energy, wisdom, and tact from Everett as a field director. One of the continual problems, he complained, was the "contamination" of new converts by unhappy older Christians. In the process, he looked for ways to resettle the "compounders" into various villages, always mindful of the McGavran plea that Christians be challenged to break out of the cultural shadows and to interact more normally with the world around them.[35]

The task of a written church constitution also remained unfin-ished through the end of the 1940s. It wasn't until 1950, under Everett's leadership, that the written constitution finally came to approval. The conscious goal of the constitution was to move away from an emphasis on missionary direction and toward empowering Indian leadership. In light of this goal, the new document was writ-ten in simple Hindi rather than a slavish literal translation of English documents, since it had to be understandable and useable for Indians. Second, it briefly stated general principles that could be revised from time to time. Third, it provided a clearer integration of mission and church, attempting to create a healthier relationship between the two. Fourth, it proposed a church that could carry on without the presence of foreigners, and included a recommendation that a provisional yearly meeting be established to give practice and experience to Indian Christians even though actual power remained with the mission. There needed to be room to learn to administer. And last, it included a doctrinal statement to put Ohio Yearly Meeting views into an Indian setting with an attempt to address Indian errors rather than American doctrinal errors. Despite the progress in breaking with the past, Everett still recognized the deficiency and the lack of involvement of Indian Friends theologians in the creation of the document.[36]

Everett Cattell and Ecumenical Ties

By February 3, 1950, Everett was attempting to interpret the mood of the Indian government toward Christian missions, not only to Ohio Friends but to others in the United States and around India. He was troubled by disagreements among evangelicals of India, some of whom had been labeled "extreme fundamentalists." They were being quoted in American Christian periodicals, with statements he felt were misleading. This, among other issues, led to his increasing leadership on a national level within India. He came to realize quickly a cleavage between the National Association of Evangelicals (U.S.A.) and the American Council of Churches (the Carl McIntyre movement, sometimes referred to as "right wing" and/or "fundamentalist" by its critics). The Friends mission had joined the Evangelical Fellowship of India, an organization that had been formed earlier, but they also held membership in the National Christian Council (NCC), an association of churches and missions for cooperation in common tasks and consultations that did not commit anyone to any particular doctrinal position or church polity. The McIntyre wing of the Evangelical Fellowship of India objected to the presence of what Everett called "a few" liberal, non-evangelicals in the NCC. The crunch came because the government of India had recognized the NCC as the body to speak for Protestant missions in the registration of missions and the recommendation of visas. Everett Cattell was no liberal, but he was bothered by the separatism and isolationism of the Carl McIntyre party.[37]

It was in this milieu that the Indian government developed its policy permitting some returning missionaries, but it would restrict new missionary visas based on several principles. First, the missionaries' services must be proven to bring advantage to India as skilled technicians, medical people, or teachers. Second, if the missionaries' only special qualifications were as religious workers, they would be refused visas. Third, all replacement visas would have to be justified anew and not merely passed to a new missionary replacement. Fourth, the government would allow returning missionaries only if there were no objections from anyone; this principle created the possibility of opening a Pandora's box of challenged visas and disgruntled minorities within churches. In the absence of a more sympathetic British government, evangelicals throughout India felt embattled and looked for ways to work together.[38]

Everett helped inform Friends and other evangelicals in India of the new regulations and helped develop strategies to best work within the new legal demands. He also assessed the effect of Communism's presence in post-war India on the missionary community. He called it bothersome, but felt the greater danger came from the orthodox Hindu party, reactionary in nature, hostile to progressive measures, and greatly opposed to evangelistic missions. The history of the years since proved Everett's assessment as correct. Communist and leftist politics have played a significant role, but Hindu loyalties were even stronger on the political scene through the 1980s and 1990s and into the twenty-first century.

Given the staunch Hindu opposition, all new visas needed to be handled "with a certain finesse," said Everett. By the word *finesse* he meant the word *evangelist* should be avoided. Instead he proposed the term "village up-lift workers," which he felt was entirely honest but less inflammatory. He urged new missionaries to combine their evangelistic skills with an awareness of adult literacy techniques and agricultural programs.[39] Everett was alert to changing times, and worked to change with them, and his administrative skills in so doing gradually brought him into national prominence.

Assessing the macro-political and religious situation in India, he wrote,

> There is something pathetic about leaders like Nehru who although agnostic in faith or in some cases still Hindu, but have absorbed Christian ideals through their British schooling are trying to project these ideals together with a basically Christian mind of character requisite to make their ideal effective. It is really pathetic to hear their speeches in which they plead with the public to cooperate in the suppression of corruption and to move toward their ideal. One wonders how long the background of British training will remain effective and whether it will soon be overcome by the basic corruption which is all about.[40]

More than fifty years later, we see the Indian experiment in democracy functioning, but still in serious trouble despite a significant economic boom since 1995. Sectarian violence among Hindus, Muslims, and Sikhs breaks out occasionally and caste patterns remain firm in most rural areas. Bureaucratic corruption is widely reported. A genuine basis for national unity seems elusive. Will the new "global economy" create a bypass around basic Indian disunity? That is yet to be seen.

Most evangelical missions in 1950 struggled with how to face changing relationships with Indian churches. Everett advocated the registration of both mission and church as separate entities in a July 11, 1950, letter, but then in an August 13, 1950, letter he said the opposite. He feared the mixed motives of some leading Indian Christian leaders who seemed to want the clout of property ownership. The Indian government fretted it was a set up for transferring foreign assets to front organizations within the country, a concern which carried some degree of truth. Yet Everett had contended earlier that what they were doing was intended to strengthen national control and stability under the laws of India.[41]

Through the 1940s, we see glimmers of the next stage of ministry Everett Cattell was about to undertake, and by the end of the decade, he had developed much experience with cultural adaptation, dependency, evangelistic strategy, and persecution. He was widely known throughout the country for his irenic spirit, his love for Christian holiness and integrity, and his ability to preserve clear goals in difficult times. His concern for Bundelkhand never wavered, but he began to sense a broader call to himself and to the Friends Mission. Perhaps part of the remedy for Bundelkhand lay far outside of that region and was related to Christian ministry to all of India.

Reflections:

In what ways did dependency became a large problem in mission/church relations in India?

What steps did Everett Cattell try to take to reduce the Indian church's dependency upon the West?

How did Christian workers try to prepare new converts for persecution, and how did they help when persecution came?

What do we learn about "faith missions" from Everett Cattell in his controversy with his home mission board?

What were the marks of "statesmanship" in the ministry of Everett Cattell? Are there ways this kind of leadership is especially useful and necessary?

chapter 13

A Statesman to the World

OUTSIDE OF THE WORLD OF FRIENDS, Everett Lewis Cattell was by far the best-known Friends missionary of the twentieth century. His interdenominational influence began first in India and continued into his life back in the United States. Of the missions leaders we have seen already, Everett Cattell had the most modest track record in church growth—a small handful of churches and a few hundred Christian believers in a highly resistant region of north India. In contrast, Arthur Chilson served as a sort of "David Livingstone" among Friends to attract great attention to Africa, establishing ministries that extended to six nations and hundreds of thousands of new Quakers. Esther Smith planted a significant Friends presence in Central America that now embraces four nations and has commissioned its own cross-cultural missionaries. But it was Everett Cattell who became the true world player and a Friends spokesman for international Christian missions.

How did this huge transition take place, launching Everett from isolation in backwater Bundelkhand to America and world evangelical prominence? What can we learn from the missionary theory and practice he exhibited at the end of his career? Which lessons can guide Friends into another century as important players in the church of the Global South as it expands?

Dealing with Dependency—Once Again

Bundelkhand Friends battled for survival through yet another crisis in church/mission relations in 1952. Everett agreed with Cliff Robinson and others that a rash of reversions to Hinduism in Bundelkhand was directly related to their mission policy of salaries and support to workers, combined with the history of support for orphans. Many of the reversions, they believed, happened because new converts felt they were being denied the privileges that had been given to older Christians. Such policies were "still not indigenous."[1] Anna Nixon charted progress toward indigenous self-support and self-propagation, which, by 1954, gave more authority to church leaders, placed a limit on missionary involvement in the organizational structure of the church, and helped increase the number of tithers within the Indian churches.[2, 3] And to Everett Cattell the problems of Bundelkhand, while serious, were frequently the same problems of poor mission policy found elsewhere in India, something that he still believed could be overcome.

An All India-Strategy

By the early 1950s, the need for an association of committed evangelical missions and churches for all of India came to a head. By that time, Everett's clear declarations and leadership were widely recognized and appreciated throughout India and he was offered the position of executive secretary of the Evangelical Fellowship of India. The mission council statements shifted from "we can't spare him" to "we must bow to the inevitable."[4] While the mission board in Ohio resisted this new role for him at first, they eventually accepted the entreaties of fellow evangelicals of India and from its own India mission council. For his part, Everett and others came to believe that while stymied in Bundelkhand, they now had open doors elsewhere that might eventually bring church health and growth back to Bundelkhand itself. In the meantime, God was calling Ohio Friends to minister in new ways in India.

The "all-India strategy" of Ohio Friends was applied first to Everett Cattell but shortly to others in the mission staff. While Everett continued to speak at conferences in various parts of India, he established an office in Chhatarpur for the Evangelical Fellowship of India. He remained a Friends missionary while spending significant time on ecumenical evangelical efforts. Shortly, however, doors opened for Friends missionary Robert Hess to minister at Union Biblical Seminary; and for Anna Nixon to develop Christian education materials for the Christian education department of the Evangelical Fellowship, and for her to teach at the seminary. Cliff Robinson worked first with India Youth For Christ and later in movements for prayer and evangelism. Dr. Ezra DeVol and his wife, Frances, became pioneers with the United Mission to Nepal, a neighboring

Hindu nation just emerging from political isolation. Anna Nixon stressed the focus of this all-India strategy as "leading the leaders" to Christ and training Indians for positions of prominence throughout India.[5] Later, Max and Ruth Ellen Banker "plunged in" to help lead an All-India Evangelical Fellowship Conference that met in 1955 in the nearby city of Jhansi in Bundelkhand, with more than three hundred in attendance.[6] While the prominence of these Friends leaders in India—Everett Cattell included—did not last for decades, their unique role during pivotal years in Indian church history is probably without parallel among Friends missions throughout the world during the twentieth century.

Everett Cattell and the Evangelical Fellowship of India (EFI)

This new involvement for Friends began with Everett Cattell's acceptance of leadership in the Evangelical Fellowship of India. The organization was formed in January 1951 and Everett came to feel that "the all-India call for me takes precedence over Bundelkhand" even though he correctly feared others would follow his lead and leave Bundelkhand, since "our mission has more than its share of all-India caliber."[7] For revival to come to Bundelkhand, it probably had to come to all of India first, he believed. This meant he was away from Chhatarpur as much as nine months out of twelve, and he never returned to village work, although Catherine continued in evangelism and they still considered Chhatarpur their home.[8]

The impetus behind the new ecumenical organization was to promote joint action and common cause against both liberal theology and hyper-conservatism. At the beginning, the greater concern was the Carl McIntyre-inspired American Council of Churches (ACC) in the United States. Many evangelicals wanted to "unitedly [disassociate] themselves from the excesses of the ACC men," he wrote.[9] Everett Cattell found himself receiving the confidence of many National Christian Council (NCC) people "in a way that few evangelicals do," he acknowledged with some embarrassment, wondering if he was compromising.[10] Along with many others, he found himself uncomfortable with those at either extreme of the theological spectrum.

Everett, for example, advocated that the Evangelical Fellowship of India be home for both Arminian and Calvinist theology—typically split by one of the great theological divisions that separated evangelicals in India and in other places of the world. His meetings with Dr. Norton Sterrett of the Reformed Presbyterians led them to believe that at the highest point of their doctrinal concerns they were united on "the sovereignty of God and free will of man, the need for instantaneous cleansing and the further need for daily cleansing by the blood of Christ, and on other issues that [initially] seemed to divide them."[11] Statements like this helped guide the formative stages of Union Biblical Seminary and other cooperative efforts throughout India. Everett was present for the seminary founding in 1956[12] and he also helped form the United Mission to Nepal in 1954.[13] His close relatives, the DeVols, eventually joined the United Mission after an illustrious tenure in Chhatarpur during which time the hospital made progress toward greater self-support and extended medical aid into new areas of Bundelkhand.[14] So the first display of Everett Cattell as a missionary statesman came during his last years in India.

Many have puzzled how a small group like the Friends could rise to such prominence in interdenominational cooperation. Why did Friends move so quickly into positions of influence throughout India in the 1950s? How did Everett help bridge theological divides that traditionally caused impassible barriers for evangelical cooperation? Anna Nixon, for one, conjectured that being small and with a pacifist tradition, evangelical Friends were considered "safe" and trustworthy—people without ego to defend. Without them, there might have been a greater tendency to juggle for positions of influence.[15] While that may well have been a factor in India, the high level of training, capability, and talent of Everett Cattell, Cliff Robinson, Robert Hess, and Anna Nixon cannot be denied.

Everett Cattell on Holiness and Mission

A second way Everett became known worldwide was through *The Spirit of Holiness*, a book first published by Eerdmans in 1963 but with roots that date back to his missionary years. Everett wrote this book, which became the most widely read of his writings, to present a "contemporary understanding of sanctification and Christian perfection for a broad evangelical audience."[16] The book presented holiness with balance and moderation, emphasizing the Christian disciplines for holy living. It was reprinted in 1977 and continues to be read.[17] In it, one can see both the Wesleyan and Quaker influence, although Everett took some exception to the Wesleyan theology with which he grew up.

Two of his earlier books, *The Self-Giving Missionary* (1951) and *Christ Prays For You* (mid-1950s) reflect holiness theology but in the context of the cross-cultural missionary experience. Holiness was a part of Everett Cattell's missionary theory and practice. While *The Spirit of Holiness* dealt especially with personal sanctity and an experience of the Holy Spirit in general, the two lesser-read books written earlier spoke to India. On the one hand he was struggling with a spirit of dependency upon the West by the Indian church, and on the other hand he accused the West of a lack of spiritual dependency upon God.[18] He stressed that freedom from materialistic constraints might release a huge amount of power to have "nothing but God," a traditional holiness concern, freeing the church to have a passion for godliness and for the lost.[19]

Rejection by the world may be necessary, he wrote, for the full power of God to be released. The rejected man of God is poised for great usefulness.[20] There was little power in an impatient Moses (striking the rock), no power in a compromising Aaron (the golden calf), but great power in an interceding, praying Moses and in Christ the suffering servant in the garden at prayer for his disciples. Both the Old Testament Moses and the Jesus of John 17 identified with God's people in a self-giving, painful way.[21] A theology of obedient suffering was a recurring Cattell theme, one he was to experience even more deeply before leaving India.

Christ Prays For You was revivalistic. Everett yearned for a purification of the Indian church. He believed that corruption within the Indian church was the greatest hindrance to a genuine evangelistic breakthrough, but he also looked for a biblical holiness free from "some of the objectional [*sic*] extremes which have often characterized the Holiness Movement."[22] Holiness is humility—not the building of missionary or church empires. Holiness is engagement with the world: We never can run away. Holiness means alienation from the world: We will be hated.[23] John 17, the scriptural basis for the book, was for Everett a theology of self-giving, sacrificial service by Christ, the very model for missionary servanthood.[24] This was not "irradication" holiness, a term he also rejected in *The Spirit of Holiness*, but rather a "relational" holiness. Maintaining a relationship with Jesus through the Holy Spirit was the answer to governing human impulse, human temper, and the human nature often identified (incorrectly, he said) as the "carnal nature."[25]

True holiness meant being "one in Christ," said Everett, who saw himself as a reconciler, bringing warring factions of the body of Christ into harmony.[26] He believed congregational unity—an openness to learn from Christians of other persuasions and the avoidance of strife—was a crucial part of God's will for the Christian.[27] The lack of Christian unity produces barriers and tensions that impede the completion of the Great Commission.[28] The way of holiness is the way of the cross. For the one who wants God to be glorified, "it means going with Him through the trials of the cross,"[29] but glory will not happen without being "with him" in his suffering. Holiness and the missionary experience were intertwined. Everett's missionary policy of seeking unity with others through ecumenical efforts and identifying with hurting people in compassion and justice ministry was an outgrowth of holiness theology.

Everett Cattell ended his *Spirit of Holiness* with a call to put love into action, specifically the kind of love Christ displayed for humans when he went to the cross. God is love, and he who loves God totally will display the virtues of godliness, not merely an inward piety, but an active, outward obedience.[30] Carole Spencer believes that Everett Cattell helped Quaker evangelicals of the twentieth century "recover their spiritual roots and modern identity through his unifying vision for Quaker holiness."[31] In so doing, he dealt freshly with Scripture without legalism and without resorting either to "modernism" or "fundamentalism." Thus, he gave Friends missions not only a theory and practice, but a core identity in holiness theology that will likely continue into the future. It could hardly be clearer that, to Everett Cattell, missions was Christian activism and not merely revivalistic pietism. Holiness meant obedience to the voice of God in service.

A Painful Farewell

Everett delighted in holiness preaching around India and worked hard with the Evangelical Fellowship of India, but in 1957 he accepted an invitation to become the general superintendent of Ohio Yearly Meeting of Friends. Before the Cattells departed from India, however, a series of painful events left them reeling. First, an Indian evangelist refused discipline and criminal court suits were leveled against Everett and other Friends leaders. Simultaneously, the Cattells' son David; David's wife, Jane; and David and Jane's baby daughter, Lisa; were killed in a car accident in Ohio. At the time several of the Bundelkhand missionaries were sick with typhoid, and Everett suffered physically through the court case, often forced to stand with an ulcerated leg that caused major discomfort. He was accused of defamation, giving armaments to robber bands, and overseeing illegal conversions. These were serious charges and a threat loomed heavily over the entire mission staff that the legal procedures would drag on for months and years, the common practice in India.

With the news of David Cattell's death, the court recessed briefly. The family staggered through a memorial service in Chhatarpur for David with Indian friends and church members who knew and loved him. Catherine Cattell's chapter in *From Bamboo to Mango* covering these events was named simply "Cloudburst." Leaving Bundelkhand without Everett for what she knew would be the end of her missionary service in India was a wrenching experience all by itself, but the grief was triply hard because of death and betrayal.[32] Catherine, in her way, felt she heard God's voice and counsel on how to respond. Very systematically and directly, she listed four points of instruction from God: 1) Do not talk about the situation continuously; but 2) be willing to talk about it at times; 3) avoid dramatization in any way; and 4) do not ask the question, "Why?"[33]

EVERETT L. CATTELL

The Cattells were stern but practical in their approach to deep suffering. Bad things happen to good people, but Everett and Catherine tried to trust without fully understanding, and they tried to avoid bitterness and resentment, all the while affirming the presence of God ("even there") in their deepest pain.

Loyal friends urged Everett to leave India quickly before the messy and volatile trial began, and to miss the whole ugly scene. He refused because he saw it as a legal test case in a fragile young democracy for establishing the right of the church to discipline leaders. He wanted to see it through to the end. But Catherine and their physically fragile daughter, Mary, made a painful journey ahead of Everett to Calcutta and Taiwan, where Everett was eventually able to join them, actually delayed only a week as the court case amazingly came to a speedy end. With time, the favorable conclusion was upheld through appeals and became something of a landmark case in Indian jurisprudence at the time.[34]

Everett Cattell as a Missiologist

Toward the end of his life, Everett Cattell published his missionary thoughts in an often-ignored book entitled *Christian Mission: A Matter of Life*[35] in the hope that it would be a tool to renew the worldwide vision of Quakers to cross-cultural ministry. A careful reading gives the reader a sense of Everett's concern for truth, for theological balance, and for a sense of compassion for the poor—all things that motivated him and that he considered essential to move the church to action. Each chapter of the book identifies two points of "tension" in missionary theory that he believed needed to be considered to maintain godly balance and to avoid damaging extremes. For example, there is tension between conversion evangelism and social service, between quantity and quality, and a tension between undertaking something small enough to be manageable while humbly recognizing the immensity of the task.

Was he a uniquely "Quaker" missiologist? I doubt Everett Cattell ever worried much about that kind of question, as he was far more concerned about basic Christianity; in the best of the evangelical Friends tradition, he felt Quakerism represented basic Christianity well. He assumed Friends doctrine to be Christ-centered, atonement-centered, and Bible-centered. Nevertheless, at a number of key points, an identifiable Quaker uniqueness permeated his book. First, he was a practical and active man and he wanted Friends to get on with the work of witness and service. "Just Do It!" had not been invented as a marketing slogan yet, but Everett had a "just-do-it!" spirit. Be done with ideology that smacks of indifference! We are Christ's friends only if we obey (John 15:14). Everett entitled the epilogue of his book simply "Urgency." Second, conversion evangelism was always important to him, but he knew it was meaningless if not accompanied by compassion or concern for human justice. Third, like early Quakers, he believed Christians can live in deep communion with the Holy Spirit—communion that produces a spirit of holiness and peace.

Everett Cattell's Abiding Influence in World Mission

Everett Cattell presents a paradox. Although he was the best-known of Friends missiologists, he was probably the least successful in terms of numbers of converts and churches. Nevertheless, his legacy is rich in Friends missions policy and practice, as is evidenced by six points.

First in order, but not in importance, he and the staff of his era left behind a small yearly meeting of Friends in Bundelkhand, and a witness continues there to this day. It is hard to imagine its survival had there been none of the changes that took place during Everett's leadership in a failed attempt to see a major people-movement started in the region. That part of the Cattell legacy—an outpouring of the Spirit in church growth in Bundelkhand—may still be in the future.

Second, among Friends he tenaciously promoted an awareness of India and the Hindu world, and other Ohio Friends continued the tradition. A decade after his death, Friends finally began finding responsiveness in other parts of the Indian subcontinent. Now, thirty years later, eight or more new ministries from Nepal in the north, to Bangladesh in the east, to Kerala state in the far south—find their historic roots with Everett's home base: Evangelical Friends

Church—Eastern Region. At the beginning of the twenty-first century, India joined the phenomenal economic growth of Asia, and church growth and missiological study throughout the region has become more significant for Friends and for others.

Third, Everett Cattell was a scholar of Hinduism. His interest in Hinduism was both practical and academic. He studied it seriously but rejected liberal Western attempts to exalt Hindu mysticism as being in agreement with or an alternative to Christian mysticism. As a matter of fact, he believed he saw a connection between demonic possession and the Hindu emphasis upon unbridled sexuality; some cases of demonic possession with which his staff in India dealt were dominated and closely linked to the sexual practices of Hindu idolatry.[36]

On the other hand, he recognized Christians had conceptual bridges to Hinduism already built by the Spirit, but he believed it important to consider those bridges without diminishing Christian truth. For example, Hinduism was concerned about holiness, about touching the unseen world, and, preeminently, about law to improve one's spiritual destiny or karma. These are human longings which Christ addressed. Everett felt, however, that the Hindu description of these concerns never matched Christian definitions, but many people disagreed with him. He called to task some with whom he had dialogued about what he called "unconscionable carelessness about words and their meanings."[37] In the study of world religions there are always important issues of truth and the character of God. While the longings of hurting human beings point to a shared humanity, the answers given by the various world religions, said Everett, are not the same answers given by Christian faith.

Fourth, Everett Cattell's teachings on holiness are rich and provide a framework for healthy missionary attitudes, motivations, and cultural sensitivity. His concern for compassion and justice grew out of scriptural holiness. His exhortation for missionaries to leave behind their own materialism and arrogance was, for him, an issue of Christian holiness. While his holiness theology was read in the West in an environment of pietism, his convictions had been nurtured in the Asian soil of poverty and activism and so can be viewed as contributing profoundly to his theology of mission.

Fifth, not unrelated to his theology of holiness, Everett Cattell's missiology contained a profoundly Christ-centered spirituality similar to George Fox's experience with Christ, the One who speaks to the human condition. Conversion to Christ is "a deep inner change from alienation," which is a natural prelude to radical discipleship, a revolution of character.[38] Everett was impatient with fads that selectively condemn one sin and overlook others. He believed the alcoholic-beverage industry, for example, is as heartless and manipulative as the warmongers who fabricate napalm. He had a Quaker sense of integrity that drove him toward wholeness.

Finally, Everett built his concept of gospel communication around three biblical terms: *service, proclamation,* and *fellowship.* All three are normal and expected in the sharing of Christian faith. As always, he stressed biblical balance. According to his concept, *service* breaks through resistance and deep needs are revealed. Then Jesus is *proclaimed,* a call for repentance leads to conversion, and finally the new believer is incorporated into the body of Christ. The *fellowship* of the kingdom is fleshed out through loving acceptance and it leads new believers back into the world of service and proclamation. Everett Cattell's biblical triad formed a flowchart of missionary communication leading to personal and social transformation.

Back in the West as a frequent preacher and teacher, Everett taught that a healthy church looked outside itself. To become healthy wasn't the primary motivation behind mission, yet he believed it was true—a mission-minded church was on the road to success in obedience. I personally remember hearing him plead with American Friends to be involved in compassionate caring and sharing for the downtrodden poor of the world—for the sake of the giver! Everett would not have fully agreed with the idea that a Christian must be spiritually renewed *before* becoming involved in missions. The opposite is also true—that obedient mission itself *produces* renewal and fresh breezes from the Holy Spirit. We discover God's blessings only when we give ourselves away to Jesus and to the world.[39]

Closing Years as Superintendent and College President

In addition to his role as a statesman in India and his leadership of the World Evangelical Fellowship, Everett Cattell rose to prominence in the arena of Christian education after serving as general superintendent of Ohio Yearly Meeting (now Evangelical Friends Church—Eastern Region). As president of Malone College (1960–1972), he oversaw the transformation of Cleveland Bible College into a liberal-arts institution and the curricular, administrative, and philosophical changes that shift involved. The old holiness Bible-school movement from the turn of the century—a movement that nurtured Arthur Chilson, Esther Smith, Everett Cattell, and Jack Willcuts (who we will look at in the next chapter)—was taking on a new face. During the 1960s and 1970s, Everett's voice for cross-cultural ministry, for the historic peace churches, and for integrity within the evangelical movement was frequently heard with high respect in committees and plenary meetings of the National Association of Evangelicals in the United States, meetings he frequently attended. After his later years of writing and teaching around the world, and after a brief illness, Everett Cattell died in Ohio in 1981. Catherine then retired to Oregon to be near friends and her brother and sister-in-law.

Reflections:

What are the positive and negative aspects of a mission agency moving from a denominational church-planting focus to focus upon institutional service with many denominations?

In what ways did Everett Cattell connect Christian holiness with the success of the cause of missions?

What do you learn about suffering and Christian ministry? How do you respond to Catherine Cattell's approach to really hard times?

Which of Everett Cattell's contributions to missionary theory and practice seem especially pertinent and important today?

EVERETT L. CATTELL

Jack L. Willcuts

chapter 14

The Bolivia Mission

Early Life

JACK L. WILLCUTS was born April 22, 1922, in Burr Oak, Kansas, the baby brother with five older siblings, six years younger than his nearest sister. His parents, Otis and Asenath Willcuts, originally came from Iowa. Jack's forebears had been Quakers for at least four generations and the family line had earlier lived in North Carolina. Many Quakers of the mid-nineteenth century joined what was called "The Great Migration" out of the South and into the North and West to avoid involvement with slavery and slave products. The Willcuts family settled near North Branch, Kansas, a rural Quaker community near the Iowa border, and home to one of a number of Friends academies that dotted the Kansas plains at the turn of the century. Two of Jack's older sisters attended North Branch Academy at the time of his birth. Three of the Willcuts siblings became teachers, two became pastors, and one became a nurse. In their heyday, North Branch and Jewell County bustled as centers of Friends activity, but as their economic base declined, many Quaker children of Jack's era drifted away to other locations as Friends continued to migrate further west across the United States.

During Jack's formative, early-teen years, his mother fell ill, and was bedfast for nearly five years before her death (she died when Jack was sixteen). Many years later, Jack still remembered waking frequently in the night, hearing his mother mention his name as she prayed. Jack came to believe the final years of her life proved the most useful and fruitful. Later he wrote, we may say "all we can do is pray" but that is actually "quite enough."[1]

Even though Jack always referred to his childhood as a happy time, his mother's suffering with rheumatoid arthritis and her eventual death were traumatic for him and left a permanent mark. He grieved deeply, and as his father's business floundered, Jack felt rootless. He started high school in North Branch, but completed it in

Haviland Friends Academy (Kansas). Following high school, Jack stayed in the Friends settlement at Haviland, and enrolled in Friends Bible College. Father Otis's business was hit hard by the Great Depression and the Dust Bowl; business success moved to total failure. The family lost the farm, and with it the emotional bond that mother Asenath had held tightly.[2] Jack's older sister Helen became a surrogate mother to him, and Jack followed her first to Haviland Friends Academy and Friends Bible College where she taught, and later to Greenleaf Friends Academy (Idaho) when she moved there to teach.

Jack developed a reputation as a mischievous and somewhat troubled youth in Haviland. Some despaired for him and all rejoiced in a dramatic switch in attitudes when he recommitted his life to Christ. Several recalled in later years the transforming shift in demeanor and values. "Mom Card," a motherly woman who had married late in life and accepted young men boarders, took him under her wing and taught him to iron clothes, cook, and care for himself. Jack often seemed perched on the edge of trouble, and despite his lack of musical skills and his troublemaker reputation, he joined a traveling youth evangelism group and accepted their exhortations to preach, which he did with some success. After completing two years at the Bible college in Haviland, and after a visit to his sister Helen in Idaho, he began the great debate on how to complete his college education. Asbury College in Kentucky attracted some of his Haviland classmates, but someone in Idaho encouraged him to consider Pacific College (now George Fox University). So Jack traveled west to Newberg, Oregon, and enrolled at Pacific where he completed a B.A. degree in religion. At Pacific he studied well, busily competed in intercollegiate speech contests, and played basketball.[3] Jack's first pastoral work was at Rockaway Community Church (Oregon) as a student pastor during his last two years of college; he then served at Northeast Tacoma Friends (Washington) for two years—one year before his marriage to Geraldine, and during their first year of marriage.

He met Geraldine Tharrington, daughter of a Church of the Brethren preacher, during his time in Idaho while she was a senior at

Greenleaf Friends Academy. After high school Geraldine studied two years at McPherson College (a Church of the Brethren school in Kansas), transferred to Pacific College her junior year to be close to Jack during his last year of college, and then transferred back to McPherson where she graduated. Jack and Geraldine were married in Idaho on June 26, 1945, and that same summer Jack was recorded a minister of the gospel by Oregon (now Northwest) Yearly Meeting of Friends.

A Missionary Call?

During Jack's ministry at Northeast Tacoma Friends, Walter Lee, an active and aggressive mobilizer for missions, and president of Oregon Yearly Meeting's mission board, wrote a letter to Jack suggesting he consider ministry in Bolivia. While we don't know the exact content of that letter, we know something of what was happening in Bolivia at the time and that Walter Lee knew firsthand the need for direction and vision for a work that in some ways was floundering. Lee's letter was, for Jack, the "laying on of hands" that caught his attention and directed his thoughts to the world mission of Friends. What was happening in Bolivia that prompted Lee to write his letter? What was the "call" that came to Jack and to what was he responding?

To capture the context of Lee's letter, we need to go back to the life of Esther Smith. The very first contacts for Friends in Bolivia came through Central Yearly Meeting of Friends in Indiana, and through an independent visit from California in 1919 by William Abel, a student from Huntington Park Training School for Christian Workers (now Azusa Pacific University). William Abel's visit led the young Bolivian Juan Ayllon to study at Berea Bible School in Chiquimula, Guatemala, which had been recently founded by Esther Smith. Esther visited the Ayllons in Bolivia in 1929 and wrote a letter to Oregon Yearly Meeting the next year about Bolivia as a mission field. The letter was accepted at Yearly Meeting in 1930 and it was approved that Oregon Friends adopt Bolivia as a field for ministry. The Carroll and Doris Tamplin family, then missionaries in

Central America, were commissioned and sent to Bolivia the following year. The Howard and Julia Pearson family, also a part of the Friends missionary staff in Guatemala, plus two women—Helen Cammack and Esthel Gulley—formed the first Friends mission staff of Oregon Yearly Meeting in Bolivia. All of them had strong roots in Oregon. All of them were products of the early twentieth-century Holiness Movement among Friends. In Bolivia through the 1930s they struggled valiantly with only limited success in the face of huge obstacles, but enough to convince them and Friends in Oregon that Aymaras were open to the message of Christ and justified concentrated efforts. Later studies have shown that while response was still small, it was a greater response than any other mission group was experiencing in the same region. Walter Lee clung to the hope of a future harvest.

The difficulties were formidable: The extreme elevation—12,500 feet—produced much illness and physical stress to lowlanders working on the high plains. Furthermore, during much of the 1930s, Bolivia was at war with neighboring Paraguay and new converts were either pressed into the military or went into hiding, leaving mostly women and children in the few scattered congregations. The Great Depression cut into missionary support worldwide, even though it provided some opportunities for local Bolivian industries to arise to replace the almost total lack of imported goods. Local officials and Roman Catholic priests treated Protestants as seditious heretics and there was little defense against persecution. The Aymara underclass that Esther Smith met on her visit in 1929—and about which she wrote to Oregon (Northwest) Yearly Meeting—was mistreated, withdrawn, and cut off from the mainstream of Bolivian society. As World War II wore on, Esthel Gulley transferred to World Gospel Mission in Mexico for health reasons and because of a new mission-board policy that did not allow single female workers; Helen Cammack was stricken with typhoid fever and died early in 1944.

In September of that year, church administrators from Oregon, Walter Lee among them, waited upon the missionary staff and faced several unpleasant realities. Julia Pearson was sick and needed to return to the United States, which she did in November—the same month that Juan Ayllon resigned from the ministry. A serious disagreement had developed between the Tamplins and the Pearsons. A new missionary family, Ralph and Marie Chapman, arrived at about the same time, but found the unity of the remaining group totally fractured, and the Tamplins on their way to a new ministry in the Bolivian jungles with World Gospel Mission.

The visiting administrators, general superintendent Joseph Reece and mission board president Walter Lee, met with the missionary staff, mediated the staff disagreements, and came to three conclusions: 1) They needed a pastoral training school; 2) They needed staff unity and that was to be implemented by switching from governance by a mission superintendent to a more egalitarian mission council system; and 3) They urgently needed new missionaries. So it was that some time between the return of the administrators to the United States (in late 1944) and 1946, Walter Lee acted on his concern for new missionaries and wrote the letter to Jack Willcuts, asking him to consider a call to Bolivia. In response Jack sensed a simple rightness about preparing for missionary service: There was a pressing need and a respected leader thought he could meet that need. This was how he often responded to what he considered to be God's call.

As mentioned earlier, after graduating from college, Jack assumed a pastorate in Tacoma. His sister Helen made her home with him for part of that year. In June 1945, Jack went back to Greenleaf, Idaho, to marry Geraldine, and they returned to Tacoma for a second year. During those two years, Jack remained close to longtime college friends Arthur and Fern Roberts who pastored in nearby Everett, Washington; Jack maintained correspondence with them for much of his life. Jack could not escape the letter from Walter Lee, and he eventually came to believe it was this "laying on of hands" by elders of the church that was crucial in his sense of call. Jack and Geraldine began Spanish studies with a tutor in Tacoma and were commissioned as missionaries at Oregon Yearly Meeting sessions in the summer of 1946. Their departure for Bolivia was delayed for revival meetings, deputations, and waiting for shipping arrangements for their personal belongings, but they arrived in La Paz, Bolivia, on July 4, 1947.

First Impressions of Bolivia

Their first impression of Bolivian society was of the apparent slowness and lack of progressive thought among the people. "Come back tomorrow," was very trying to their patience. On the home front in the kitchen, the high altitude demanded Geraldine use pressure cookers, and cooking often went awry. Spanish and Aymara languages, strange driving patterns, rough and sometimes primitive roads, poverty, and more bombarded their senses. As new arrivals Jack and Geraldine did not have a vote in council meetings, but this did not prevent them from becoming aware of temperaments and relational stress within the missionary team. Geraldine quoted an unknown author that "the greatest disillusionment to the new missionaries is to find that all the others are just normal people too." She added, "But some of the normalcy rather astonishes Jack and me." She quickly developed a concern not to talk behind the backs of fellow staff members. "Jack and I have a policy of the closed mouth. And we hope we stick to it tenaciously."[4]

The Soul-Cry of the Aymara

Oregon Friends Mission produced an aptly named publicity piece: *The Soul-Cry of the Aymara*—and the Aymara's sense of depravation and oppression was palpable as Jack and Geraldine arrived. Jack observed that the Aymaras had been "driven high by their white conquerors who took over the arable land in the valleys."[5] While not exactly true of the whole Aymara people (they had always been highlanders), it was true that after the Spanish conquest Aymaras were forced to the least desirable areas and white hacienda owners took control of the better altiplano (high plateau) tracts through a near feudal system of serfdom. The land reform that changed all this did not begin until 1952, five years after Jack and Geraldine Willcuts arrived.

Jack joined heartily in a compassionate response to a people in need. Although he lost eighteen pounds in a matter of weeks and suffered from debilitating high-altitude headaches, he threw himself into preaching through interpreters who translated from English to Spanish and to Aymara. Both Jack and Geraldine spoke publicly in Spanish for the first time in November and then began feeling less like outsiders. The large rural conferences excited Jack: "I have never enjoyed preaching more," he wrote, and a series on "Christ the Truth, "Christ the Liberator," and "Christ the Good Shepherd" brought satisfaction to him.[6]

In September, just two months after their arrival, Jack came down with a bad case of the measles after an arduous evangelistic trip to Lake Titicaca and back that included late starts, long delays, and running out of gas.[7] Jack used his recuperation time to form his thoughts: "The Indian is suspicious, downtrodden, ignorant, exploited." Yet he marveled that the Aymaras had maintained their identity, their language, and their folkways. Jack viewed the recent purchase of Hacienda Copajira[8] by the mission and the beginning of a Bible institute in that location[9] as an opening for a great cultural and evangelistic impact. Roscoe Knight, who had arrived just two years prior to Jack and Geraldine Willcuts, had been charged with creating a more complete Bible-school program and Jack collaborated with Roscoe's plans. Jack's initial vision for his ministry centered on a "church in [each] community" and his first assignment was field evangelism and supervision of various community projects. "The Gospel works in Bolivia…when anyone is willing to abandon sin and serve Christ [and] he finds it pays in joy, peace and hope. And those three things the Aymara Indian has never known before."[10]

Cultural Responses

Life was not easy, and disease, unhygienic living conditions, and culture shock rocked them at times. "The men stare, they steal anything, nothing is private. If you are a *gringo* you have only half a chance," Geraldine wrote.[11] Jack traveled frequently for evangelism and supervision of mission schools. In between trips, he often found himself entangled in legal affairs like securing a driver's license. He learned to go patiently through the process without expecting special treatment or demanding intervention from an influential friend, which he often found to be counterproductive, creating resentment.[12]

Jack put his hand to domestic work at times—washing dishes, ironing clothes, and cooking. Mom Card back in Haviland would have been proud! Jack worked with Geraldine at home, and Geraldine found art and teaching provided an opportunity for her to work outside the home in the ministry. At home, she busied herself in settling in, cooking, decorating, and planting flowers. Jack took pride in his wife's work and would occasionally bring home flowers from the market for her.[13] Although their first Christmas abroad brought feelings of homesickness, the couple learned to cope with the heavy stress of high elevation, ministry, and disease by sharing game evenings with friends—numerous games! It was a way to maintain emotional health, and Jack made serious work of it!

Church Discipline

One of the first major stressors came in December 1947 when prominent pastor and worker Francisco Medrano was expelled from church ministry by the mission council. The action appears high-handed and paternalistic by twenty-first-century standards, even though Medrano's expulsion was likely the desire of the church as a whole. The nationals on the local church council advocated his dismissal, but the mission council took the authoritative action and it was the mission that locked the building after the dismissal letter was read.[14] The "Indigenous Society" that had been created a few months earlier was, in theory, supposed to deal with such issues, but it was clearly not functioning.[15] This significant foray into the awkwardness of missionaries wielding authority over national Christians likely had a strong impact upon Jack, as the concern for a "self-governing" national church quickly became high priority for him; in many ways this was to become Jack's greatest contribution to Bolivian missiology.

Jack struggled in the middle of the Francisco Medrano controversy.

> There seems to be no easy place…[yet] someone must stand in the gap…build the wall…even though surrounded by difficulties.…I have always admired the folks who maintain their personal integrity and keep a spiritual radiance even when a situation is adverse…I find it one thing to be surrounded by strife, degradation and problems and another to keep strife and problems from getting inside my own mind and heart. God is helping us in learning some of these lessons.[16]

The conclusion of the Medrano affair was the annulment of the Indigenous Society and "we are back in the old way of missionaries control[ling] everything," Geraldine observed.[17] Jack's insomnia was not getting better—"altitude-related," Tina Knight told Geraldine—but the stress and pain of taking steps backward away from the indigenous church ideal took a toll. Jack's *Time* magazine was his refuge, the air-mail delivered copy occupied him for a full evening every time it arrived.[18]

Missionary Family Life

By February 1948, Geraldine began experiencing severe morning sickness from the first weeks of pregnancy. The sickness persisted into March. Even though Jack and Geraldine had not announced the pregnancy to others, Geraldine wrote that she "heaved up my socks," and knew that fellow missionaries would soon guess what was going on.[19]

Jack became mission-council president, and he remained busy as evangelistic secretary and as pastor of the Max Paredes congregation. He also continued Spanish-language study. The Willcutses moved into the mission home, which was a sort of "Grand Central Station" for mission and church activities—a point of further stress to the family. Geraldine took pride in how Jack was establishing his stride in ministry, "catching on and doing all the work," attending weekly meetings, preaching, and learning Spanish. But, she said, "He comes home awfully discouraged about Spanish and the way he is not able to understand it."[20]

The mission home, located on Max Paredes street and next to the central church, was something of a clearing house for the American missionary community, even though it was located in the Indian district and away from the seat of power in the city. Government and American embassy personnel often called to ask for addresses or telephone numbers for others in the area. The Willcutses made a point to keep their home open to both Indian and foreign visitors, even if it meant enduring fleas left by the poor.[21] Jack would later counsel missionary staff to keep an open attitude about national visitors in their homes. One's *attitudes* about material possessions, he said, are more important than the exact level of *lifestyle*. To have "foreign possessions" is not as much a barrier in cross-cultural friendships, he felt, as one's protective or fearful attitude about contamination or damage.

Geraldine became the mission hostess once the couple settled into the mission home. They had prized their independence and privacy at their first apartment some distance away from headquarters at Max Paredes, but they were good sports about the change. They discovered the art of mixing gasoline with kerosene for added heat—extremely dangerous anywhere else in the world, but acceptable at high elevations where combustion was much slower.[22] Living in La Paz also meant helping those living at a distance from the city—a servant's role for both of them.[23] Those missionary friends, both within and outside the mission, were important—friends with whom to share ice cream and cake, birthday and anniversary celebrations, potluck meals and games. Geraldine worked to bring comfort and cheer to the table—a lace tablecloth, snapdragons, and on one occasion a bright bouquet of pink carnations with touches of roses and yellow carnations from Jack. Geraldine often considered Jack a thoughtful husband—he frequently earned "points" with her and a place in her letters home.[24] "I certainly have a good husband. He helps me all the time. In fact he just *does* it."[25]

By August of 1948, Geraldine faced the last two months of her pregnancy with Stuart, their first child, but also a full plate of everyday frustrations. Meanwhile, Jack was busy outside the home—annual conferences, helping a new pastor settle into the church in Palca, attending to legal issues in the city—and he also invited the local youth group into their home. Despite their numerous activities, Jack and Geraldine detested the image of the overworked missionary—one who would "go around all the time saying how busy they are...and personally I don't think we are such a busy bunch."[26] But Jack was busy. He had become mission-council president and carried a major part of correspondence for the council, and not yet one year into his missionary service. It was the attitude of calling attention to one's busyness that Jack and Geraldine wanted to avoid.

Frustrations and hard work were a part of every day. One week, for example, Jack had to walk home from the airport area of Alto La Paz and had a broken tie rod that delayed another trip. A flat tire, an empty gas tank, and gasoline shortages were other frustrations of the same week. We don't know Jack's "typical" response, but Geraldine that week chirped, "My dear husband took me out to dinner Tuesday night." That and a freezer full of ice cream, flowers for the table, and a birthday cake were duly noted. And if there were leftovers, they were used for breakfast! They always found ways to cope in the midst of frustrating circumstances.[27]

Stuart was born September 23, 1948, and to Geraldine's surprise, she felt like a first grader learning to do college work as she began the process of parenting. But she trusted that she and Jack together—along with an Aymara Christian believer who helped as a cook—could figure it out. Prior to Geraldine and Stuart's return from the hospital, Jack worked hard to get the home ready: He varnished the floors, dusted, and replaced rugs. "I think I have an exceptional husband!" Geraldine declared again.[28]

In the same week that Geraldine ran a sewing machine needle through her finger (Jack came running with first aid), Jack left Geraldine alone with the new baby and accompanied Howard and Julia Pearson to Corocoro to help them retrieve personal belongs left there.[29] Jack developed sympathy and empathy with others through the rigors of his own missionary life, and he was aware that Geraldine was being stressed heavily by his schedule. Perhaps the even more difficult times were when Jack was buying, packing, shipping, and investigating for his fellow missionaries, and he was not able to give full attention to his own family or to his intellectual gifts.

By the end of 1948, and after a quite restful vacation in Cochabamba, Bolivia, Jack found time to write his "annual letter" to Geraldine's family. "We occasionally feel rather closed in and far away," he wrote. "In many respects one['s life] here is very limited; in his reading, social life and other things." Yet Jack went on to ruminate that missionary life was fascinating and demanding with trips full of adventure and a life full of demands for development—in language, in personal dependence upon God, in practice in getting along with people—all kinds of character development! In addition to that, he said, existed the challenge of retaining the "vision and faith for spiritual leadership while living in a pagan environment." Jack's reflections reveal he was catching on that he could find enjoyment from the unusual and from the "differences" in cross-cultural living—enjoyment in the contrast with the commonplace of his home culture and in being in a setting where there was no limit on possible personal and spiritual growth.[30]

In the same letter, Jack showed how far he had come in fewer than two years on the field. Some missionaries, he noted, seemed to delight in the feelings of insecurity; some lived for the adventure or excitement; others cherished the opportunity to depend upon the Lord; and others relished the chance to tell of "the multitudinous dangers involved."[31] Jack believed those who learned to enjoy missionary life would likely persist much longer!

Missionary Tensions

As Howard and Julia Pearson neared the end of their tenure, and it became difficult for them to release their Bible-school teaching work to others and to see new methods employed. They had a rugged pioneer spirit; they lost a child in an accident in Guatemala; they understood deprivation and loneliness. Julia was a gifted teacher, Howard a faithful administrator, but loose words could fly and feelings could get hurt in several directions. Jack agonized on how best to help them enjoy their last two years of ministry before the new regulation of mandatory retirement at age fifty-five would move the Pearsons out of their positions.[32] (It probably was not a coincidence that a similar regulation had been made in Chiquimula, Guatemala, after the death of Esther Smith in 1947.) Jack and Geraldine felt the tension again when the staff, despite the disapproval of the Pearsons, agreed that Jack and Geraldine should have a vehicle for their work in and around La Paz.[33]

As the Pearsons prepared for retirement through the summer of 1950, Jack found himself counseling a Bolivian leader who held strong resentments against Julia Pearson. Wrote Geraldine, "I think perhaps they do not understand her."[34] The leader felt wronged by Julia and slighted that she never acknowledged the wrong. Jack and others found it difficult to confront Julia, so the issue was laid aside and the Pearsons left for the United States via a long steamer trip down the Amazon River. Julia's teaching had been appreciated and she was remembered by many Bible-institute graduates from the Copajira farm for her firm hand, which was tempered with compassion. Jack saw this time of transition as an opportunity to reflect on the importance of interpersonal relationships, which he always felt were paramount to successful ministry.

Catholic Persecution

The relationship between evangelical Protestants and Roman Catholics was difficult, to say the least, although with the post-war fear of communistic atheism, Catholics seemed open to anyone who professed a belief in God as a possible ally against the Red threat. Nevertheless, a New Zealand missionary was expelled from the country after a new convert destroyed his personal idols and the Catholic priest blamed the missionary. For this and similar cases, Jack became active in establishing an inter-mission organization to represent missions before the government.[35] Slanderous press reports against Friends missionaries at Copajira alleged the missionaries carried guns and demanded obedience from the peons. "Just the Catholics trying to stir up trouble," wrote Geraldine.

While the Copajira farm served as a base for leadership training and a training ground for the enlarging mission staff to become much closer to Aymaras culturally and emotionally, the entire mission staff, in time, became convinced that Copajira had become an encumbrance. The farm continually made the mission staff a target for persecution and opposition, including persecution from the Roman Catholic Church and later persecution as a political target. The nominally Catholic peons demanded a Catholic school on the farm, and they protested the takeover of the Catholic chapel at Copajira for evangelical services.

Catholics nationwide expected and demanded preferential treatment. *Time* magazine from June 28, 1948, quoted the Jesuit demand that the Roman Church receive religious freedom for itself alone as the only true church. While it would not draw the sword against others, said the article, the Church would protest against the legal existence of any other religions in places where Catholics were in a majority. And, it said, where religious minorities actually existed, "they shall have only a de facto existence without opportunity to spread their beliefs."[36] This is a position not unlike twenty-first-century Islamic demands for preferential treatment in nations where there is a Muslim majority. But it is hard to imagine such a position by the Roman Catholic Church since the Vatican II council in the early 1960s dramatically eased tensions. At the time, however, such an attitude created situations where Jack and others found themselves standing before magistrates, requesting authorization for freedom of worship, protesting beatings, and requesting investigations by police officials. Fortunately, local secular authorities often sided with the letter of the law, which supported the evangelical cause. But unfortunately, those some authorities could be easily swayed by radical Catholics in behind-the-scenes opposition. Jack's treks to court with protests against persecution and petitions for freedom of worship were frequent and prolonged in the rural area around Copajira and around the shores of Lake Titicaca.

Geraldine and her sister-in-law Helen Willcuts attended an English-language church memorial service at the local Baptist church for missionary Eugene Dabbs and other Baptists killed in an attack on Protestants near Oruro, Bolivia, in August 1949. It was something of a landmark case in Bolivian evangelical history, and marked one of the last major outbreaks of Catholic hostility.[37] Several years later the Willcuts family looked back at the Dabbs killing with fear after Jack, Stuart, Roscoe Knight and others experienced a "near miss" when a crowd of Aymaras—almost certainly at the instigation of the local Catholic priest—threatened them during an evangelistic meeting at an altiplano community named Karhuisa. They fled by a back road and escaped unscathed but shaken, remembering that Dabbs and the Baptists were fatally injured by stones and clubs under very similar circumstances.[38]

Ecumenical Contacts

By April 1948 Jack was busy helping to establish an inter-mission organization to address such issues as Catholic opposition.[39] Jack also established personal relations with other missionaries and mission groups—Baptists, Central Friends, Bible Society, Bolivian Indian Mission, and World Gospel Mission. Perhaps Jack did this no more so than others, but he lived in the city for much of his first term of service and that allowed for more such contacts. He accepted invitations to speak at the local English congregation and even the local Baptist youth group.[40] His closest ties were often with people associated with the holiness tradition, including the Salvation Army, Central Friends, and World Gospel Mission, yet Jack was never narrowly sectarian in his sentiments about sanctification, and he had friends in the broader expatriate Christian community.

Jack and the mission council were involved in a small way in the founding of Radio Cruz del Sur, a Canadian Baptist-owned radio project. Lutherans gave a technician, Bible Seminary Friends donated a location, and Oregon Friends made a small monthly donation. Jack did a ten-minute sermon read weekly by a Bolivian for the radio station, since apparently it was illegal for a foreigner to speak on the radio.

The La Paz Missionary Fellowship met monthly by this time and became the avenue for several joint projects.[41] Jack was elected president of the group in November 1949; One of his responsibilities was to help form a united voice before the Bolivian government.[42]

Beginning in November 1949, Jack accepted requests from time to time to preach at the English-speaking La Paz Community Church that met in the prominent downtown Prado Baptist Church. Other times he would turn down the invitation and point to his other responsibilities, which included pastoring the Max Paredes Friends Church and a heavy travel schedule.[43] It was obvious Jack enjoyed preaching in English and found a certain pastoral liberty doing so, but his primary calling was still to Aymara Christians. As president of the missionary fellowship, Jack attended every monthly meeting even when Geraldine, late in her pregnancy with daughter Susan, could only send along her salad and stay home with Stuart.[44] Jack preached there again for Thanksgiving and after Christmas in 1950; he preached there quite frequently for a man his age, age twenty-eight.[45]

Political Instability

Meanwhile, from 1947 through 1951 during the Willcutses' first term of service, all of Bolivia suffered regular cycles of political instability every three to six months. President Gualberto Villarroel had been summarily executed in his own presidential palace just a year earlier in 1946 and his body hung on a lamp post in the central plaza as had been the body of fascist dictator Benito Mussolini in Italy in 1945. The conservative military and political forces that took Villarroel's place faced an explosive situation through the years 1946 until 1952 when they were finally overthrown in a violent and popular revolution after ignoring the will of the people in a free election. For Jack and Geraldine, post-World War II politics influenced Bolivia as German and Jewish stores popped up around the city, carrying imported but expensive outside consumer goods. Villarroel was anticommunist but tainted by fascist tendencies, as was strongman Juan Perón in neighboring Argentina. Both were nationalists who aroused the ire and opposition of the elite traditionalists, leaving Bolivia and the missionaries in a state of perpetual uncertainty.

In May 1949, violent revolution came to the gates of the Max Paredes church and mission property where the Willcutses lived. A traffic police officer was killed and rocks were thrown at the church. The Willcutses were vacationing away from the city at the time, but the threat seemed especially real.[46] Later the same month, Aymaras, likely urged on by communist agitators, went on strike in the city, demanding higher wages. Jack and his family had food on hand, were locked in, and felt basically safe, but one young man from the church was killed in the street by a stray bullet.[47]

Jack coped by seeing humor in national affairs. He wrote,

> The new president [of Bolivia] got into office on a technicality as the real president made the grave mistake of leaving town over the weekend for a rest. The man now in office was his vice president so he just slipped up a notch. The papers reported that the former president resigned because of a bad heart, but I think he resigned anticipating a bad heart if he didn't. I admire the former president for his ability to get out of office in one piece. To get to be president here is not as difficult as getting out of the job once in. Bolivia has had 23 presidents in the last 50 years and only two are alive to report. They are real souvenirs.[48]

Turmoil continued through September; evangelism trips and missionary arrivals were jeopardized and rebel groups appeared in other parts of the nation.[49] Rumors of government bankruptcy filled the air in March 1950, and labor strikes filled the city streets in May while inflation ran unchecked.[50] Thoughtful Bolivians of the era, disgusted with the graft and charade of government, eventually set in motion a movement that toppled the non-elected governments in 1952. But the stability didn't come until decades later.

Meanwhile, the Friends and some other mission agencies found themselves in an awkward position. Their personal sympathies lay with the oppressed Aymaras who seldom were allowed to vote, and who were treated either as urban beasts of burden or as rural serfs virtually tied to and traded with the land. Nationalist aspirations became confused with communist propaganda. Even though

221

apolitical and neutral in every uprising, the missionary community—identified as mostly North Americans—became enemies to the new wave. Uncertainty reigned in La Paz and in Copajira. The Friends missionaries favored justice for the Indians, but doubted the Marxist-inspired politicians sweeping the country would provide it.

The Beginnings of a Missiologist

Jack Willcuts's early years show a mixture of traits. He was a bright, joyful child whose emotions had been darkened by the loss of his mother; a perplexed teenager struggling to find his place in the church; an athlete who won speech contests; and a latent scholar who found his place not in the rigors of academics but in the world of applied theology as a missionary and pastor.[51] While never completing academic programs beyond college, he worked hard to overcome limitations through a rigorous personal discipline to establish goals and maintain focus. He was gifted in writing, for example, so he disciplined himself and studied to improve his gift through correspondence courses. His preaching was characterized by careful word choice that grew out of his writing. His good humor lifted many, even though at times he found himself feeling heavy and withdrawn. He was competitive at almost any sport or game, but found it difficult to leave work behind and relax when on vacation. Through this mixture of giftedness and struggle, Jack Willcuts became a productive leader who could share a vision and point out new directions for his missionary and pastoral colleagues.

As with each of our other three Friends missiologists, Jack Willcuts cannot be defined in simple terms. His missions theology and practice was colored by his childhood and early formation in the world of western Friends (those of Kansas, Idaho, and Oregon). The Holiness Movement that we have seen in the lives of Arthur Chilson at Cleveland Bible Institute, Ruth Esther Smith at Huntington Park in California, and Everett Cattell at Marion College in Indiana also impacted Jack Willcuts at Friends Bible College (now Barclay College) in Kansas. Arthur and Esther were unique pioneers and Everett was a statesman and thinker. What were Jack's unique contributions? Was it his good humor? Was it his sense of call to "churchmanship"? Or was it his special kind of trust in the Holy Spirit to build the body of Christ through an autonomous structure that would take hold of a culture and make it over in Jesus' name?

Reflections:

What do you think of Jack Willcuts's approach to God's call to missions "through the elders of the church"?

Which of Jack and Geraldine Willcuts's first impressions or first experiences are most memorable to you? How is the Willcuts's setting similar to that of the Cattells' in India?

Why might it seem especially awkward for missionaries to wield discipline over church members in a cross-cultural setting?

What about a missionary lifestyle would be most difficult for you? Why?

What similarities, if any, do you see between Everett Cattell's ministry and Jack Willcuts's ministry?

What approach to ministry do you think missionaries should adopt in the face of political and civil unrest and threats of violence?

chapter 15

The Churchman at Work

WATER SERVICE in the city of La Paz was irregular the week before Susan Willcuts was born in 1950. It was hard to schedule baths and once a bath was taken, it was hard to feel clean since the water was dark with sediment. Jack was off to altiplano churches at Chunavi and Puerto Perez. Church ministry was going better now that Jack was mostly recovered from a bout of hepatitis that plagued him through the month of May. Not too many months earlier it had been typhoid. Both diseases were endemic in the region.

Some church leaders had become discouraged when Jack was absent during his illness, but upon his return classes for workers were once again held every Wednesday. The church leaders used materials that workers could turn around and teach directly to others.[1] As the jaundice effect of the hepatitis gradually disappeared from Jack's body, the date for Susan's birth drew near, and Jack was in town on June 20 when the baby came. Susan was delivered by a young American Dr. Brown who was called in at the Methodist Clinic. It was a difficult breach delivery after eight hours of labor—perhaps a week or two early—but Susan was strong and healthy.[2]

Baby Susan

But there was one problem: Susan's right ear was completely closed and doubled over. Some believe fetal development can be adversely effected by high elevation, but reasons for the condition were un-clear. The solution, however, was very certain: A plastic surgeon in the United States could fix the ear and her hearing would most likely be normal. Despite challenges like this, Geraldine reported "[We are] happy in our work and trying to do our best for the Lord."[3]

Susan's birth marked a turning point that influenced the family's future for some years to come. Jack and Geraldine did not feel a release from their call to serve in Bolivia, but their commitment was to family above ministry, so they began forming plans to meet Susan's medical needs within a few weeks. Perhaps they would make an appeal to a specialist in Los Angeles; maybe they would go directly to Mayo Clinic in the Midwest; or maybe simply doctors in Portland, Oregon, would care for Susan. The mission board granted permission for them to leave immediately at the end of their term, or perhaps sooner, to attend to Susan's health needs,[4] and the likelihood of the Wilcutses being in the United States for more than one year began to take shape. The last year of their term of service was marked by a whirlwind of trips, consultations over the national church organization, medical help for leaders and Christians, and many house guests.

The Willcuts family felt a quiet and gentle satisfaction within the whirlwind, however. Jack wrote with what appears to be Quaker plain speech—a lack of exaggeration or romanticism:

> The past three-and-a-half years have been pleasant ones and worthwhile. More than 100 people have been saved from liquor, immorality, absolute hopelessness and soul degradation through the light of the glorious gospel of Christ....The work has grown to more than 1000 from around 600 when we arrived in 1947....Work of this type cannot be accurately estimated now as to real success or failure and we have at times been quite discouraged and homesick.

Discouragement, however, was small in comparison to "a far more exceeding and eternal weight of glory," he said. With the chaos of the beginning of the Korean War, the confrontation of world powers, and the fear of nuclear holocaust in the minds of world leaders and Americans everywhere, Jack took confidence in eternal truths and eternal promises.[5]

Serving the Whole Person

Jack viewed his Christian ministry as a union of helping and proclaiming. He and others of the mission staff considered the Copajira Farm not only a place to train pastors but a place to demonstrate better farming methods, better animal stock, and better seed. He and Geraldine delighted in seeing Aymaras follow the missionary example and irrigate before starting the cultivating cycle, something they did for the first time in 1957. The tradition had been to put the fiesta system first, rather than agricultural survival. The evangelical example broke that pattern.[6]

Jack routinely allowed his life to be interrupted by the medical needs of others. "Indescribable filth" sometimes led to major, open-sore infections—sores that responded to penicillin and sulfa. Even with very little medical training, the missionaries could do good things.[7] Taking a believer to the hospital was a common event. "Not a little of our time is taken up in handling medical cases." Jack helped people make contact with good doctors whenever possible, and in a jocular mood wrote home that,

> I handle nothing more difficult than hang-nail cases. Speaking of hang-nail cases, though, the worst was a fellow who came to the door with his hand completely gone, just hanging by some cords. He was throwing dynamite sticks into the air to discourage the hail clouds, and neglected to let go in time. Only a tourniquet saved his life.[8]

Jack felt some evangelical missiologists missed the important role of touching the whole person with the gospel.

Years later, back in the United States after completing studies in church growth and co-writing a book on the subject, Jack came to feel that Friends had a perspective on ministry that made them stand somewhat apart from many other evangelicals.[9] He believed ardently in evangelism and leading people to Christ. But God's greatest "harvest," he wrote, is not just needy people but the "harvest is the work of God *through his people* [emphasis added]."[10] In other words, kingdom ministry happens when God's will is done on earth, and evangelism, compassion ministry, and social reform are all God's will for his people. He wrote that in the United States, daycare, nursing-home care, pastoral and psychological counseling, a refugee ministry, and even the church library show that God is ruling.[11] In Bolivia God's rule through his people happened when people turned to Christ, when better agriculture was practiced, when education was shared, and when Aymara men and women were empowered by God to raise their faces and hearts toward God in dignity and grace.

Another opportunity for serving the whole person came in dealing with the unusually high mortality rate among Aymara babies. The missionaries attempted anything that could be done to help a mother who had recently given birth, such as introducing the mother to a capable nurse for advice and guidance.[12] Jack and Geraldine recognized the frequent lack of trust Aymaras had for them. The Aymaras ignored medical advice and often accepted death as inevitable and without hope. "There is nothing to be done," the people often said. So when an emergency baby delivery confronted Geraldine one day, she served as a nurse and cut the umbilical cord, "praying all the while," and hoping there would never be a second time![13] Living in the city, however, with medical treatment more readily available, Jack and Geraldine stood in the center of conflict between medical science and animistic fatalism.[14] Medical services were available but often ignored by people who assumed the spirit world alone controlled illness. Meanwhile, in the rural areas where doctors did not exist, something as simple as typhoid vaccinations and small-pox vaccinations became part of school exams and tent evangelism as Jack and others traveled.[15]

In the mid-1950s, an unusually poor harvest threatened the Bolivian altiplano countryside with famine. The American agency CARE began giving handouts with no long-range development plan. Results were so poor, the mission decided to refuse the aid.[16] More recent studies have shown the mission was right. Handouts in many settings have proven to have a negative effect rather than a positive effect in improving health and sometimes even determining survival.[17] Jack was not oblivious to the pitfalls of unbridled charity that can stifle initiative and create unhealthy dependency. His whole push for a vital and self-supporting national church depended upon local initiative.

The Last Missionary Pastor

Jack was the last official missionary pastor in the work of the Oregon Friends Mission at the central Max Paredes Friends Church in LaPaz. For two or three years, Jack preached on Sundays, led weekday services, counseled, met with the youth society, made hospital visits, prayed for the sick, and attended church-council meetings. Geraldine sometimes taught Sunday-school classes and frequently rehearsed with young people for programs and events. Living next door to the church meant a steady stream of visitors and being constantly "on call." Jack attempted to have national leadership working alongside him whenever a church discipline issue arose.[18]

With time, however, being "pastor" meant that while he was present for activities during the week and served as an authority figure, he could also be gone on many Sundays. Sometimes this happened for as many as four consecutive Sundays when he would perform weddings or settle church difficulties elsewhere.[19] He crossed Lake Titicaca, traveled south and west across the altiplano or into the tropical Yungas valleys. When he was gone from La Paz, an active and capable associate pastor led services. Such lengthy and exhausting travel for a "settled pastor" is hard to comprehend, but his role became that of a superintendent rather than a pastor.

When the Willcutses left for furlough in May 1951, Jack was replaced at Max Paredes exclusively by Aymara pastors. This had been a mission-council goal for some time, and something of a contrast with other mission agencies in the area at the time. One mission, after a series of difficulties, agreed that only *missionaries* would pastor their churches. While the Max Paredes congregation—the largest and most influential of the Oregon Friends churches—had its own history of instability and faulty leadership, Jack and the council felt it important to move to a higher level of indigenous direction. The inherent paternalism and sense of mission control was heavy with a missionary in the role of pastor. Jack and the council knew they needed to move beyond it.

The Churchman as Thinker

Jack was a scholar and reflective person by temperament but accomplished his academic growth through independent study, not through standard academic programs. As he prepared for a first furlough, he developed a longing for graduate studies in theology and ministry, and he briefly considered the possibility of biblical seminary in New York or Asbury Seminary in Kentucky. He was eager to make his life count: "There comes a time when one is obliged to make lasting decisions as to what he wishes to accomplish and contribute in life....We have prayerfully and deliberately agreed that our main goal in life is to be dedicated to missionary and ministerial work...in education, pastoral work or missionary service."[20] This is the first reference I find of Jack desiring further study, a great longing that Jack never fully satisfied. It seems he quietly laid aside the longing after Susan's birth, when family needs—which the Willcutses placed above ministry—became more defined.

An Oregon Pastorate

Lents Friends Church in southeast Portland, Oregon, welcomed the Willcutses in the fall of 1951 and there Jack enjoyed the closeness of relationships between a pastor and his people. He found the freedom to teach and articulate pastoral concerns and the freedom felt good. Living in Portland also allowed for Susan's medical needs to be addressed.

In 1954 the Willcutses had to make a decision—return to Bolivia or stay in the Lents pastorate. Jack delighted in telling the story of going to Elizabeth Braithwaite, a saintly and prayerful elder, for advice. After listening to the list of pros and cons on the decision, she responded somewhat impatiently: "Well, Jack, what do you really want to do? Both of the courses to follow are right, not evil, it is just a choice of directions. What do you want to do?" Jack responded that they wanted to return to Bolivia if the Lord would let them. She then closed her Bible and stood up with an air of finality. "No use to pray more about that," she smiled. "When your heart is right with God and the door is open...no use wasting time talking to God about it....Don't forget the song 'Trust and Obey' means action as much as waiting." The decision was made: back to Bolivia for unfinished work.[21]

Meanwhile, Back in Bolivia

During Jack and Geraldine's absence from Bolivia—1951 to 1954—momentous events took place both for Bolivian Friends and the nation. Understanding the context surrounding these events is important in understanding the rest of Jack Willcuts's story.

During the Easter conference—April 9-13, 1952—a major social convulsion swept an unpopular military regime headed by General Urriolagoitia out of power, and called veteran politician Victor Paz Estenssoro from exile to the presidency. In a few days of fighting, the Bolivian army was overcome by defections and armed civilian militias and the revolutionaries took control. Bolivia was suddenly "in the hands of a radical political movement with popular political support and a legitimacy based upon having won the last election."[22]

Paz Estenssoro, who had been elected more or less fairly in the voting of 1951, had been denied office by an entrenched military that feared the economic, political, and social reforms promised by Paz Estenssoro and his partisans. Once in office, the new president decreed sweeping reforms, more remembered for their idealism than their full reality: 1) nationalization of the tin mines; 2) agrarian land reform; 3) universal suffrage; and 4) universal education.[23] For decades to come, ethnic Aymaras and Quechuas thought of Victor Paz as something of a political messiah, granting them rights and dignity never before experienced. Paz Estenssoro had flirted with strong communist elements and continued to show socialist tendencies, but his greater sympathies proved to be toward nationalism rather than toward worldwide communism. He is remembered not so much for installing social tranquility (which did not happen), but for establishing hope and promise for oppressed people.

Is Spiritual Hope Influenced by Politics?

Within the Bolivian tumult, the Friends mission had the huge advantage of being slightly ahead of the political curve. During the 1940s, the mission had instituted its own land reform and granted farm acreages to the Copajira peons—more land than demanded by the land reform decreed in 1952. In education, the mission supervised and financed a small network of schools for Aymaras, some that had been hotly resisted by landowners eager to maintain their feudal control. Of all the reforms by the Paz Estenssoro government, the most meaningful to the indigenous population was the ownership of farms, allowing serfs to gain title to ancestral lands and take control of their own economic destiny.

On the spiritual side, by 1951 the mission was well on its way to establishing a Bolivian-led church in which Aymaras were to govern, propagate, and finance themselves. Dignity was expected and inherent in the plan. What we know now only in retrospect was that the 1950s and 1960s would prove to be the time of most rapid growth for the newly formed Bolivian National Friends Church. Political forces appear to have colluded providentially with spiritual forces.

But at the time of the April 9, 1952, revolution, the missionaries were simply annoyed, frustrated, and fearful as the fighting and shooting of yet another revolution swirled around the Easter conference site at Max Paredes. Many of the conference sessions were canceled, but a number of attendees were stranded inside the grounds as a captive audience. Toward the end of the week the gunfire subsided sufficiently to allow part of the program to be resumed, and the conference was able to give serious consideration to the primary item of business on the agenda—approval of the new national church program and plan for the organization of a quarterly meeting, yearly meeting, and executive council. "This was a great answer to prayer," read the mission-council minutes in May 1952, and that "in the midst of revolution this church was born, with not one injury done to the large group...gathered at the Mission property." There was a *mesa directiva* (executive council) meeting later and Ralph Chapman reported "a great blessing in seeing that [the] group evidenced a feeling of responsibility in the direction of their church."[24]

We have no way of knowing what "approval" meant to Bolivian Friends at the time, but certainly some caught the vision that ownership was *theirs*, not the mission's, that *they* were in charge and not the missionaries; and that the Holy Spirit was guiding *them directly*, and that they did not need to go through a council of foreigners for direction. What many people present at that Easter conference did not fully realize was the strange coincidence of a secular social reform that was so closely timed with the beginnings of a national church. Suddenly the concept of *indigenous* church was *national* church and the sweeping changes in Bolivian politics were all under the banner of *nationalism*. Political nationalism essentially meant Bolivia for the Bolivians and resources for Bolivians, not for foreigners. Bolivians were to be masters of their own destiny and dignified enough to care for themselves. At least that was the rhetoric and the ideal, even though in many ways the ideal still remains to be achieved even in the early twenty-first century.[25]

Jack Willcuts was not even present in Bolivia at the precise moment and he was certainly not the only one beating the drum for an indigenous church that was self-governed, self-financed, and self-propagated. The Indigenous Church Movement was at its prime among evangelical missions in the 1940s and 1950s, and the Church Growth Movement of Donald McGavran supported and extended many of the same goals. The mission council in Bolivia had several times tried but failed to secure broad Aymara support for their Indigenous Society plans through the 1940s. The Oregon Friends Mission Board ardently believed indigenous Bolivian leadership needed to be encouraged and empowered. So what was Jack's role in all of this? Jack tried to work himself out of a job, and indeed he became the last missionary pastor at Max Paredes. The primary purpose of the Copajira project was to train pastoral and church leaders. Jack, with the approval of the council, had essentially written the first Constitution and Discipline (*Estatutos* in Spanish) for the Bolivian Friends National Church (*Iglesia Nacional Evangelica Los Amigos*—INELA), gifting it with a Friends statement of faith, Friends terminology, and outline of a basic organizational structure that persists nearly sixty years later. Jack Willcuts just happened to be the most articulate spokesperson for the national church and helped focus the attention of the Northwest home base, the missionaries, and the Bolivian leaders upon this crucial step.

There is more than a little irony in that Jack Willcuts, who had been the most ardent champion of the national church before his 1951 furlough, was actually absent when the national church program was approved by a large assembly of Bolivian Friends Christians. Maybe all the better, because his absence reflects the mission council's full consensus to do everything possible to empower the national church. More and more the mission needed to step away from the governance, financial support, and even unilateral evangelism that had kept them in a fairly strong paternal relationship with the emerging Bolivian church. Could they move from a "parent" stage of missions to a "partnership" role, working alongside national leaders? Could they make the shift as fast as the political revolution, which happened in one week in April 1952? Or was there more to it than that? How did this all come about and what can be learned from it?

Reflections:

Although they were church leaders, Jack and Geraldine Willcuts believed that the family came first, and their practice reflects that belief. Is that a strong position or does that weaken the sense of a missionary call? How did their conviction affect their ministry?

Reflect on the section subtitled "Serving the Whole Person." How did Jack Willcuts define kingdom ministry in ways he felt were especially important for missionary theory and practice?

Does it seem crucial that missionaries have a scholarly and reflective attitude toward their work? If yes, why?

In what ways were Bolivian political events and Friends Church development linked in the revolution of April 9, 1952? What was the great answer to prayer that came out of that revolution?

How, specifically, did nationalistic politics seem to create an unusual atmosphere for developing an indigenous church?

chapter 16

The Creation of a National Church

AS WE HAVE SEEN, the year 1952 saw the official creation of a national church, but in retrospect we almost immediately ask the question, is a *national* church the same as an *indigenous* church? Did political *nationalism* become mixed up in the concept? Was the creation of this church good, or not so good? And what was Jack Willcuts's role from 1952 onward? The development of the Bolivian national church proved to be a major step forward not only for Bolivian Friends; it also became a model for other evangelicals within the nation of Bolivia, and contributed to the development of Friends churches in other places of the world.

Bolivian mission council minutes and letters don't discuss political nationalism, but certainly nationalism was a dominant theme throughout Latin America in the 1940s and 1950s. As Victor Paz Estenssoro and his MNR party assumed power (the *N* stood for *nationalistic*), they sought self-determination, independence, and cried out for Bolivian dignity. While the dominant leadership of the MNR party still came from the upper-class elite, they were open to a broader political spectrum and an awareness that the large Aymara and Quechua populations of Bolivia needed to be brought into the political process in some way. Wisely, the Eisenhower administration in Washington, D. C., opted to maintain dialogue with the MNR and accepted Bolivian nationalism as something different from international communism. (In contrast, in Guatemala the American Central Intelligence Agency at the same time supported a proxy force that overthrew a socialist nationalist government there, fearing the influence of international communism.) In Bolivia, the American government supported the MNR reforms at least in limited ways. On the church front, the creation of a national church allowed for local leadership to take greater responsibility and to begin thinking of the organization as truly Bolivian. This was by no means a brainchild of Jack Willcuts alone; a short history of the mission reveals attempts to strengthen national leadership, with several aborted endeavors at an *indigenous* organization.

Pre-1952 Dreams

In a most unusual file marked in Jack Willcuts's handwriting and archived with his personal papers, scraps of undated notations, gathered together, show something of a history of Bolivian mission dreams and hopes for the development of an autonomous Bolivian church. One piece of paper proposed a National Society structure "*beneath* the direction of the Missionary Council" [emphasis added], that was to complete projects under the direction and approval of the mission council. In this scheme of things, the mission council reserved the right to change any official that did not work for the good of the group. Internally, the group was to function democratically, but would include two missionaries named by the mission council. But suspicion and lack of confidence in Bolivian leadership is latent and powerful. Perhaps this was the kind of organization that national leaders rejected and never fully supported for a number of years.

The same file also included a primitive, handwritten constitution (perhaps written by a Bolivian) that lists the small cluster of churches that existed in 1945 bearing the name of the "Society of Bolivian Evangelical Friends." The written objectives included the cultivation of spiritual life, evangelism programs and education, and the unification of the churches *in joint cooperation with the mission* [italics added]. The Statement of Faith was basic and not controversial. The document provided for an executive council with a president, vice president, secretary, and treasurer.[1] Both of these documents suggest a date prior to 1950 and present a fairly limited vision, little trust, and little independence for national leadership.

Other fragments of notes from the archival file seem to reflect the same pre-1952 era that used the terminology *Indigenous Society*. These notes laid out this vision: The mission would maintain the Copajira Bible School and sponsor regional quarterly and annual conferences as its primary responsibilities. The Indigenous Society had the unclear and rather secondary role of uniting with the mission (assisting the mission?) in the maintenance of the work. Workers would be recognized by the Indigenous Society, not by the mission. The churches would send representatives or delegates to plenary meetings of the Indigenous Society. Minutes of the meetings of the executive council would be read at the various annual conferences, but no one would travel in the name of the Indigenous Society without the expressed approval of the Executive Council and its two missionary members.

This Indigenous Society functioned briefly in 1947 and discussed disciplinary issues, tension between the mission and churches over properties ("what belongs to the church and what belongs to the mission?"), the taking of offerings, and the working together of the mission and Indigenous Society throughout the field. Issues of authority and independence were not well addressed. The Indigenous Society was something other than the mission council, but something far less, it seems, than an independent expression of the body of Christ. The emphasis was on governance under the tutelage of missionaries.[2]

A next step forward is represented in a statement of bylaws—also found in the same file—that may have been intended to guide a Constitution and Discipline (*Estatutos*) that was to be yet another document. The "National Society" was to be scriptural, should have the purpose of encouraging a more natural and rapid development of evangelism, should prepare the type of foundation for the future church that would permit legal incorporation and the holding of properties, and should be the means of channeling mission funds for education purposes and for the training of national leadership. It included job descriptions for the members of the executive council (the mesa directiva) that was to be under national direction with a lone missionary advisor present. The mission did reserve a role for missionaries to collaborate with national leaders. It appears the mission was trying to move toward a more equal partnership with Bolivian Friends.[3]

At this point in the early 1950s, the mission questioned whether pastoral salaries should be channeled through a central treasury. Also at this point, the mission planned to turn evangelism and local church direction to the National Society while schools would continue under the direction of the mission. The mission hoped to start a secondary school and a teacher-training school, and to improve school buildings. They were apparently moving in the direction of the mission, building up auxiliary institutions while the national church would build up the churches and a Friends yearly meeting. The mission intended to explain and promote the national church plan everywhere and to urge national church funding and support.

The National Church Takes Root

From May 1952 forward, the Bolivian mission council received regular recommendations and requests from the executive council of the national church. The mission was trying hard to recognize and honor the new organizational structure that had just been approved by the church even as the MNR political party took control of Bolivia. Letters from the mission to the national church marked the beginning of a more respectful relationship, and the number of contacts and scope of discussion only increased through to the year 1958. The 1952 council minutes records an almost immediate consensus that deeds to church properties be placed in the name of the national church "after a reasonable length of time...[to] demonstrate...ability to administer properties." The council was ready to promise this, but wanted to exclude from that promise the titles to the Copajira farm and any missionary residency.[4] No such actual church-property transfers took place, however, until the securing of the official incorporation papers for the national church, which finally came in March 1956[5]—a date now duly honored by the Bolivian Friends Church as the beginning of official governmental recognition.

Despite much goodwill and progress, the Copajira titles became a point of serious contention for nearly a decade. From the perspective of the national church, should not these valuable properties become theirs if the national church was to be in charge? The mission, however, feared the national church was not nearly mature enough to handle the major finances involved in the Copajira operation. Furthermore, the mission questioned how the mission could work and live in security if irresponsible church leadership were to mishandle properties where missionaries resided. Both parties—the national church and the mission—wondered how the mission could channel funds to the national church for evangelism or schools when the mission was still directing those programs. The lines of relationships were complex.

Early in the process, the council decided that schools should be funded and administered separately from the churches.[6] It seemed the mission during the 1950s was pushing for responsibility and initiative by Bolivians while still holding the "purse strings." The brew for misunderstanding and mistrust was thick indeed! Nevertheless, the council prayed regularly and ardently for national church leaders, and leadership became a bit more independent. The national church conducted some conferences without missionaries present, and the council regularly discussed how to channel more of its efforts through the national church structure. For example, rather than the mission taking unilateral action, the national church directed payments to pastors and evangelists.[7]

The question of who should direct the schools—missionaries or nationals—also bounced back and forth, as did dissatisfaction by the missionaries over the lack of spiritual direction or spiritual purpose for the grade schools. The council believed the schools were not fulfilling their spiritual purposes.[8] A number of "unspiritual" teachers were dismissed, and with the mission firmly in charge of salaries for pastors and teachers, it seemed reasonable that the decisions be made by the council. As the nation of Bolivia attempted to spread education more broadly following 1952, the handful of Friends day schools likely played a positive role and seemed worth maintaining—they provided the only education available for their communities, and placed Friends as positive progressives in the eyes of community and national leaders.

The Willcutses' Second Term, 1954–1957

Despite stress, there had been growth in national church leadership during Jack and Geraldine's three and-a-half years in the United States while Jack pastored and the family attended to some of Susan's medical needs. Upon their return to Bolivia, they happily noted that nationals arranged the welcome service for them at Max Paredes, and a Copajira graduate led the service as pastor. If life in the church was a bit different, governmental red tape and bureaucracy had not improved. Geraldine complained gently, "Bolivia is not exactly as we remember it. It is worse!"[9]

At first the Willcuts family lived in La Paz and spent a few weeks at Copajira for classes from time to time, but eventually they moved to Copajira for their last eighteen months in Bolivia. In his first term, Jack had visited the church districts regularly by himself, encouraging local accountability and fellowship. Even though he now shared that responsibility with others, Jack still visited the quarterly meetings frequently, and resumed his role as a counselor for the mesa directiva.[10]

During both short visits and a longer residency there, the Copajira farm was somewhat of a new experience and more pleasant than La Paz for the family. The children had playmates and space to enjoy life. Geraldine was freer from the nearly constant hosting of visitors. Business details Jack alone had cared for in La Paz were now assigned to others at Copajira, and Jack spent time traveling, reading, and writing. He thought maybe he was gaining weight! He tried to read everything he could find about the national-church movements around the world. He knew the council had much work to finish before seeing the "national church project" through to a more stable and successful position.

The four quarterly meetings (district conferences) were set up as an official part of the national-church organization at the 1955 Easter conference. They had functioned informally for a number of years, but now became a part of the national-church structure.[11] Jack was delighted by this, another first, and he attended many of these conferences for his remaining time on the field. He held the quarterly meetings in high esteem and viewed them as crucial for building field unity and maintaining strength of the local congregations. Evangelistic tent meetings and quarterly-meeting business meetings were at times merged, and Jack's role as secretary of evangelism and promoter of the national church clearly ran together.[12]

Later in 1955, Jack read a paper to the mission council expressing a deep concern. Progress had been made on promoting a national Friends church, but he was strongly aware of a need for greater consistency.[13] The mission council received his paper with "sympathetic unanimity." The goal was stated clearly. How to achieve the Three Selves ideal, however, was not so clear and was proving to be painful and slow. For much of that council meeting there was "constant reference" to Jack's paper: "The Lord is definitely leading us in this," the minutes declared. The group saw the indigenous church was Bible-inspired and Pauline in method. Promoting the national church was the right thing to do! Their faith was aroused and they contemplated several drastic moves: 1) Transfer schools to the church so instead of being "mission" schools they would be "church" schools with local school boards under a Bolivian-church secretary of education; 2) Promote tithing and self-support for pastors, and take the first step by immediately announcing that pastoral salaries from the mission would be discontinued after Easter conference, 1957; 3) Promote self-support of buildings.[14]

Promoting the National Church

What were the difficulties they faced in promoting a truly independent national church? For one, pastors depended upon the mission for salary and benefits. One pastor's wedding conducted at Copajira, for example, required considerable financial and material help, both from the mission and the Willcutses themselves. They were troubled by the precedent but helped anyway.[15] It was painful to watch beloved Bolivian pastoral friends in physical need, but Jack came to believe it was also dangerous to help too much.

A second difficulty was educating the constituency back in the United States on the nature of a self-supporting church. It feels good to help others, but doing so is not always wise. In 1957, Jack wrote a dynamic and stirring article in *Northwest Friend* about personal sacrifice by Bolivian nationals who relied on their own resources to minister. This sacrifice, to him, was a necessary "cost" to have a national church—a cost that should be accepted and prayed over by those on the outside. Jack's article received such a strong response from readers, and Jack had to deal with the outpouring of offers for financial help for needy pastors mentioned in the article. Many North American readers wanted to find ways to help the needy pastors—something that was actually contrary to Jack's intention in the original article. In a follow-up article, he explained that he had wanted to arouse prayer for the Bolivian pastors—not to solicit funds directly. He went on to explain several proposals to help pastors toward bi-vocational self-support, and he mentioned that people could give small gifts for these efforts without serious damage to the goal of a self-supporting Bolivian yearly meeting. He turned down direct financial gifts to individuals, however, explaining that "even as a parent must one day stand aside and let his growing child learn by experience, so must a mission of twenty-seven years one day entrust to nationals the financial and directive matters of a growing church. It is not always easy but necessary."[16]

"Being Americans," he continued in his article, "we like to plunge into an evident need with funds and a vigorous program. What God may desire, during this time of inevitable testing and sacrifice for the new indigenous church, is a praying people at home able to hold back the power of the devil in a heathen land until the church is firmly rooted."[17] Can generosity kill the spirit of an emerging national church? Jack said yes. Many writers in the later twentieth century came to agree with him.

A third difficulty lay in the churches looking first to the missionaries rather than to national church leaders for help in church discipline. In early 1955, two school teachers were placed under discipline *by the mission* for sexual immorality.[18] On another occasion a year later, Jack was called to intervene in two cases of church discipline near Lake Titicaca, while at home Geraldine found herself the disciplinarian of unruly grade-school children at the Max Paredes church.[19]

A fourth difficulty was the placement of pastors. Not only did many pastors expect the mission to support them financially, they often expected help to relocate[20] and a supportive presence when their authority was questioned. That meant Jack was still working to extricate himself from the role of field supervisor to pastors, a role designated for the mesa directiva in the church constitution, not for the mission. At Max Paredes, for example, Jack found himself in the culturally awkward position of asking for anyone with complaints to speak in regard to the calling of a new pastor. No one spoke, so the call was ratified.[21] A few years later, no one would ever have imagined pastoral placement was the work of a missionary rather than national-church leaders, but the change did not happen automatically.

A fifth difficulty Jack felt was the church's dependency upon the mission for tent evangelism and regional conferences. One step forward was to provide transportation for equipment and personnel, but to leave nationals in charge of the actual preaching and teaching. The implication: Though leadership grew stronger, the national church still found itself in a dependency relationship. On yet another occasion, Geraldine observed that, "these days the pastors and brethren do most of the preaching, but Jack has to speak several times and direct everything to see that it goes well."[22] Jack certainly continued a nurturing ministry on the quarterly-meeting level. In the 1955–1956 church year, he attended twenty quarterly-meeting sessions— each one about three days long—filling a minimum of sixty days.[23] This was, on the one hand, church maintenance, but on the other hand was an effort to solidify and strengthen churches to do their own evangelism. It was without question a period of significant church growth.[24]

A sixth concern was living arrangements for the missionaries. The three-story Hadley Hall at the Max Paredes property had been remodeled into two apartments plus a guest apartment. Now Jack and Geraldine began wishing they had *less* of a missionary presence or, better yet, none at all at Max Paredes! Geraldine wrote,

> If our work is to be indigenous and national, we should move clear away…to another part of the city. [The Aymara Christians] see all our things, furniture, machines, jeeps, etc. etc. and they don't see why we can't continue to support them as before. Jack has written a paper about this to the Board at home…We are sure that the Board will agree to Indigenous work, they have up to now, so we will wait until we hear from Walter Lee.[25]

This particular seed to move away from Max Paredes may have been planted, but the board did not quickly agree to Jack's proposal. Financial investments at Max Paredes were heavy and the idea of walking away from free rent on mission property seemed poor stewardship at that time.

During the mid 1950s, national church leadership was spotty; church leaders at times proved their dedication and commitment, but at other times abandoned their responsibilities and assumed the missionaries would pick up the slack. In other words, true emotional "ownership" for the church was hardly in place, even though a national church functioned in theory. For example, many considered the regional and annual conferences directed by the mission to be mission business, not national church business. The concept of quarterly sessions for worship and business under the direction of the national church to hear reports, pray and encourage one another, enact church discipline, and take offerings for regional projects was new, and a necessary part of the *Estatutos*. Through the Willcutses' second term in Bolivia, one of Jack's major tasks was promoting district quarterly meetings and installing regional authorities so governance and expansion could be meaningfully continued.

The Moment of Spiritual Ownership

To capture a fuller picture, perhaps we need to fast-forward from 1958 to 1962. The great concern to see an autonomous yearly meeting did not come to fulfillment quickly. Bible-school classes at

Copajira were suspended because of turmoil among the students, and then in mid-1961 the entire farm and school complex was hastily evacuated under the cloud of serious political and social threat. This meant a serious financial loss to the mission, even though much of value was removed before the final evacuation. No injuries occurred, but there were people who wanted to kill the missionaries, and the staff feared for their lives at times.

In response to the loss of Copajira, the mission staff redeployed to new locations along the shores of Lake Titicaca, to Peru, and to the north-Yungas area around Caranavi. Tensions persisted between the mission and the national church over pastoral salaries, benefits for teachers and pastors, and the expectations of many churches for buildings and programs—all of which the mission struggled to reduce and redirect. Misunderstandings and harsh words were frequent. National-church presidents served for a period of time and then left in discouragement. Finally, in 1962, a vote by national church leaders demanded that if the mission was not interested in accepting their requests, they would sever relations and go looking for help elsewhere. During meetings with mission leaders from Oregon, the mission agreed to withdraw all missionaries but two families, who would remain briefly to handle financial affairs, wind up business, and prepare to leave. During those months, contacts between mission and church were quite limited. The moment tested the missionaries' faith in the whole concept of a national church.

In the turmoil that followed and in a meeting of the national church in 1963, a new mesa directiva was elected and a seven-point proposal from the national church was drawn up for the mission to consider as a "program of cooperation." It was a proposal entirely prepared without mission assistance or presence. The national-church proposal did not mention pastoral salaries, and a number of other demands were conspicuously missing. From the perspective of the mission, this became a significant turning point. Leaders had begun to refer to *their* church and took the active leadership to prove it. From that point forward, national-church presidents traveled and communicated needs between the central mesa directiva and the churches. They busied themselves with the spiritual and material support of new preaching points, established churches, and quarterly meetings. The national church felt increasingly confident and supported by its own constituency. Missionaries moved away from the Max Paredes property in 1965, and the church looked to their own leaders rather than the missionaries to solve their problems. More and more, the national leaders talked about what was within their reach and what initiative they could take *without* mission involvement—precisely the vision Jack Willcuts and others had hoped for. In retrospect, mission staff and mission administrators—Jack Willcuts included—could see answered prayer and guidance by the Holy Spirit, even though at the time that seemed anything but certain.

In 1965, Pacific College classmates David and Florence Thomas returned to Bolivia for a profitable time of consolidation for the national-church structure, long after Jack and Geraldine had assumed new positions in the United States. David and Florence responded years earlier to a personal letter from Jack Willcuts urging them to apply for missionary service in Bolivia.[26] Jack saw in David the kind of quiet, indirect, yet fearless leader he felt was needed to move the national church forward. While Jack was the last missionary pastor at Max Paredes, the Thomases, who Jack recruited, were the last to live in the mission-owned residence at Max Paredes. The Thomases and others were convinced by that time that missionary presence close to the offices of the mesa directiva was counterproductive. David Thomas masterfully shared ideas, encouraged others, and then stepped back to await others' action. His persistence was unusual and his selfless, unassuming humility won him many friends. Mesa directiva members responded with sacrificial labor that increased their stature among the churches.

The spiritual ownership the Bolivians accepted from 1963 forward revealed—by 1973—that the national church had functioned as an autonomous yearly meeting for the prior ten years and that it was the responsibility of Northwest Yearly Meeting (previously Oregon Yearly Meeting) to recognize that maturity. Programs partnering with the mission in education and evangelism would continue for another twenty-five years, but the critical issues of stress and conflict between church and mission were greatly lessened or disappeared altogether. Northwest Friends welcomed the INELA into the worldwide family of Friends yearly meetings. In 1973, Jack Willcuts, as Northwest Yearly Meeting superintendent, had the privilege of signing the document recognizing INELA as part of the worldwide family of Friends yearly meetings, bringing to completion his ardent concern for a Bolivian Friends national church.

Reflections:

How was the pre-1952 "Indigenous Society" of Friends different from the later "national church" vision for a Friends church in Bolivia?

What important steps did the Bolivian Friends mission council take to help the national-church structure become firm?

What were the difficulties the Bolivian Friends mission council faced in promoting a truly independent national church? Which of these difficulties would have been the most difficult for you, personally? Why?

Discuss the concept of "spiritual ownership" described in this chapter. What do you feel are the key elements of missionary practice that allow a national church to fully embrace an expression of the body of Christ within a new culture?

chapter 17

Passing the Mantle of Leadership

JACK WILLCUTS never quite recovered from his missionary years, which ended in 1958, and he liked it that way! For the rest of his life he frequently referred to his cross-cultural experiences, and his function as a missiologist actually peaked in years after he left missionary service.

Although he felt called back to the Northwest where he eventually assumed a wide variety of responsibilities—primarily pastoral—his life in South America left him committed to nurturing leaders. His Bolivia years, although relatively brief, had given him skills in supervision and administration, helped him become a better writer, and made him forever loyal to his denominational connection. He admired and appreciated fellow worker Roscoe Knight's call to a lifetime of cross-cultural evangelism and yet felt cross-cultural ministry was not his lifetime call.[1] In contrast he felt a call to a settled pastorate where his particular intellectual gifts in preaching, writing, and organization could reach their full potential. He felt Friends had something crucial to offer the evangelical mosaic around the world and he wanted to call Quakers in the north back to their roots. He once again began considering work in the United States.

Back in 1956, two years before leaving Bolivia, Jack shared with visiting general superintendent Dean Gregory his sense of unsettledness, and Dean suggested Jack become "a yearly meeting worker" of some sort. Jack began to feel this was their last term in Bolivia. Mission board chairman Walter Lee thought they should continue. But Jack, always attentive to direction from church leaders, was far less certain.[2] He was not one to push himself into positions, but always asked for counsel from others. So, just like the letter from Walter Lee that turned him toward Bolivia, a letter from the board of publications in 1957 drew him back to the United States. He soon accepted their invitation to become editor of *The Northwest Friend*, a position he began in the fall of 1958. He continued his journalistic and editorial work even after *The Northwest Friend* was incorporated into a national magazine, *The Evangelical Friend.* Jack encouraged the moving of the denominational printing press to Newberg, Oregon, to be close to George Fox College, and the family accepted a part-time pastorate nearby. Fellow missionary Ralph Chapman also became a part of the new team in publication. The Willcutses were ready to make the cultural shift back to North America.

Before leaving, however, and as Jack and Geraldine wound down their service in Bolivia, the growing complexities of cross-cultural ministry were mirrored in their December 1957 Christmas letter: "Ten years ago last July 4 we arrived in Bolivia. Then, we knew very little about being missionaries. Now, we feel we know even less."[3] Yet 1947–1957 had been an unusually fruitful time in Bolivia despite great stress: "The challenge of a personal call and concern more than counterbalance the inconveniences," they wrote. The Bolivian Friends Church had grown from eleven congregations to seventy-eight, from three hundred believers to a community of more than 2,500. During that time span sixteen grade schools were established, and a 3,000-acre farm and Bible school had been developed where more than two hundred Aymara leaders had studied.[4] It had been an immensely satisfying team effort and it would continue to be an important, formative part of Jack's ministry for the rest of his life.

The Rest of the Story

Jack Willcuts's remaining years of ministry played themselves out in the Northwest from 1958 to September 23, 1989, when he died suddenly at the age of sixty-seven, on son Stuart's birthday. During those thirty-one years in the United States Jack wrote avidly, pastored compassionately, and practiced "churchmanship" in conferences and on boards and committees. He was gifted with discernment,[5] loved his work, and reveled in his calling.[6] In terms of his long-range role as one who stated missionary theory and put it into practice, this was a time for reflecting on and re-applying what he learned, and passing to another generation a concern for a world without Christ. What was "the rest of the story" of Jack's missiology, and how did he encourage others to go forward in missions? What were his abiding contributions to the world of Friends missions?

Lasting Contributions in Missions

Jack Willcuts's span of years abroad—eleven years, with a three-and-a-half-year break in the middle for home leave—were brief in comparison with the missionary service of Arthur Chilson (thirty-seven years), Esther Smith (forty-one years) and Everett Cattell (twenty-one years). Nevertheless, he left a significant mark on Friends missions, in part because of a global influence from his new positions in the United States. Writing letters, spreading good humor, promoting an egalitarian view of women in ministry, refining mission-council governance (out of which grew his concept of "team ministry"), practicing wholistic ministry, setting an example through churchmanship, and developing a coherent and consistent philosophy of the national church were major contributions that came from his life.

Jack the Letter Writer

As a general superintendent and through his service with the board of missions, Jack nurtured leaders through writing letters. Missionaries for three decades enjoyed his good humor and passed his letters from one to another. South American missionaries especially delighted in his ability to empathize with their isolation and physical stress; he reminded them that they were "the most prayed over people in the Yearly Meeting." To a Christian development worker in Africa he recalled a gift of two White Rock chickens in a community in Bolivia back in 1957 and on a return administrative visit many years later discovered most everyone in the area had White Rock chickens![7] To a language teacher in Japan, he chatted about the church at home and encouraged her to be faithful in personal witness. Always the encourager, he stressed the positive and gave only passing references to difficulties.

Crossing Cultures with a Laugh

Every cross-cultural worker finds his own way to ease stress, but good humor is almost always a part of that formula, and that was certainly true for Jack Willcuts. Jack enjoyed the unusual that became the usual. A child fell out of an upper berth on a train and survived without injury. What can you do but laugh! He noticed that a decrepit Jeep had wheels that tracked like a puppy—one was not sure if it was coming forward or turning a corner. Then there was the Jeep model that presumptively took the name "Hurricane Jeep," but, said Jack, the Jeep had become "a mere gaseous breeze!"[8]

"Laughter is a truly spiritual experience," wrote Jack later, citing Ecclesiastes 3:4—"a time to laugh."[9] Laughter, he said, sets people apart from animals. "It puts people at ease. It releases tension. Laughter is a conduit for bringing in spiritual truth."[10] "Blessed is the person who can tell a good joke well,"[11] he said, and this was a skill he worked seriously (pun intended) to develop. Yet in his playfulness, he was always eager to clarify truth.[12]

Jack and the Role of Women

Jack Willcuts was a traditional Quaker when it came to his view on the role of women in ministry, and fellow workers who preceded him in Bolivia also shared this aspect of the Quaker tradition. In the first generation of the Bolivian mission, Doris Tamplin, Helen Cammack, and Esthel Gulley startled Aymaras by riding mules and motorcycles long distances to preach and teach. Much like the Friends women in Guatemala and the Chilson daughters in Urundi, they gathered first children and then adults together for classes and public evangelism and worship. Doris Tamplin, a recorded Friends minister, was the official pastor at Max Paredes for a while. Julia Pearson, also a minister, was always the more active preacher and teacher in her family and the first students at Copajira remembered for decades the rigors and disciplines of *Dona Julia*. The spirit of Esther Smith and her mostly female colleagues in Guatemala was alive and well in Bolivia when Jack and Geraldine arrived!

Married female missionaries, while allowed by the board to give first priority to family, were invited and encouraged to teach in both urban and rural settings. If missionary women were present at a rural conference, they were always expected to lead women's or children's classes, or both. The example of the egalitarian American marriage was powerful. And from time to time, changes were observed in the local culture: the Aymara wife given a seat of honor alongside her husband, the husband and wife who walked together instead of the wife trailing behind, the Christian family who sent their daughters to school. These were unusual happenings in their day.

With time, the pattern changed and nationals—not just missionaries—led in the cultural innovations, but the requests for missionary women to teach continued for many years.[13] The mission staff was conscious that the social role of women was being elevated. The Copajira Bible School became a site for regular women's classes[14]—classes especially for young women who were usually illiterate and given menial field jobs herding pigs until they were old enough to marry! Aymara women through the 1940s and 1950s were still, for the most part, marginalized socially and culturally.

The *señorita* classes of 1957 at Copajira brought seventy-three young women together for instruction.[15] Jack preached and Geraldine and others taught. The missionary women had the uncomfortable role of enforcing the rules for naïve young women away from home.[16] At the end of the classes, the girls were sent out to give testimony in local communities. Since it was still an era of persecution, one girl was bit by a dog and other girls had sticks and stones thrown at them, but they responded well, even though, wrote Geraldine, "so many of the Indians do not think it is necessary for the girls to learn."[17] After a few weeks of classes, a closing song and tearful goodbyes sent the girls on their way. The students were welcomed back for two additional years, and those who completed three years were honored with a diploma. Geraldine noted that by the time the students received their diplomas, they were reading and writing—something generally unknown among Aymara women.[18] Clearly the mission was implementing a cultural shift.

On the home front, Jack was a thoughtful husband and tried to live out a positive example of treatment of women. He shared family responsibilities with Geraldine, and completed domestic chores such as cooking, ironing, and house cleaning as needed.[19] On occasion, Jack took on other tasks usually reserved for women in his era, encouraging Geraldine to teach and work at her art. At the Co-pajira Bible School, both missionary men and women taught, al-though the men took the majority of the teaching and women took the majority of the domestic chores. At the beginning of the 1957 school year, for example, Jack preached the opening chapel messages and taught eighteen hours each week while Geraldine taught for seven hours each week. At Copajira, Geraldine felt more fulfilled with more time to teach and time to be closer to fewer people. "How nice it is," she wrote, "no one at the door, no offices to visit and haggle over affairs."[20] To her, the last eighteen months at Copajira—with fewer expectations to host out-of-town guests and fewer errands to run—were opportunities and blessings[21].

As a strong supporter of women in ministry, Jack penned a tribute to the late Charlotte L. Macy, a Friends minister:

> While there keeps creeping back into the evangelical church the curious notion that leadership and ministry is for men only, it is good to have a fresh, effective example of the truth that qualifications for ministry rest not upon one's masculinity but upon character, gifts, and the graces of God in anointing those whom He chooses [both men and women].[22]

Jack and the Mission-Council Concept

Jack Willcuts did not invent the field-mission council, but he did describe it to a whole generation of Friends missionaries and ex-plained how it was supposed to work. It had been a formative part of his missionary experience and eventually became the basis for what he articulated as "team ministry" in local churches in the United States. It was a Friends core conviction, he believed, that God by the Holy Spirit guides the body of Christ toward his will, in unity, and in creative uniqueness. While the basic biblical material in the book of Acts is built around the apostolic and Pauline missionary band, Jack's concept of the body of Christ was welded to that from the book of Ephesians. Jack believed that mission moves forward when

Christ speaks, when Christ's people listen to one another, and when Christ's people faithfully encounter new cultures.

Friends in Bolivia knew a successful missionary enterprise demanded some kind of local governance, as did Friends in Africa and Central America. Everett Cattell was given great personal authority as superintendent of the field in India. Hudson Taylor's experience with China Inland Mission decades earlier had been publicized broadly: The successful mission is one that can make flexible decisions locally. It is the missionary who best understands the culture, comprehends the opportunities, and senses the dangers. Nevertheless, while many mission decisions need to be made on the field, there is the opposite error of erratic and inconsistent efforts if there is no long-term oversight with the "big picture" in mind, and where accountability is unclear. An effective home board must do far more than raise money and recruit candidates. Otherwise, each new missionary will tend to start over without learning or building upon the past, or—worse yet—build his or her personal empire. One of Jack Willcuts's greatest insights was that an effective mission is not merely an association of independent missionaries on a field, but an interactive team.

Traditionally, a home board struck a balance between home and field governance by naming a field superintendent who acted on behalf of the donors to select recruits and fund their passage. The field superintendent was empowered to make and implement many local decisions. Arthur Chilson, Esther Smith, and Everett Cattell were all field superintendents. While all three had staff meetings and developed a sense of teamwork, Everett eventually moved his team much closer toward making local decisions as a group of equals. Nevertheless, a superintendent at his or her best was still nearly always in a position of authority over fellow missionaries, and at worst, could be downright dictatorial. Communications with the home base depended upon the abilities of the superintendent. Feelings among the field missionaries and their superintendent were often tense.

This issue of communications and the role of a field superintendent was one the primary reasons for the visit by a team of Oregon Friends administrators to Bolivia in 1944. They faced a conflict between the Tamplin and Pearson families and a breakdown of communication. To resolve it and to move forward better, they established a "council" of missionaries to transact business and communicate discussion and decisions to the home board. With Friends egalitarian values in place, the field council became increasingly a body for discussion of a wide range of concerns, and no one person was considered an authority over others on the team. Everyone was given access to correspondence and everyone was invited to write personal letters to the board.[23] The group suggested job assignments and placements, and many decisions were made locally. The home board accepted most recommendations made on the field. Occasional administrative visits were intended to help cast a new vision, clarify long range goals, and determine new major directions.

Looking back on the beginning of the council system, Jack viewed the establishment of the council system as a healthy way to avoid resentments and feelings of being misunderstood:

> Invariably where there was a field superintendent or director, there was resentment on the part of missionaries or frequently the superintendent himself, because of the chain of command arrangement. Missionaries were trying to circumvent the field superintendent in communicating their complaints or concerns to the home board….Not only was this unfair, it was also counter productive in allowing individual initiative to be encouraged and a feeling of trust to be built.[24]

In Bolivia, Jack was early named to the role of council chairman, despite his youth and inexperience. It is likely that Jack was given this position in recognition of his skills in leading a discussion; the group's desire was *not* to have an authoritarian leader! One suspects Jack, like Everett Cattell in India with Esther Baird, knew how to show respect to the elder Pearsons and win their approval. Yet he also quickly earned the loyalty of the Chapmans, Knights, and Cammacks, who were his close peers in their youth and newness to the field.

In later years back in the United States, Jack became an outstanding spokesperson and defender of the mission-council concept. As an administrator, he pressed the mission staff to make the council concept work—to do the hard work of maintaining healthy relationships, of listening well to all perspectives, and taking ownership of decisions. He saw this as biblical governance of the body of Christ, and a major part of the Quaker ethos. Jack was unswervingly committed to an egalitarian model, empowered to make many decisions on site, but ultimately responsible to a home board that guided the mission toward the broad goals. A council chairperson, he said, was not to be a less significant version of a superintendent, but a spokesperson for the group and a clerk who could sense the guidance of the Lord. Everyone was to have a voice and it was important to gather ideas and listen.[25] The mission council (or the church team) should display a variety of gifts and become a training ground for new workers.[26] A council was a small Quaker meeting that met for worship and business, looking and listening for the Holy Spirit to guide vision, relationships, and actions. A council clerk was empowered to listen to the Spirit directly, but also to the Spirit's voice through the voices of others.

In later years as he articulated a model for team ministry in the local church in North America, he echoed three themes he first discovered in Bolivia: 1) egalitarian decision making, 2) servant leadership, and 3) group identity and loyalty. During his American years as pastor and superintendent, Jack frequently reminded his colleagues that people can overcome almost any obstacles by nurturing open and warm relationships. If that kind of unity is not present, he said, not much else is possible. Within the mission council, there was no place to run away and hide—differences had to be faced and dealt with. Loyalty to the group was paramount.

These concepts, which were self-evident on the mission field Jack believed to be biblical and true everywhere Christians work together. His pastoral-team concept was quite like a mission council in Bolivia! The Bolivian Friends mission experience meant frequent council meetings. There was a high level of discussion and group decision making. The Willcutses personally gave credit to the Lord for the way a system of governance by council—rather than by a missionary superintendent—made life easier.[27] While the mission council was never a perfect arrangement and disagreements arose from time to time, the council's strong sense of loyalty to one another and loyalty to the basic cause of evangelism, leadership training, and building up of an indigenous church movement was never questioned.

How did the council find God's will in the particulars of those goals? They followed the long Bolivian mission tradition of worshiping together, believing that one starts finding God's will by corporate worship, rather than by an authoritarian dictum. To some, this seems "soft" and uncertain and hardly a way to move forward. Jack took issue with that, however, and wrote that he preferred to "run scared" with some uncertainty and to maintain a high level of vulnerability and dependency upon God rather than be proudly self-assured and turn the guidance of the Spirit into a pat formula.[28] Could that have been a truth he discovered in the cross-cultural setting where missionaries have fewer clear points of reference, where there are fewer precedents, and where the cultural differences make us ill-at-ease? What can we do when things seem so uncertain? "Being a Spirit-moved people," he wrote, "is worth considering and praying about."[29] It may be scary, but to wait as a group to be moved by the Spirit is far better than to rely on the decisions made by authoritarian human beings or the independent lone ranger. This Quaker distinctive, he felt, was one of the "unique qualities of the Quaker faith [which is] actually one of the greatest attractions of our church."[30]

Wholistic Ministry

Simple service to human beings enhances and validates the verbal proclamation. The two elements will always appear together. Sometimes service comes first and functions to open doors and make people receptive to hear God. Other times service and verbal proclamation occur simultaneously. At yet other times, acts of service follow proclamation as the newly formed body of Christ finds itself called to serve in love. Jack was aware of this positive relationship, and among Friends in his latter years he strongly encouraged maintaining it. In Bolivia, it had meant better crops and better health care. In the United States, it meant child care, outreach to the poor and elderly, and peace work.

During a 1981 visit to Bolivia, Jack noticed a dramatic social shift in the culture of the Aymara peons he first met in 1947. When he met them, they labored for the landowner for four days a week without pay. More than thirty years later, he visited a chocolate factory where some young Aymaras were entrepreneurs—processing, packaging, and marketing for international sale. A young Christian man named Emilio, from the church in the Chunavi community, had studied cooperatives in Israel and built the chocolate business as a cooperative with participants who were committed to tithe, work with honesty, and maintain quality of product.[31] Jack clearly remembered an honest peon named Benjamin from Chunavi community who refused to steal from his landowner; Benjamin became a leader at the Chunavi church. This kind of validation of the Christian mission was especially close to his heart.

The Missionary as Churchman

"You can take a boy out of the Quaker church, but you can't take the Quaker faith out of the boy," wrote Jack.[32] His intense loyalty first to the body of Christ and second to his family of Friends led him to believe it was worthwhile to spend time helping the church thrive. He became a staunch supporter of the establishment of the Evangelical Friends Alliance that later became Evangelical Friends Church International, linking together evangelical Friends from around the world.

Instead of maligning "church machinery and church committees" he reminded his readers that a well-organized congregation will reach more of the lost and bless more Christians than a disorganized congregation. He wanted workers conversant with how a church functions.[33] One of the most important parts of that function is profoundly theological: "Christ is the head of the Church, and to sever ourselves from His leadership in this society either organizationally or spiritually detaches the true Christian from the lifeline of teaching and the fellowship he requires."[34] With Christ as head, "the church is a sacred institution, and it is never more impotent than when it forgets this fact."[35]

Jack continued to work out his "churchmanship" concern in his book *Friends in the Soaring '70s: A Church Growth Era.* He was addressing the church in his home culture, but his exhortations have clear applications for cross-cultural missions. He prodded Friends to establish goals, make meetings count, and build commitment to a meaningful, covenantal membership. He advocated the use of small groups, stronger direct evangelism, the creation of multiple social ministries that would connect Christians with the needs of their community, and a more concerted effort at leadership development for Friends. That list of recommendations, when read forty years later, still sounds amazingly contemporary. Some strategies never wear out.

A Philosophy of the National Church

There is little doubt that Jack Willcuts's culminating effort was to develop a national church. This effort brought together his concern for cultural sensitivity, his attention to churchmanship, and his love for Friends. It was his greatest contribution to Quaker missiology. Jack was convinced that the emerging church called Friends in Bolivia truly *was* Quaker in essence. He cited a Bolivian church leader who was asked, "Why are you a member of the Friends church?" Rather than saying he was a member because his parents were, or that it was Friends who brought the gospel to his community (both true), he pointed to characteristics that were important to him: 1) a church free of class distinctions where missionaries treated him as an equal; 2) a church body bound together by love and trust, not by rules, rituals, or church government; 3) a church that taught a simple gospel of holiness that is for every Christian. The young Bolivian's loyalty was to Friends, despite invitations and pressures to leave Friends.[36]

On the surface, the Bolivian national church of Friends was guided by the so-called "indigenous church method," but Jack Willcuts's interpretation of it was far more than a simplistic "turning over the work to the nationals"—a phrase often used in that era. Jack and the mission council advocated for self-support, self-governance, and self-propagation not to be merely *Bolivian* but to be *the church*. The church, however, naturally takes on cultural form, just as did Christ when he came to earth. But an earnest trust in the Holy Spirit meant that the emerging church could be trusted. Later missionaries admitted errors and lack of trust, but the vision became increasingly strong through the 1950s and up to 1963 when the "moment of ownership" made the national church more truly Bolivian. Leaders like Carmelo Aspi (the first Bolivian teacher at Copajira) and Antonio Mamani (one of the first Copajira graduates) became two outstanding national church presidents after 1963. They functioned as genuine superintendents, serving the church and nurturing leaders. This had been Jack's vision, and vision of the entire Bolivian Friends Mission Council, including Roscoe Knight, Ralph Chapman, and David Thomas, who contributed greatly to the completion of the vision.

With Jack Willcuts we end our study of Quaker missiologists of the twentieth century. Jack was not an Arthur Chilson pith-helmet pioneer. He did not approach the forty-one-year tenure of Esther Smith. He never became recognized as a world leader among evangelicals in the same way as Everett Cattell. He aspired to none of the above, but he did aspire to be truly human, truly obedient, and truly clear, and he believed he could best do that by being truly faithful to his Quaker heritage. Of the four missionaries, he was probably the one most sensitive to national-church aspirations, and his work in building an autonomous body of Friends became a model studied widely.

Reflections:

Think about "lifetime" calls for missionaries. What is the value of serving for long periods of time (like Arthur Chilson, Esther Smith, and Everett Cattell did? Do you think it fair to place Jack Willcuts's call in the same category?

In what ways did Jack Willcuts effectively nurture and encourage young and new Christian workers?

What important Quaker values were attempted through the mission-council concept that Jack Willcuts encouraged and promoted? What benefits might this model have, both within the Western world and overseas? How practical or impractical is this concept?

What do you make of Jack Willcuts's stalwart denominational loyalty? Is this a thing of the past or is it something to be retained? How does this relate to the kind of ecumenical Christian leadership exercised by men like Everett Cattell and Jack Willcuts?

Why may the model of a self-directed "national church" and Jack Willcuts's vision for such a church model be especially crucial in the twenty-first century?

Conclusions

chapter 18

Timeless Principles and Practices

Looking Back

CAN THESE FOUR twentieth-century missionaries teach us something for missions in the twenty-first century? Arthur Chilson of Kenya and Urundi was a Quaker David Livingstone for the early twentieth century. R. Esther Smith demonstrated strong administrative skills. Everett Cattell magnanimously served the global evangelical church and Jack Willcuts advocated the necessity of a national church being autonomous both in spirit and structure. Are these lessons to learn again? Certainly personalities and talents varied widely from Arthur Chilson the mechanic to Jack who thought of himself as "all thumbs"; from the polished and tactful administrator Everett Cattell to Esther Smith, who (while not tactless or crude), stressed the personal warmth of human ties in a very Latin American way. Arthur and Esther were consciously Friends pioneers, building the church more from scratch than Everett and Jack, who arrived many years after the first works had started. Pioneers are more solitary and independent, more likely to cultivate idiosyncratic behavior, while Everett and Jack moved more seamlessly between mission field and mission home base. It is not surprising that Arthur and Esther died on their fields of service, while Everett and Jack spent their last years serving the church profitably within their home cultures.

Similarities among these four actually may be far stronger than their differences. All preached and taught with great vigor and attention to biblical preparation. All had meaningful ecumenical ties outside of Friends circles and believed in the unity of witness with fellow Christians. Yet throughout their lives they loyally supported and encouraged the Friends movement. All believed Christian conversion was best understood in terms of an encounter with the living God through Christ, an event always seen in a change of life. Public testimony and verbal statements of faith could be helpful, they felt, but spiritual and moral transformation was the bottom line. It was more important to walk the walk than to talk. As traditional Quakers, they maintained that orthodoxy and orthopraxis are intertwined—one must have faith *and* live it out. They expressed great concern for the integrity of life and witness, and all were in one way or another profoundly influenced by the Holiness Movement among Friends.

We can assume all four knew how to laugh well. Most missionaries who last long have learned to cope through good humor. Jack, for one, worked at telling jokes well and could throw back his head and roar in laughter. Arthur enjoyed active games and played jokes on people in his conversations. Everett is remembered for his cheery smile that balanced his intellectual intensity. Even the proper Miss Smith was pleasant, enjoyed people, and could see the lighter side of life. The stereotypical image of a glowering, angry, puritanical missionary simply does not fit these four. The fruit of holiness among these Friends included joy.

The Work of a Pioneer

What can we learn from people who blaze new trails and look for innovations? First, it is simply true: Missions often (although not always) requires stepping into untested waters, a willingness to experiment without much precedence, and the courage to take a stand in new places. We will always need pioneers. Most missionaries do their own personal version of pioneering when they learn a new language. In addition to learning new languages, Arthur Chilson worked long, hard, physically demanding hours. Esther Smith built relationships around tea cups and cookies, and rode a mule over much of southeastern Guatemala and parts of western Honduras. Everett Cattell spent weeks at a time camping from village to village and endured the even more strenuous work of facing legal accusations from hostile upper-caste Hindus who opposed social change. Jack Willcuts did physically exhausting evangelistic travel through extreme elevations and put himself in harm's way to preach, but even so, his greatest contribution was a pioneering effort to develop a national-church structure. Pioneering takes place in myriad ways. Pioneer virtues include: 1) a strong self-esteem matched by a firm reliance upon God that helps the person stand alone; 2) clear-headed goals and a willingness to do physically and intellectually challenging tasks to achieve those goals; and 3) above all else, a readiness to try something new and to learn from the process.

Early pioneer missionaries are often viewed negatively in the twenty-first century. Some assume the pioneers were so intent upon conveying their message that they tried to conquer cultures and impose change by force. The reputation of harsh egomaniacs who slash and burn innocent nationals in disregard of personal relationships is, for the most part, simply false, as is substantiated by some recent secular studies. Such studies of David Livingstone, for example, suggest some improprieties not well proven, paint him as a sensitive and caring person.[1]

The India missionary staff made significant and sometimes wrenching changes in their approach in the 1940s as did the Bolivia Friends staff at about the same time. Writers from all four fields frequently acknowledged their errors and tried to make corrections. Anna Nixon, a valued colleague of the Cattells in India, is famous for her response to criticism of Western missionaries: "Yes, we made mistakes, serious ones, but praise God, the church is there!"[2] Humble pioneers leave others to find the balance and wholeness they fail to fully achieve. Anna Nixon did not make excuses for mistakes, but rather a statement on human fallibility while expressing deep appreciation for those who came along behind as instruments of the Spirit to perfect the church. Josephine Still made the same declaration about Guatemalan Friends leaders, people in whom she had great confidence to build and extend the church far more than did the missionary pioneers.[3] The best pioneers know the better work is done by those who follow. Jack Willcuts carried the same burden as he promoted an indigenous and autonomous church in Bolivia, believing a truly Bolivian church would be a far stronger church.

The Message of Christ

These pioneers believed and practiced that Christ—his life, his death and resurrection, and his ongoing presence as a teacher and friend—was the center of their message. Whether couched in terms of "the way of salvation" or "a personal relationship with God," Christ was at the center of the message and was never eclipsed by a secularized message of social reform. The tensions between social reform and salvation preaching were indeed present, but the work of Friends in the Global South and east was likely more balanced on this issue than it was in the missionary homelands of the north and west. It is true that the Chilsons vigorously opposed some non-evangelistic staff persons sent from the United States to Kenya—persons they believed had lost the faith. This did not mean they rejected compassionate service, social action, and social reform in favor of emotional revivalism. To the contrary, they continued to extend medical, educational, and industrial service that resulted in social change. In exactly the same era, the Guatemala Friends missionaries protested relations with Friends in the United States who they believed were not Christ-centered, not because they saw no place for education, an equal role for women, or justice for the poor, but because they feared the loss of the message of a Jesus who transforms sinners. In later years Everett Cattell and Jack Willcuts frequently engaged in dialogue—in the United States and elsewhere—with those who did not consider themselves Christ-centered. Everett and Jack never once doubted the importance of Christ but engaged in dialogue, longing to see a healthy Friends movement that was "evangelical in nature and worldwide in scope," a phrase frequently used by evangelical Friends during the 1950s and 1960s. Both Everett and Jack participated in activities of the Evangelical Friends Alliance, the predecessor of the Evangelical Friends Church International, and saw it as at least a partial fulfillment of the vision for an evangelical and international Friends movement.

Evangelistic Practice

Oral proclamation of the message of Christ was the twentieth-century norm among evangelical Friends. Street preaching, tent preaching, preaching in rented halls, home Bible studies, home visits, and evangelistic teams were all common and were carried over from the late nineteenth century. The greatest fruit almost always came through the efforts of new Christians sharing their faith face-to-face with family, friends, and fellow workers in field and factory. Indian evangelists stood along the roads and engaged people in conversation; Bolivian Aymaras used flannelgraphs to tell Bible stories at the gate of the church; Guatemalan youth and adult teams traveled incessantly; Kenyan and Urundian school teachers doubled as pastors to disciple new converts in their communities. The expatriate missionary example was to build relationships, to extend unconditional love, to share faith, and to call for a response. This gentle, non-coercive approach was eventually articulated in Everett Cattell's *Mission: A Matter of Life.*

Persuasion was measured and careful, allowed for questions and answers, and gave the evangelist time to sense where God was already working in people's lives. Friends missionaries often reported that God had gone before them, prepared hearts and planted seeds that they helped water, cultivate, and harvest. Was conversion an intellectual response or was it a spiritual and emotional encounter? Everett Cattell and Jack Willcuts considered it both, preaching to the mind but expecting a response of the heart. We know less of Esther Smith's and Arthur Chilson's preaching styles, but both were deeply schooled in the Bible-training programs of the Holiness Movement. They were taught to provide much teaching for the intellect while appealing for an emotional and spiritual response, which, it was believed, would bring moral transformation by the work of the Holy Spirit. All four believed in Christian experience as a hallmark of Quaker holiness and their fellow missionaries were of one mind on the subject.

The Messenger and the Social Sciences

Another way to profit from history is to appropriately honor the use of the social sciences. Missions have long tended to be ahead of the rest of the church in integrating the social sciences into their ministry, but the subjects of this book had little access to this field. Now, however, studies in sociology, political science, and cultural anthropology are commonplace. As Western colonialism first expanded in the eighteenth and nineteenth centuries and then retreated in the twentieth century, the need for cultural sensitivity overseas became especially evident. It was not always easy to stand separate from the political imperialism of Europe and North America, although Friends tended to be harsher critics of their home governments than some of their fellow evangelicals. Missionaries made frequent and glaring mistakes, but successes still pointed to a spiritual wisdom and power found only in the Holy Spirit.

To employ the social sciences is not to say the social sciences dictate the answers, but rather to let the social sciences become tools to analyze, to understand, and to predict the impact of change. Paternalism and lack of cultural understanding surfaced at times for Friends missions in the twentieth century Friends-missionary movement. Western practices may have been substituted for healthy local customs. Those things happened, but to a lesser degree than is assumed by the secular world, and were combined with an attitude of empowering others to make corrections. As a matter of fact, the churches of Central Africa have adopted worship styles far more reflective of a gregarious and active culture, allowing for greater joy and spontaneity. So have churches of Latin America and Asia—each nation and ethnicity with great distinction. The rise of national-church structures among Aymara-speakers in Bolivia acted strongly to preserve indigenous language, culture, and leadership style in that nation. Aymara identity continues and is actually experiencing something of a nationalistic renaissance in the Andes in the early twenty-first century, and evangelicals in Bolivia do not feel estranged from that cultural renewal. Friends in Nepal often worship seated on the ground with drums as their primary musical instruments. Latin American leadership style may, on the one hand, seem hierarchical and rigid to some, yet behind the scenes, we discover sensitivity to consensus and process. Lastly, contemporary ethno-theology is worthy of profound consideration both in the West and in the Global South. The employment of the social sciences should continue to move forward, especially to better inform theology and biblical teaching.

Wholism

North American evangelical Friends early in the twenty-first century find themselves in a profoundly different world from that of Arthur Chilson, Esther Smith, Everett Cattell, and Jack Willcuts. World political alliances, population increases, and the plethora of new nations attempting to join the world community have been influenced by Christian missionary education, health care, and cultural reinforcement. Many in the West remain largely oblivious to the fact that Christian missions in Latin America, Africa, and Asia have helped shape these global changes. Furthermore, within the field of Christian ministry, the evangelical movement has moved firmly toward a stronger integration of word and action. For example, evangelical Friends broadly accept that effective ministry includes preaching and teaching leading to personal conversion, but evangelical Friends also believe witness must be combined with compassion and a concern for justice and peace. Christian missions actively pursued a wholistic vision throughout the twentieth century, despite the fractures, separations, and debates on the subject in the West. The disagreements among North American Friends over the relationship between social activism and conversion evangelism were never as great as in Central and South America, India, and Africa.

Friends educational enterprises—especially in Africa and Latin America—contributed to social change; young women were educated and young men and women rose from humble beginnings to positions of influence. Other global writers have admitted that Christian missions, rather than supporting colonialism, actually empowered the nationalists who clamored for independence and freedom from colonial powers.[4] Among them have been Friends-educated students. The serious issues of what kind of social change is appropriate and how to advocate for change have been faced more often in the Global South. Some of that advocacy has filtered back to the North, but there is still more to observe and learn. This is one way the twenty-first-century church of the West can learn from the past.

Human Equality

Another hallmark of twentieth-century Friends missionaries was a firm belief in human equality. Their spiritual ancestors, whose history they knew, had served as "conductors" and "stations" to speed Africans north and away from slavery. Everett Cattell was born in an area of eastern Ohio deeply committed to Quaker activism and anti-slavery. Esther Smith spent many years of her early adulthood with the inner-city poor, who she believed to be redeemable and capable of a full and rich Christian life. On her trip to Bolivia, she immediately noted the great human potential among the Aymaras, just as she was attracted to the poor of San Francisco and Chiquimula. The Holiness Movement at the turn of the twentieth century taught Friends to believe that the poor were loved by God and that a deep experience with Christ would motivate and move people toward healing. The Bolivian Friends mission repeatedly championed the Aymara underclass (as did the Urundi Friends missionaries with the Hutus) and Jack Willcuts believed these oppressed people would one day govern their own national church with dignity and honor. Everett Cattell agonized deeply over the Indian caste system and delighted when steps were taken toward caste reconciliation and recognition of equality within the body of Christ. He stalwartly opposed the labor forced upon the miserably low-caste Chamar people, and believed the gospel would support and encourage them to live in equality with other Indians.

Esther Smith's team of missionaries was mostly women, and the team would never have even considered the issue of whether women are equal to men in ministry; they just assumed it. Arthur Chilson shared ministry with his wife, Edna, also a recorded minister, and his two daughters became missionaries in their own right. Everett Cattell worked alongside Esther Baird, Anna Nixon, and other highly capable, recognized female ministers of the gospel, not to mention his wife, Catherine. Jack Willcuts promoted women in ministry and within the Bolivian missionary team. Like the teams in Kenya, Urundi, Central America, and India, Jack gave focused attention to oppressed and underserved women.

Guidance of the Holy Spirit and Prayer

The Spirit-oriented faith and practice for which Quakers are known was present in their twentieth-century missions. Group discernment rather than an individual's sense of guidance marked Friends decision making, although concerns often arose from a single person. The practice of a church body corporately commissioning a missionary was the standard Friends process. A Cleveland Bible Institute ad hoc committee, for example, blessed Arthur Chilson, Edgar Hole, and Willis Hotchkiss before their epic voyage of discovery to Kenya and before they came under the care of a denominational board. R. Esther Smith heard God's call to Chiquimula while walking down a street in Oakland, California, and California Yearly Meeting confirmed that leading and sent her, along with others, on her way to Central America. Both Everett Cattell and Jack Willcuts responded directly to the discernment of the church and its elders and joined a missionary team because of that encouragement. When considering new steps in ministry or the opening of new fields, Friends relied on extensive prayer and waiting on the Lord. Esther Smith was famous for her "calls to prayer" that brought the Chiquimula staff together at random times to deal with crises. The mission-council systems in all the fields upheld the ideal of finding the will of God for the group through worship and waiting. This reliance upon community approval saved the Friends movement from many of the abuses of independent missionaries who had little or no accountability.

Simplicity

Can we claim Friends missionaries lived simple, humble lives among the poor and dispossessed in the twentieth century? For the most part, yes. The Kenyan missionaries lived and slept among the common people and struggled alongside their African porters, carrying their own packs. Arthur Chilson could be exacting and maybe even imperialistic in his demands of mission employees, but he was not afraid to get "down and dirty" and surprised his African friends by his lifestyle, which was a contrast to nearby colonial administrators.

LESSONS FOR THE 21st CENTURY

Esther Smith left "no will and no property" after her death. She undoubtedly had a few clothes and a private box for memories, but nothing of commercial value; she had no estate whatsoever. What she used in daily living belonged to the mission. Everett Cattell shared his meals around the campfire in the harsh Indian countryside, and found the depth of conversations and fellowship his greatest possession. Jack Willcuts instructed a generation of missionaries after him to openly share their homes, furniture, and meals with the poor, believing that generous sharing was the key to overcoming the differences between relatively affluent Westerners and the poor of the Global South. He believed it was the *attitude* of simplicity that is the most important, not the exact parity in lifestyle.

A Concept of Christian Leadership

One is struck by the total lack of pretense or the thought that these four Friends missionaries of the twentieth century were building personal religious empires. Many of them had personal traits that could have earned them money and prestige in the United States. Their leadership skills were noteworthy, and they might have built religious followings and institutions to enhance personal fame. But it didn't happen. A strong sense of humble servanthood pervaded their lives—even the lives of Everett Cattell and Jack Willcuts, who served in high positions in churches back in the United States. Servanthood was the first mark of the Christian leader, and the godly example of the servant was his or her greatest virtue. The desire and call for independent, indigenous leadership became sharper in the lifetimes of Everett and Jack, but the vision was always there from the first.

Although a servant, the missionary was expected to move under God's power, not serve as a doormat. Clarity and plain speech ("say what you mean without exaggeration and mean what you say with integrity") were the human parts of speaking with power, but there was always a longing for the "anointing of the Holy Spirit" for God's power to connect with people. A leader could use words powerfully and move people toward truth, either in public preaching and teaching or in small-group mission-council discussions. Everett

Cattell and Jack Willcuts were especially effective with their fellow missionaries, but so were Arthur Chilson and Esther Smith as they declared their visions for ministry.

These Friends missions largely moved as teams, believing that God leads the body and not just individuals. Within the mission councils, they tried to practice the time-honored Friends beliefs about a harmony that leads to unity. As the missions moved toward governance by a council rather than by a superintendent, the sense of consensus decision making grew considerably and became the norm, especially in Bolivia and Central America. The Cattells faced sharp differences—at least in style and practice—with the older generation of India missionaries, but likewise there were differences in Bolivia in the 1940s between the younger and older missionaries. Disagreements among the Guatemalan team arose from time to time, but the pattern in each case was to pray, wait, and expect unity. In Central America, a council system was instituted after the death of Esther Smith. Less is noted about inter-missionary relations in Kenya from 1910 to 1930 during the Chilson days, but we know that the mission commissioned workers with a wide variety of abilities, and many of them supported one another in their various tasks. The mission certainly worked to build one East Africa Yearly Meeting, which maintained an essential unity for decades before sharp dissention and disunity appeared within the Kenyan national church in the 1980s and onward. In those earlier days, leadership was expected to bear the fruit of spiritual unity within the church.

Friends and the Broader Christian Church

These four groups of Friends missionaries—in Africa, Central America, India, and South America—each had influence and leadership beyond their own circle of denominational churches and pastors. In the beginning there had been comity agreements in each of the four fields. For example, in Guatemala, Presbyterians, the Central America Mission, Friends, and Primitive Methodists each carved out a section of the nation as their area. While today comity agreements seem archaic, somewhat imperialistic, and unworkable, in their time they were an expression of trust, mutual respect, and economy of resources. Friends therefore took their places geographically and tried to faithfully "occupy" the areas accepted. In Bolivia there were tacit agreements with Central Friends, Baptists, and Methodists. In Kenya, the agreements were with Africa Inland Mission, Anglicans, World Gospel Mission, and others. In Urundi, comity areas were marked out for Danish Baptists and Anglicans, and later for World Gospel Mission, Free Methodists, and Pentecostals. In India, the Friends mission went to Bundelkhand at least partially because no other mission had claims there and the area had been left without Christian witness. Comity agreements are unlikely to reappear, but a spirit of cooperation and awareness of the work of others is greatly needed.

Friends interdenominational leadership took different forms. The most common was for missionaries to preach and teach for other churches occasionally, but fellowship organizations, joint projects for education, pastoral training, evangelism, and publishing also provided opportunities for interdenominational leadership. Early Kenya missionaries took leadership in Bible translation as did Friends in Bolivia where mission agencies pooled resources for an Aymara Bible translation and other literature. Friends often took positions of prime leadership in these interdenominational projects.

Inter-agency fellowships formed in each of the four regions and Friends always participated. Arthur Chilson served as chair of such a group in Urundi for a while, as did Jack Willcuts in Bolivia and Everett Cattell in India. Everett rose to the position of executive director of the Evangelical Fellowship of India and led in the creation of an all-India strategy for the Friends mission there, believing their efforts in education and Christian Education publications were crucial for the entire subcontinent. What would bless believers everywhere, he said, would bless Friends churches as well. In the 1950s, in the closing years of Everett's work in India, a few Friends missionaries, led by Everett, held key leadership positions throughout the nation. The Friends India Mission established an historic precedent that other evangelical Friends have admired as an example of service to the broader body of Christ.

As noted earlier, it was probably the Quaker reputation for peace, reconciliation, and humble service that won Friends the trust of others. More than reputation, however, their significant aptitudes and integrity brought invitations to lead and represent fellowships of expatriates. People who build personal empires do not receive that kind of confidence from their peers. Neither do people who are insecure in loyalty to their own spiritual family. This generation of Friends leaders were firmly Friends and yet openly friendly and generous to others.

A Vision for the Church

This study has especially stressed Jack Willcuts's vision of "churchmanship" and the creation of an autonomous national church free to express itself biblically under the guidance of the Holy Spirit. Yet each of the other Friends fields we have studied experienced something similar—a belief that God is in charge of building his church and that God's "Word will not return empty" (Isaiah 55:11). Christ's church will be built despite indifference, persecution, illness, or failure.

Such a vision requires a gripping confidence in the Holy Spirit to take charge. Noteworthy indigenous Friends churches have developed in three of the four fields—Central America, South America, and East Africa. The same cannot be said of Bundelkhand, India, where the church is much smaller. In the broader picture of India, however, the church is making striking forward movements and Friends have contributed to that regional growth. Furthermore, the persistence of Eastern Region Friends' interest in the entire subcontinent has aided in the raising up of eight additional ministries, some of them in three neighboring nations. All of these ministries are led by East Asians who are planting Friends Churches and developing a loyalty to the Friends movement.[5]

Passing the Missionary Baton

None of our four subjects lived to see the creation of indigenous Friends missionary societies within their fields, although perhaps Esther Smith came closest as the Chiquimula Tabernacle Church supported a missionary family in Bolivia for more than six years. Interestingly, Central American Friends made the plunge in the late 1990s by sending workers to Nicaragua and later to Southeast Asia. South American Friends and African Friends have crossed borders to neighboring countries with the gospel, but the possibility of sending bi-vocational workers to Asia, Europe, or the Americas is still largely unrealized even though the potential is huge. The tiny church of Bundelkhand has supplied workers to many places of India, and the new Friends ministries scattered over the Indian subcontinent are awakening to how strategically they are placed on the world scene.

What will the next generation of missions bring? Perhaps a rainbow of ethnic color, people from the North and Global South working together, or Western and Eastern cultures participating in a variety of partnerships. Networks and "contacts" will be the order of the day and more of these non-Western missionaries will be bi-vocational yet intentional, trained, and focused on accountability and reporting. Some will sail right under the radarscope of religious and political hostility to the gospel, and others will suffer persecution and isolation. Some will sow seeds, others will cultivate, a few will gather the harvest, and many more will perfect and contextualize the new churches. Intense expressions of religious fervor will break out, similar to the revival in Guatemala in 1918 to 1919; such an outpouring of the Spirit may puzzle the workers and drive them to their knees to find the will of Christ. Others will agonize over indifference and apathy that will likewise drive them to prayer.

Arthur Chilson and his colleagues Edgar Hole and Willis Hotchkiss explored, wandered about, and found both a place to settle and "a great people to be gathered." The next generation of missionaries—many of them from the Global South—may find themselves doing the same. Like Ruth Esther Smith, young women from Eastern Europe or Asia will hear the call of God and decide they want to give the rest of their years to building relationships, loving people, and training up workers in another ethnic group or nation. Young Bolivians or Peruvians will become world statesmen for Christ and will join the broader church that transcends denominational lines. Africans and Asians will capture the vision of interdependent movements of churches—national churches in their home continents and elsewhere! They will depend on God and not upon foreign resources, and they will move ahead aggressively with initiative and confidence.

As a North American, I am a child of my Western cultural tradition. But God is not done with me—or us. Our place and our callings have not changed, yet we are increasingly aware that our place is more modest in the cosmic view than we previously envisioned. Hopefully, we are less arrogant and self-centered than we used to be. I pray it is so. It will take all kinds of missionaries to complete the Great Commission. We in the Global North and West clearly hold great economic resources, and we need to use these faithfully and well to help and not hinder God's work in the world. But important resources of spiritual life and cultural creativity abound elsewhere, and God will use these as well.

Our four friends—Arthur Chilson, Esther Smith, Everett Cattell, and Jack Willcuts—saw great potential for Christ in the peoples of Asia, Africa, and Latin America. Wouldn't they take delight in knowing their examples stirred exploits in mission far greater than their own?

Reflections:

In what ways were these four missionaries—Arthur Chilson, Esther Smith, Everett Cattell, and Jack Willcuts—very similar people?

What important lessons can we learn from a pioneer missionary?

How do you think these four leaders would respond to the accusation that Christ-centered Friends missions have shown little or no social concern?

How would you characterize evangelistic practices of Friends missionaries in the twentieth century?

In what ways have Friends shown cultural sensitivity in missions through the twentieth century?

How have Friends missions been different because of Friends' convictions on human equality?

How would you describe the Friends ideal of a missionary as a leader?

What are the advantages of a strong, non-Western missionary force?